GLOBAL HISTORY OF THE PRESENT
Series editor | Nicholas Guyatt

In the Global History of the Present series, historians address the upheavals in world history since 1989, as we have lurched from the Cold War to the War on Terror. Each book considers the unique story of an individual country or region, refuting grandiose claims of "the end of history," and linking local narratives to international developments.

Lively and accessible, these books are ideal introductions to the contemporary politics and history of a diverse range of countries. By bringing a historical perspective to recent debates and events, from democracy and terrorism to nationalism and globalization, the series challenges assumptions about the past and the present.

Published

Thabit A. J. Abdullah, *Dictatorship, Imperialism and Chaos: Iraq since 1989*

Timothy Cheek, *Living with Reform: China since 1989*

Alexander Dawson, *First World Dreams: Mexico since 1989*

Padraic Kenney, *The Burdens of Freedom: Eastern Europe since 1989*

Stephen Lovell, *Destination in Doubt: Russia since 1989*

Alejandra Bronfman, *On the Move: The Caribbean since 1989*

Nivedita Menon and Aditya Nigam, *Power and Contestation: India since 1989*

Hyung Gu Lynn, *Bipolar Orders: The Two Koreas since 1989*

Bryan McCann, *The Throes of Democracy: Brazil since 1989*

Mark LeVine, *Impossible Peace: Israel/Palestine since 1989*

James D. Le Sueur, *Algeria since 1989: Between Terror and Democracy*

Forthcoming

Kerem Oktem, *Turkey since 1989: Angry Nation*

Nicholas Guyatt is lecturer in American history at the University of York.

About the author

James D. Le Sueur received his PhD from the
University of Chicago. He is the author of *Uncivil
War: Intellectuals and Identity Politics during the
Decolonization of Algeria* and the editor of several
books, including *The Decolonization Reader*
and the critically acclaimed English translation
of Mouloud Feraoun's *Journal, 1955–1962:
Reflections on the French–Algerian War*. A leading
authority on Algerian and French history, his work
investigates a broad range of subjects, including
colonial and postcolonial history and theory. He is
currently filming a documentary and completing
a book about exiled writers from Muslim-majority
countries in Europe and North America. He is
professor of history at the University of Nebraska,
Lincoln.

Algeria since 1989: Between terror and democracy

James D. Le Sueur

Fernwood Publishing
HALIFAX | WINNIPEG

Zed Books
LONDON | NEW YORK

Algeria since 1989: Between terror and democracy was first published in 2010

Published in Canada by Fernwood Publishing Ltd, 32 Oceanvista Lane, Site 2A, Box 5, Black Point, Nova Scotia B0J 1B0

<www.fernwoodpublishing.ca>

Published in the rest of the world by Zed Books Ltd, 7 Cynthia Street, London N1 9JF, UK and Room 400, 175 Fifth Avenue, New York, NY 10010, USA

<www.zedbooks.co.uk>

Set in OurType Arnhem and Futura Bold by Ewan Smith, London
Index: ed.emery@thefreeuniversity.net
Cover designed by Andrew Corbett

A catalogue record for this book is available from the British Library
Library of Congress Cataloging in Publication Data available

Library and Archives Canada Cataloguing in Publication:
Le Sueur, James D.
    Between terror and democracy : Algeria since 1989 / James D. Le Sueur.
Includes bibliographical references and index.
ISBN 978-1-55266-256-4
    1. Algeria--History--1990- 2. Algeria--Politics and government--1990-
I. Title.
DT295.6.L48 2007   965.05'4   C2007-905184-7

ISBN 978 1 84277 724 4 hb
ISBN 978 1 84277 725 1 pb
ISBN 978 1 84813 535 2 eb (Zed Books)

ISBN 978 1 55266 256 4 pb (Fernwood Publishing)

Contents

Acknowledgments

Thankfully, throughout the process of writing this book, I had the good fortune to have a lot of sound advice and help. And, although those who have helped me see through this book bear no responsibility for any of the book's flaws, they do share collective responsibility for any success the book sees. I have been humbled by their patience, insights, commitment to rigorous inquiry, insistence on clear writing, and, most important, their friendship and support.

Since this endeavor took many years to write and research, I'd like to begin by thanking those involved in the research necessary to complete the book. First and foremost, I'd like to thank Prem Paul, Vice Chancellor for Research at the University of Nebraska (the faculty's real champion at the University), and Laura Damuth, of the University of Nebraska's Undergraduate Creative and Research Experience (UCARE) program. Through the generous support of the UCARE program, I have benefited from the assistance of several brilliant and tenacious research assistants who vigilantly sought out documents, books, newspaper articles, and other relevant sources. Without their help, this book would never have been possible. Those UCARE students that I'd like to praise are: April Kirkendall, Isabelle Koch, Dené Oglseby, Jennifer Pahlke, Maegan Stevens-Liska, and David Thomas.

Writing this book was also a collective experience. I'd first like to thank Ken Barlow, commissioning editor at Zed Books in London. Without Ken's patience, flexibility, and support, this book would never have been realized. Next, it is impossible to imagine this book without Nicholas Guyatt. First, because Nick invited me to write the book for his "Global History of the Present" series with Zed Books, and second because he stuck with me throughout the long process of preparing this text. As series editor, Nick is truly irreplaceable. He is without question the smartest and most dynamic editor and colleague I have had the pleasure to work with. His undaunted encouragement, keen observations, honesty, and unrivaled ability to understand both the big picture and the unique significance of the story told in this book literally kept me going. Moreover, his determination to see the book reach a broader audience by focusing on clear prose clearly impacted the design and the delivery of the material. Next, my colleagues John Entelis, John Ruedy, and Jennifer Bryson also deserve praise for their willingness to advise me on either parts or the entirety of the manuscript at key moments. Finally, I'd like to thank my friend Jennifer Pahlke. Like Nick, Jen read every single draft of this book from beginning to end and made an invaluable contribution to the text. Jen's insights and willingness to help no matter what (even as she was on her way back to the US from France on her way to start her PhD at Yale) can never be repaid. I am truly indebted to her for her generosity at every step of the way, both in the research and the writing phases.

Throughout the past few years, I have also had the opportunity to conduct extensive oral history interviews for a documentary film I am producing, and these conversations have helped me clarify many key aspects of the story told in this book. Among those who granted me interviews that I'd like to thank here are: Henri Alleg, Slimane Benaïssa, Anouar Benmalek, Aziz Chouaki, Anita DeFrantz, John Entelis, Anwar Haddam, Alec Hargreaves, Reda Hassaine, Gilles Kepel, Yasmia Khadra, Malika Mokaddem, Hugh Roberts, Paul Silverstein, Benjamin Stora, Alec Toumi, and Marie Virolle. Similarly, William Lawrence was always willing to discuss ideas or issues addressed in the book, and his advice was invaluable.

I had the opportunity to test out several sections of this manuscript as public lectures. I would therefore like to thank Jane Moss for inviting me to Colby College's Goldfarb Center to try out what would become the conclusion of this book. John Calvert at Creighton University gave me the opportunity to present the basis for Chapter Eight in a public lecture. My colleagues Danny Postel and Hamid Akbari gave me the chance to present other sections of this book before it went to press to a wonderful audience at Northeastern Illinois University. And the faculty at West Point gave me one final opportunity to try out key aspects of this story just before publication.

I'd like to thank Lorna Scott Fox for her much appreciated assistance in preparing the book for publication.

Finally, I'd like to thank my group of friends at the local Starbucks in Lincoln, whose daily indulgences and great Americanos kept me going as I sat for months and months at "my office" by my favorite window, writing and revising this book.

Chronology

1827–1953

April 30, 1827 – The *"coup d'éventail"* (Pierre Deval, French King Charles X's consul in Algiers) is hit with fly swatter by the Ottoman Hussein Dey.

June 1827 – Beginning of French blockade of Algiers. Charles X sends Prince Jules de Polignac to Algiers, and, in return, Hussein destroys French posts at Bône and Le Calle.

July 5, 1830 – The French capture Algiers.

August 2, 1830 – Charles X abdicates. The Duc d'Orléans is subsequently crowned as King Louis-Philippe.

July 22, 1834 – Louis-Philippe issues Royal Ordinance designating Algeria a military colony.

1837 – Treaty of Tafna signed by General Thomas Robert Bugeaud and the Algerian resistance leader, the emir Abd el-Kader, acknowledging Abd el-Kader's sovereignty over a considerable portion of Algeria. The treaty is broken by Louis-Philippe two years later.

November 18, 1839 – Abd el-Kader formally declares war against the French.

November 1840 – General Bugeaud is appointed governor general of Algeria. He initiates a total war approach against the Algerian resistance, which results in widespread human rights abuses.

February 1844 – Creation of the Office of Arab Affairs (Bureau Arabe).

December 1847 – Alexis de Tocqueville publishes his "Report on Algeria," commissioned by the French government, in which he urges France to use less violent means of subduing the Algerian people.

December 21, 1847 – Abd el-Kader surrenders to the French general and commander of Oran Province, Louis de Lamoricière, who guarantees Abd el-Kader safe passage to either Alexandria or Acre.

February 1848 – Revolution in France and abdication of Louis-Philippe. The Second Republic is declared. The French renege on promises made to Abd el-Kader (the condition of his surrender). He is placed under house arrest at the Château d'Amboise.

1848 – Algeria is divided into the three French *départements* of Oran, Algiers, and Constantine.

1851 – Coup d'état by Louis-Napoleon Bonaparte (Napoleon III)

October 1852 – Emperor Napoleon III visits Abd el-Kader at the Château d'Amboise and orders his release.

1860 – Napoleon III declares a *"Royaume Arabe"* or "Arab Kingdom" in Algeria, which the European settlers resent.

1860 – Unrest in Syria. Abd el-Kader's intercession helps spare the lives of thousands of Syrian Christians, for which Napoleon later inducts him into the French Legion of Honor.

1863 – In a move widely criticized by European settlers as being too pro-Muslim, Napoleon's *senatus-consulte* declares tribes of Algeria owners of land they had traditionally occupied.

1865 – The *senatus-consulte* declares the end of war on Arabs, and creates a separate legal status for non-Christians in Algeria. Although Napoleon intended to protect Muslims with this action, the law codified the second-class status of Algerians.

July 19, 1870 – Franco-Prussian War (July 19, 1870–May 10, 1871) begins when Napoleon III declares war on Prussia.

September 2, 1870 – Napoleon III taken prisoner during the Battle of Sedan after his army is defeated.

September 4, 1870 – Third Republic declared. Insurrection in Paris, while France continues war against Prussia.

1870 – The Crémieux decree naturalizes the Algerian Jewish community, but does nothing to alter the inferior legal status of the Muslim majority.

Fall 1870 – Insurrections throughout Algeria, instigated by settlers rejecting the French government's interference in Algerian affairs.

1870 – *Code de l'indigénat* (proposed by settler delegation in French parliament) creates a legal framework for discrimination against Algerian Muslims and renders them second-class citizens.

1870–71 – Uprisings throughout Grand Kabylia, which bring harsh military punishments.

January 21, 1871 – Paris falls to the Prussians.

March 1871 – Paris Commune begins and lasts for two months.

May 10, 1871 – Treaty of Frankfurt ends the Franco-Prussian war.

1881 – French law separates religion from education.

1881 – France invades Tunisia.

1883 – French troops (including Algerians) sent to Madagascar.

1884–85 – European powers gather in Germany for the Berlin Conference, to draw up a map of official colonial powers in Africa.

1906 – French incursions begin in Morocco.

1908 – Young Algerians delegation meets with Prime Minister Georges Clemenceau in Paris to discuss the possibility of reforming the colonial system in Algeria.

1912 – French law enacted that imposes conscription on Algerian Muslims.

August 1914 – Germany declares war on France.

1919 – Treaty of Versailles.

1926 – The nationalist organization, the Étoile Nord-Africaine (ENA), founded in Paris. Led by its general secretary, Ahmed Messali Hadj, the group publicizes its agenda to liberate Algeria.

1929 – ENA is dissolved and banned by France.

1933 – Messali Hadj re-establishes ENA.

June 1936 – Muslim College created in Algeria, establishing a separate representative body for Algerian Muslims.

1937 – Foundation of Parti du Peuple Algérien (PPA), following the renewed dissolution and banning of the ENA.

November 1942 – Allied landings in Algeria.

May 1943 – Resistance leader, General Charles de Gaulle, arrives in Algiers to lead the Free French operations.

May 8, 1945 – The French massacre thousands of Algerians at Sétif and Guelma. Algerians estimate that 45,000 were killed, the French government proposes a total of 20,000. Messali Hadj and other prominent leaders arrested. These events drive the Algerian resistance into clandestinity.

April 1946 – Ferhat Abbas founds Union Démocratique du Manifeste Algérien (UDMA).

October 1946 – Messali Hadj establishes Mouvement pour le Triomphe des Libertés Démocratiques (MTLD), which later recruits an armed wing known as the Organisation Spéciale.

1954
Spring – The Comité Révolutionnaire pour l'Unité et l'Action (CRUA) is founded.

November 1 – Guerrilla war begins against the French. CRUA becomes the nationalist organization thereafter known as the Front de Libération Nationale (FLN).

December – Messali Hadj, marginalized by FLN, creates a rival guerrilla organization, the Mouvement National Algérien (MNA). The two formations compete for control over Algerian nationalism.

1955

January – François Mitterrand, France's minister of the interior, vows to restore order in Algeria and authorizes full use of military force to crush the insurrection.

February – Jacques Soustelle appointed by Prime Minister Pierre Mendès France as governor general of Algeria.

April 18–24 – Bandung Conference (Asia-Africa Conference) held in Indonesia under the leadership of President Ahmed Sukarno. Participation of FLN. Bandung led to the creation of the Non-Aligned Movement.

September – Algerian Communist Party officially banned by French government.

1956

February – Jacques Soustelle leaves post of governor general and Robert Lacoste is named as his replacement; the post is renamed "minister resident," allowing Lacoste more direct power.

October – Airplane carrying Ahmed Ben Bella, Hocine Aït Ahmed, Ferhat Abbas, and other FLN leaders over Algeria forced to land. Leaders on board arrested and held until conclusion of the war.

1957

January – "Battle of Algiers" begins when General Massu is granted police powers in Algeria. This action transforms the military campaign considerably.

June – Mélouza massacre. FLN denies responsibility, but later admits to the murder of over 300 Algerian civilians at Mélouza.

June – Arrest of Maurice Audin, member of Algerian Communist Party and professor of mathematics at University of Algiers. He is disappeared by French military. Henri Alleg, editor of *Alger Républicain*, also arrested.

July – Senator John F. Kennedy makes impassioned speech calling on France to end the war in Algeria.

1958

February – Henri Alleg's *The Question* published in Europe. The book causes an international scandal over the French use of torture, which Alleg, as a victim, outlines in great detail.

May – Political conditions in Algeria deteriorate.

May 13 – General Massu creates Committee of Public Safety after assuming control over government in Algeria, and calls on de Gaulle to take power in France with a military coup d'état. French military threatens to take over Paris if de Gaulle is not brought to power.

June 1 – Despite widespread opposition in Paris, de Gaulle illegally assumes powers over French government. Coup d'état becomes a reality.

1959
September – De Gaulle makes it clear he will pursue self-determination for Algerians in a national referendum.

1960
January – Conservative French settlers revolt against French government, put up barricades in Algiers.

September – Organization of the Petroleum Exporting Countries (OPEC) founded in Baghdad.

1961
January – French voters pass referendum on de Gaulle's handling of Algerian situation.

May – Organisation Armée Secrète (OAS), an ultra-right, pro-colonial paramilitary organization, created with the intention of overthrowing de Gaulle and keeping Algeria French.

September 8 – De Gaulle survives OAS assassination attempt.

1962
March – Evian meetings between FLN and French formalize the terms of ceasefire; OAS responds with a wave of terror in Algeria.

March 15 – Mouloud Feraoun and five other leaders of Centres Sociaux murdered by OAS in an attempt to disrupt the peace process.

March 18 – Evian agreement signed.

March 19 – Ceasefire goes into effect.

July 5 – Algeria declares independence.

July 22 – Ahmed Ben Bella seizes control of government.

October – Algeria inducted into United Nations. Ben Bella, as prime minister, attends ceremonies in New York.

October 22 – US President John F. Kennedy makes television appearance informing US citizens of presence of Soviet missiles in Cuba. Ben Bella expresses sympathy for Fidel Castro and alienates the Kennedy administration.

1963–87

September 1963 – Ben Bella elected to first five-year term as president.

October 1963 – Sands War begins between Morocco and Algeria.

October 17, 1963 – Hocine Aït Ahmed, founder of Front des Forces Socialistes (FFS, a Kabylia-based opposition party) is arrested.

December 1963 – National Society for the Transportation and Commercialization of Hydrocarbons (Sonatrach) created.

June 19, 1965 – Houari Boumediene stages military coup against Ben Bella.

July 1969 – Algeria joins OPEC under leadership of Sonatrach director, Sid Ahmed Ghozali.

October 1973 – OPEC oil crisis begins: OPEC members announce oil embargo in protest at US military support of Israel in Yom Kippur war.

June 1976 – Boumediene's National Charter adopted by national referendum. Places emphasis on socialist model for economic growth, and confirms Islam as state religion.

December 27, 1978 – Boumediene dies unexpectedly from a rare blood disease.

February 9, 1979 – Colonel Chadli Bendjedid chosen to succeed Boumediene as president.

November 4, 1979 – 53 Americans taken hostage in the American embassy in Iran, by Islamist supporters of the Iranian revolution.

April 1980 – Rioting in Tizi-Ouzou, capital of Kabylia, amid demands for recognition of Berber identity.

January 19, 1981 – "Algiers Accords" ends the Iranian hostage crisis. Americans are flown first to Algiers, then released in Germany.

1982 – Algerian crackdown on Islamists at the University. Abassi Madani, Abdellitif Soltani, and Ahmed Sahnoun placed under house arrest.

June 9, 1984 – Algerian government passes "Family Code," greatly diminishing the status of women. Under this legislation women can be prevented from traveling without male supervision; men are allowed up to four wives without consent of previous spouse(s), and to repudiate wives at will.

1985 – Algerian state lifts ban on *raï* music.

Mid-1986 – Collapse of oil prices begins, with catastrophic economic consequences for Algeria.

1988

October 4 – Riots in Algiers and other cities.

October 7 – Islamists organize peaceful demonstration in Algiers, meeting with violent military response.

October 10 – In wake of riots and military killing of hundreds of civilians, President Chadli promises to liberalize the political process.

December 22 – President Chadli re-elected.

1989

February 14 – Iran's Supreme Leader, Ayatollah Ruhollah Khomeini, issues fatwa against Salman Rushdie.

February 15 – Soviet withdrawal from Afghanistan complete.

March 9 – Front Islamique du Salut (FIS) founded.

September 14 – FIS recognized by government as an official party.

1990

June 12 – First free elections held. FIS win nation-wide local elections, well ahead of FLN.

August 2 – Under Saddam Hussein, Iraq invades Kuwait. Saudi royal family requests military support from US President George Bush.

August 7 – US commences Operation Desert Shield.

November 29 – United Nations authorizes the use of force to remove Iraq from Kuwait and issues deadline of January 15, 1991 to withdraw.

1991

February 24 – Desert Storm coalition forces commence ground assault on Iraq.

March 3 – Ceasefire declared in First Gulf War.

April – Strikes begin throughout Algeria. Situation deteriorates quickly.

June 5 – President Chadli declares state of siege, which enforces curfew.

June 27 – Date for which first round of parliamentary elections set, with second round scheduled for July 18. Both are soon postponed.

June 30 – Abassi Madani and Ali Belhadj arrested.

July 15 – Madani and Belhadj sentenced to 12 years' imprisonment.

August–September – Hassiba Boulmerka and Noureddine Morcel win women's and men's World Track 1,500-meter competitions in Japan.

September – Algerian dinar devalued by 22 percent.

December 26 – FIS win first round of parliamentary elections in landslide victory (188 of 232 possible seats).

1992

January 11 – Second round of scheduled national elections canceled. Parliament dissolved and President Chadli forced to resign by generals.

January 14 – Army stages coup d'état and imposes five-man junta (Haut Comité d'Etat, or HCE).

January 16 – Mohamed Boudiaf returns from exile in Morocco and is given command of HCE.

January 22 – FIS leader Abdelkader Hachani arrested under authority of HCE.

February 9 – HCE declares state of emergency.

March 4 – FIS banned by HCE.

June 29 – Mohamed Boudiaf assassinated.

July 19 - Belaïd Abdessalam becomes prime minister.

August 9 – Hassiba Boulmerka wins Algeria's first Olympic gold medal, for the 1,500-meter race, at Barcelona Games.

August 10 – Algeria declared a "war economy."

August 26 – Bombing of Algiers airport.

1993

February 13 – Failed assassination attempt on General Khaled Nezzar.

February 26 – Al Qaeda detonates bomb in World Trade Center in New York.

March 27 – Algeria suspends diplomatic relations with Iran and Sudan after accusing them of sponsoring terrorism.

May 26 – Tahar Djaout shot in the head in Algiers (dies on June 2).

August 22 – Kasdi Merbah assassinated.

October 30 – Groupe Islamique Armé (GIA) issues warning against all foreigners.

December 1 – GIA-issued deadline for all foreigners to leave Algeria or face certain death.

1994

January 30 – Liamine Zeroual appointed president of HCE.

April – European firms announce commitment to invest large sums in Algerian drilling of Algerian oil fields.

April – Algerian dinar devalued by 40 percent.

April 10 — International Monetary Fund (IMF) confirms that it will help stabilize Algerian economy.

September 26 – Berber singer/activist Matoub Lounès kidnapped by GIA. After massive protests, he is released on October 10.

September 29 – Cheb Hasni, a rising star of Algerian *raï* music, assassinated.

November – Key opposition party leaders meet in Rome to discuss what will become the Sant'Egidio Platform.

December 24 – Air France flight 8969 hijacked in Algiers. Two days later, plane is diverted to Marseilles. All four hijackers are killed and remaining hostages freed.

1995

January 13 – Sant'Egidio Platform, sponsored by Sant'Egidio community, signed in Rome. A major effort to end the carnage in Algeria and to restore the democratic process, the Platform calls for the repeal of the ban on the FIS, among other things. The HCE immediately rejects it. Key participants: Hocine Aït Ahmed with Ahmed Djeddai (for FFS), Ali Yahia (for Algerian League of Human Rights, LADDH), Rabah Kebir and Anwar Haddam (for FIS), Abdelhamid Mehri (for FLN), Louisa Hanoune (Algerian Workers Party), Ahmed Ben Bella and Khaled Bensmain (Movement for Democracy in Algeria), Ahmed Djaballah (al-Nahda), Ahmed Ben Mouhammed (Contemporary Muslim Algeria).

July 11 – FIS leader Abdelkai Sahraoui assassinated in Paris.

July 25 – GIA bomb explodes in Saint-Michel RER station, Paris, killing eight people and wounding 80 more.

August – Algerian government announces plans to hold presidential elections on November 16. Radical Islamists threaten to wage campaign of total war if government proceeds with elections.

August 17 – GIA bomb explodes at Arc de Triomphe in Paris.

September 7 – GIA bomb detonates in Jewish school in Lyon.

October 6 – Paris's Maison Blanche metro station bombed by GIA.

October 17 – Musée d'Orsay–Saint Michel line of Paris metro bombed by GIA.

November 16 – General Zeroual elected president with healthy voter turnout, despite threats by radical Islamists.

1996

March 27 – Monks of the Notre Dame de l'Atlas monastery at Tibhirine abducted. It is announced two months later that they have been killed.

May – Osama Bin Laden, expelled from Sudan, returns to Afghanistan.

June 25 – Bomb devastates US military housing site in Saudi Arabia.

June – Al Qaeda propagandist Abu Mus'ab al-Suri breaks ties with nationalist GIA emir, Djamal Zitouni, over GIA's merciless killing of Algerian civilians/Muslims, which al Qaeda claims deviated from acceptable Islamic doctrine.

November 13 – New Constitution, banning parties based on religion and ethnicity and limiting the president to two five-year terms, put into effect.

1997

January 28 – Abdelhak Benhamouda, Algerian labor union leader, assassinated.

July 15 – Former FIS leader, Abassi Madani, released from custody.

July 19 – Former FIS leader, Abdelkader Hachani, released from prison.

September 21 – AIS (Armée Islamique du Salut) announces ceasefire with government forces.

December 30 – *Wilaya* of Relizan massacres.

1998

February – Osama Bin Laden and Ayman al-Zawahiri issue fatwa calling for killing of Americans.

May – Former GIA field commander, Hassan Hattab, announces creation of the Groupe Salafiste pour la Prédication et le Combat (GSPC). Vows to fight a cleaner war against the Algerian regime, and end indiscriminate attacks on Muslim civilians.

June 25 – Matoub Lounès assassinated.

July 5 – Law making Arabic the only official language of the country goes into effect amid wide-scale protests from Berber community.

August – Al Qaeda bombs US embassies in Kenya and Tanzania.

September 11 – President Zeroual announces that he will leave office before the end of his first term.

October 12 – Al Qaeda bombs USS *Cole* in Yemen.

1999

April 14 – All six candidates running against Abdelaziz Bouteflika request meeting with Zeroual to protest against election irregularities. Zeroual denies their request, and, in response, all rivals call for a boycott of the elections. Bouteflika carries the elections the following day.

April 26 – Bouteflika sworn into office for his first term as president.

June 26 – Bouteflika moves forward with "Law on Civil Concord": a plan to offer national referendum granting limited amnesty to some of those involved in terrorist actions.

July–November 2000 – Algerian spy Reda Hussaine agrees to spy for MI5 on Abu Hamza's Finsbury Park Mosque in London.

September 15 – In a popular national referendum, Bouteflika's Law on Civil Concord passes.

November 22 – Abdelkader Hachani assassinated in Algiers.

December 14 – Ahmed Ressam caught crossing the Canadian border in Washington state by US Customs and the Millennium plot is discovered, setting off nation-wide man-hunts for other radical Islamist cells in Canada and the US.

2000

January 11 – Despite protests by human rights groups, Bouteflika grants amnesty to former members of the AIS.

2001

January 18 – European Parliament issues resolution lamenting that Algerian state had not responded to claims about the disappeared.

April 21 – Algerian police kill young Berber boy in Tizi-Ouzou, sparking riots throughout Kabylia.

July 12 – Bouteflika visits George W. Bush at White House. Discusses, among other things, possibility of more US military aid.

September 11 – Al Qaeda attacks against the US.

October 4 – In concession to Berbers, Bouteflika promises to recognize Tamighizt.

2002

October 12 – Al Qaeda kills over 200 people in bomb attack on tourists in Bali.

2003

March 20 – US President George W. Bush commences invasion of Iraq and the Iraq war begins.

May 13 – First group of European tourists kidnapped in the Sahara Desert freed.

October 8 – After internal power struggle, GSPC replaces Hassan Hattab with Nabil Sharawi. Hattab continues to maintain that he controls GSPC.

October 23–25 – US Assistant Secretary of State for Near Eastern

Affairs visits Algeria and confirms that US will supply Algeria with limited military support.

2004

March 11 – Bombs detonate in Madrid commuter trains, killing nearly 200 and wounding more than 1,400.

March 16 – Mastermind of 2003 Sahara tourist kidnappings, "El Para," caught by rebel group in Chad and offered for ransom.

April 8 – Bouteflika elected to second term as president.

June 20 – GSPC leader Nabil Sharawi killed by Algerian security forces. Succeeded by Abdelmalek Droukdal.

2005

April – Ahmed Ressam sentenced to 22 years in jail for his involvement in Millennium plot.

June – US-led Trans-Sahara Counterterrorism Initiative begins. GSPC carries out cross-border attack against Mauritanian forces.

June 17 – American officials place GSPC on "Tier Zero" terrorist list, defining it as a major global terrorist network.

July 5 – Italy complains openly about existence of GSPC cells within country.

July 7 – British Muslim suicide bombers attack London's transport system, killing 52.

August 22 – Amnesty International criticizes Bouteflika's proposed referendum on national reconciliation.

August 28 – French journalists Christian Chesnot and Georges Malbrunot kidnapped by terrorists in Iraq. France launches full diplomatic effort to secure their release in December.

September 29 – In a national referendum, Algerians pass Bouteflika's Charter for Peace and National Reconciliation that grants amnesty to nearly all terrorists and full amnesty to all agents of the state.

2006

February 12 – US Secretary of Defense Donald Rumsfeld meets with Algerian officials.

June 7 – Leader of al Qaeda in Iraq, Abu Musab al-Zarqawi, killed in Iraq safe house.

September 11 – GSPC links itself officially with al Qaeda.

December 11 – GSPC bombs convoy carrying Brown and Root Condor employees.

2007

January 24 – GSPC formally announces name change to Al Qaeda au Maghreb Islamique (AQMI).

February 13 – Massive AQMI synchronized bomb attacks in police stations across country.

April 11 – Three AQMI suicide bombers kill themselves in Casablanca, Morocco.

April 12 – Devastating AQMI suicide bombings destroy prime minister's office, the minister of interior's office, Algiers police station.

September 22 – AQMI founder, Hassan Hattab, turns himself in to Algerian authorities and applies for amnesty.

September – AQMI suicide bombing.

December 8 – AQMI suicide bombing of Coast Guard post at Dellys.

December 11 – AQMI bombs Algerian Constitutional Council and United Nations offices in Algiers.

2008

August 19 – AQMI suicide bomber attacks police academy.

October 28 – Bouteflika speech announcing request to revise the constitution to allow him to run for a controversial third term. Unlike reconciliation agreements, this is not brought to a national referendum. The constitution is amended as per Bouteflika's request on November 12.

2009

January – CIA Algiers station chief accused of rape. US President Barack Obama promises swift investigation.

April 9 – Bouteflika elected to a historic third term.

The principals

Hocine Aït Ahmed (1926–): A historic co-founder of the FLN in 1954, he was captured by the French military in 1956 after a plane carrying FLN leaders was illegally forced to land. He spent the rest of the war in custody. After independence he opposed Ben Bella and the FLN's hegemonic one-party stance. In 1963 he founded a Kabylia-based opposition party, the FFS, but was arrested by Ben Bella's government that same year. He escaped from prison in 1966 and lived in exile, first in France and then in Switzerland, until returning to Algeria in December 1989. He oversaw the legalization of the FFS as an opposition party after the democratic process was opened. He supported and signed the Sant'Egidio Platform in 1995. He withdrew as a candidate for president in 1999 due to claims of election rigging by the military, but ran again in 2004 and 2009.

Ali Belhadj (1956–): Born in Tunisia, he began his career as a high school teacher and the imam of the Al-Sunna Mosque in Algiers's Bab el-Oued district. Representing the Salafist wing of the FIS, he and the more moderate Abassi Madani were considered joint leaders of the FIS from 1989 until their arrest by the military authorities in 1991. He was tried and found guilty of crimes against the state. He was conditionally released from prison in 2003 after promising to refrain from all political activity. He was re-arrested in 2005 after he made statements in support of Iraqi insurgents, but was again released in March under the provisions of the Charter for Peace and National Reconciliation.

Ahmed Ben Bella (1918–): Served in the French military during the Second World War. A historic founder of the FLN, he was based in Cairo until he was captured in 1956 when a plane carrying FLN leaders was illegally forced to land by the French military. After independence, he became prime minister in 1962 and was elected (in an uncontested race) to become Algeria's first president in 1963. In 1965, Colonel Houari Boumediene overthrew him in a bloodless coup d'état, and kept him under house arrest until 1980. In 1980 he went into exile, returning to Algeria in 1990. While in exile, in 1984 he founded the MDA, a moderate Islamist party, which he revived in Algeria after coming back to take part in Algeria's first democratic elections. He was present at the Sant'Egidio Conference in Rome and a signatory of the Rome Platform. His party was officially banned in 1997.

Chadli Bendjedid (1929–): Served as Algeria's third president from 1979 to 1992, following the death of Boumediene. After the overthrow of Ben Bella, he occupied important government posts, including key military command positions. Re-elected to the presidency in 1985 and 1989, he oversaw the controversial Family Code in 1986 – which greatly restricted women's freedoms – as a concession to conservative Islamists. Following the riots in October 1988, he quickly opened up the political process and pledged to enforce liberal economic reforms. He enacted the 1989 Constitution that formalized Algeria's commitment to reform, and introduced a multi-party system. He lost the confidence of the military after the FIS swept the local elections in 1990 and the first round of the national parliamentary elections in 1991, and was forced to resign after the military coup d'état in January 1992.

Mohamed Boudiaf (1919–June 1992): A member of Messali Hadj's PPA, he remained a fervent nationalist during the colonial era and throughout decolonization. He was captured in 1956, along with other FLN leaders, when the plane he was traveling in was forced down by French military. He rejected the FLN's single-party stance after independence, but was forced into exile in Morocco by the FLN's ruthless tactics. In 1992, after 27 years in exile, he returned to Algeria at the request of the government to accept the chairmanship of the newly created ruling council (HCE). He was assassinated by his bodyguard on June 29, 1992.

Houari Boumediene (1932–December 1978): Joined the FLN in 1955 and directed the ALN, the party's armed wing, from 1960. Took power in a military coup d'état in 1965 that led to the imprisonment of Ben Bella and consolidated the FLN's hold on power. He ruled as an autocrat, but instituted major reforms that focused on a socialist economic model in an effort to create a vibrant industrial-based economy. He accelerated arabization in primary and secondary schools. Under his leadership, Algeria became a leading member of the Non-Aligned Movement. In 1976, he oversaw the implementation of the National Charter that, among other things, re-enforced Islam's place as the state religion but also the state's control over religious institutions. Under his leadership, the Algerian state imposed strict limits on democratic freedoms, including freedom of the press.

Abdelaziz Bouteflika (1937–): Elected president in 1999. Re-elected in 1994, and to a controversial third term in 2009. A veteran of the war of liberation, he served as minister of youth and sport and minister of foreign affairs until 1978. He went into exile in 1981 to avoid being prosecuted for corruption, and continued to live abroad until after 1989. Marginalized in the post-Boumediene reshuffle of the old guard, he became the military's favored candidate to succeed General Liamine Zeroual as president. In 1999 and in 2005 he successfully sponsored controversial amnesty referendums designed to foster national reconciliation and thereby end terrorism.

Tahar Djaout (1954–June 1993): A leading journalist and poet, he was known for his criticism of both the Algerian military state and the Islamists. The author of several important novels, he founded the review *Ruptures*. He died on June 2, 1993, after lying in a coma for a week following gunshot wounds to the head.

Louisa Hanoune (1954–): A vocal critic of the FLN's authoritarian policies, she was harassed and imprisoned by the regime before political opposition was legalized in 1988. She opposed the 1984 Family Code, and supported the Berber rights movement. She was involved in the creation of several workers' parties throughout her career as a union activist, and she currently leads the PT. In 2004, she became the first woman to stand for president.

Hassan Hattab (1967–): Founded the militant Islamist group, the GSPC, in 1998 following his decision to break with the GIA. He officially surrendered to Algerian authorities in October 2007.

Matoub Lounès (1956–June 1998): A prominent Berber activist and singer who opposed the government's arabization programs, he was kidnapped by a GIA group on September 24, 1994, only to be released after nation-wide protests against his abduction. Published his autobiography, *Rebelle*, in 1994. Despite orders by his captors to quit singing or face certain death, he continued to record CDs highly critical of both Islamists and the state. He was assassinated on June 25, 1998, and the GIA later claimed responsibility for his killing.

Abassi Madani (1931–): A veteran of the war of liberation, he spent most of the decolonization period in prison, after a bomb-planting conviction in 1954. He received a PhD in education from the UK, and returned to Algeria to teach as a professor at the University of Algiers. In 1989, he emerged as a leading political Islamist when he co-founded the FIS. Considered a moderate, he advocated the application of shari'a law. He was arrested in 1991 and convicted of crimes against the state. He was confined to house arrest in 1997 and released in 2003. He has since gone into exile in Saudia Arabia and Qatar, and advocated a boycott of the 2009 presidential elections.

Khaled Nezzar (1937–): A veteran of the war of national liberation, he remained in the military after independence and held key posts at the ministry of defense. Following Boumediene's 1965 coup, he continued to rise through the ranks of the Algerian army. As a general, he played a leading role in the military's excessive response to the October 1988 disturbances. In July 1990 he was named minister of defense, and in that capacity was one of the generals responsible for forcing Chadli Bendjedid to resign in 1992. He became a member of the HCE, and in 2002 he filed a libel suit against a former Algerian officer, Habib Souaïdia, in a Paris court.

Khalida Toumi (1958–): Known throughout the 1990s as Algeria's leading feminist politician and vocal critic of the government's limitations on women's rights, she was forced underground after a failed assassination attempt by radical Islamists. She taught mathematics until deciding to devote herself to a career in politics. From 1996 to 2001, she was a leading member of the secularist Berber party, the RCD, led by Saïd Saadi. She was appointed by President Bouteflika in May 2003 to the post of minister of communications and culture, which she continues to hold today.

Liamine Zeroual (1941–): A member of the ALN during decolonization, he rose through the ranks after independence to become a general in 1988. He resigned from the armed forces in 1990, after a disagreement with Chadli Bendjedid. Following the 1992 coup d'état, he was named minister of defense in 1993 and then named head of the HCE in January 1994. He was elected president in November 1995 but resigned from the presidency before his first term expired. He was succeeded as president by Abdelaziz Bouteflika in 1999.

Abbreviations and acronyms

AIS	Armée Islamique du Salut / Islamic Army of Salvation
ALN	Armée de Libération Nationale / National Liberation Army (armed wing of FLN)
APC	Assemblées Populaires Communales / Popular municipal assemblies
APW	Assemblées Populaires de Wilaya / Popular provincial assemblies
AQMI	Al Qaeda au Maghreb Islamique / Al Qaeda in the Islamic Maghreb
CRUA	Comité Révolutionnaire pour l'Unité et l'Action / Revolutionary Committee for Unity and Action
DCE	Direction du Contre-Espionnage et de la Securité / Office of Counter-Espionage and Security
DGSE	Direction Générale de la Sécurité Extérieure / Head Office of Foreign Security
DRS	Département du Renseignement et de la Sécurité / Department of Intelligence and Security
DST	Direction de la Sécurité du Territoire / Office of Territorial Security
ENA	Étoile Nord-Africaine / North African Star
FFS	Front des Forces Socialistes / Socialist Forces Front
FIS	Front Islamique du Salut / Islamic Salvation Front
FLN	Front de Libération Nationale / National Liberation Front
GIA	Groupe Islamique Armé / Armed Islamic Group
GIGN	Groupe d'Intervention de la Gendarmerie Nationale / National Gendarmerie Intervention Group
GSPC	Groupe Salafiste pour la Prédication et le Combat / Salafist Group for Preaching and Combat
HCE	Haut Comité d'Etat / High Committee of State
LADDH	Ligue Algérienne de Défense des Droits de l'Homme / Algerian League for the Defense of Human Rights

MDA	Mouvement pour la Démocratie en Algérie / Movement for Democracy in Algeria
MDJT	Mouvement pour la Démocratie et la Justice au Tchad / Movement for Democracy and Justice in Chad
MIA	Mouvement Islamique Armé / Armed Islamic Movement
MNA	Mouvement National Algérien / Algerian National Movement
MSP	Mouvement de la Société pour la Paix / Movement of Society for Peace
MTLD	Mouvement pour le Triomphe des Libértés Démocratiques / Movement for the Triumph of Democratic Freedoms
OAS	Organisation Armée Secrète / Secret Armed Organization (sometimes known as Organisation de l'Armée Secrète / Organization of the Secret Army)
OAU	Organization of African Union
OPEC	Organization of Petroleum Exporting Countries
PPA	Parti du Peuple Algérien / Algerian People's Party
PSI	Pan Sahel Initiative
PT	Parti des Travailleurs / Workers Party
RCD	Rassemblement pour la Culture et la Démocratie / Rally for Culture and Democracy
RND	Rassemblement National Démocratique / National Democratic Rally
RPN	Rassemblement Patriotique National / National Patriotic Rally
SM	Sécurité Militaire / Military Security
Sonatrach	Société Nationale pour la Recherche, la Production, le Transport, la Transformation, et la Commercialisation des hydrocarbures / National Company for the Location, Production, Transformation, Transportation and Commercialization of Hydrocarbons
TSCI	Trans-Sahara Counterterrorism Initiative
UDMA	Union Démocratique du Manifeste Algérien / Democratic Union of the Algerian Manifesto
UGTA	Union Générale des Travailleurs Algériens / General Union of Algerian Workers

For Sef and Sofia

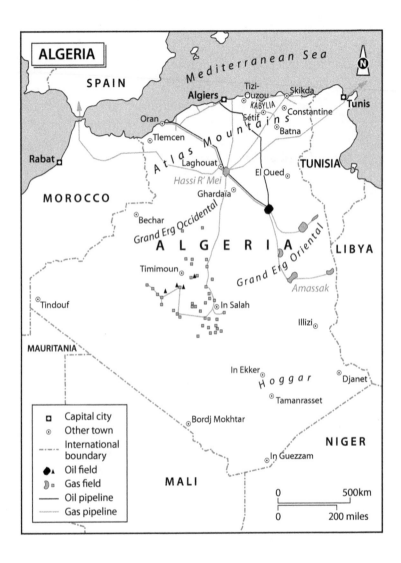

Introduction: democratic reform, terrorism, and reconciliation

In a 2006 essay broadcast on American National Public Radio, former US Secretary of State Warren Christopher paid homage to Algeria for its role in ending the Iranian hostage crisis.[1] He entitled his essay "A Shared Moment of Trust," and in it he noted that Americans owed Algeria a special debt of gratitude. For him this debt symbolized the very essence of diplomatic trust and has remained the high point of his long and distinguished career. The reason was simple. It was only by trusting the intervention of Algerian Foreign Minister Abdulkarim Ghuraib at the end of 1980 and during the first three weeks of 1981 that the Carter administration could secure the release of all remaining 52 American hostages in Iran. Effectively, only Algerian diplomacy, which resulted in the "Algiers Accords" on January 19, 1981, and the transfer of the hostages to Algiers the next day ended 444 days of American national anguish. As the sole government in the world capable of negotiating between President Jimmy Carter's crippled administration and the emboldened Ayatollah Khomeini-backed revolutionary Islamists, Algeria had pulled off one of the greatest diplomatic feats of the twentieth century.

Contrasted against the failed hijacking of Air France flight 8969 (when Algerian terrorists attempted to blow up a plane over the Eiffel Tower on Christmas Eve, 1994), the 1995 Paris bombings, and the December 1999 attempted bombing of Los Angeles International Airport during the Millennium celebrations (when an Algerian terrorist trained in Afghanistan by al Qaeda was caught with a car filled with explosives trying to cross the US–Canadian border in Washington state), Algeria's earlier status seems distant and almost nostalgic. The change in Algeria's fortunes between 1980–81 and the early to mid-1990s represented one of the biggest shifts in postcolonial history, as well as the emergence of an altogether different kind of political problem. The 1994 hijacking, 1995 Paris bombings, and 1999 Millennium plot by Algerian terrorists were calculated strikes at key Western targets and served as important precursors to 9/11. Indeed, by the 1990s Algeria's previous fortunes seemed to have unequivocally reversed, and many foreign governments, the European Union, and international human rights organizations called on the state to end the terrifying conflict between the military and radical Islamic terrorists and to conform to international human rights norms.

Ironically, both Algeria's success with the Iranian hostage negotiations and its failures of the 1990s hinged on its fierce reputation forged during decolonization and was sealed by its leadership during the postcolonial period. From 1962 to 1988, Algeria had occupied a paramount position within the Middle East, North Africa, and the "Third World" because it had been able to use the very carnage of decolonization to present itself as a strong nation. However, the Front de Libération Nationale's (FLN) revolutionary heritage, embodied in the violent theories of authenticity articulated most clearly by the adopted revolutionary Frantz Fanon, culminated in the state's vision of the nation that pitted unity against individuality, authoritarianism against liberalism, national identity against ethnic and regional differences, and Arabic against other indigenous languages and French. As a result of this combative program of postcolonial identity politics, for the first three decades after independence challengers to the FLN's hegemonic notions of identity were suppressed and largely neutralized by an oppressive regime that brooked no opposition. This heavy-handed statist approach led directly for dramatic calls for change in the 1980s and ultimately set the stage for the catastrophic events of the 1990s.

Democratic reform

The irony and lessons from Algeria's descent in the late 1980s and 1990s are clear. After serving for several decades as the Middle East's most important negotiator (as highlighted by the spectacular diplomatic breakthrough in Iran) and one of the leading states of the Non-Aligned Movement and of the postcolonial era, Algeria found itself as the example par excellence of what can go wrong in the process of political reform. Algeria's perfect storm showed officials floundering to head off a showdown with two equally determined opponents: political Islamists and liberal reformers. Both clusters (comprised of a wide array of political views) unanimously called for a rupture with the FLN's postcolonial status quo and for an immediate re-ordering of society. Each opposition party argued that it best represented the very idea of Algeria itself and claimed to hold the unique solution to Algeria's woes. To be sure, the ruling elite had given their challengers ample evidence that a new idea of the nation was now necessary, because the FLN had long since outworn its welcome as guarantor of liberty. Hence the decades-long insistence on the one-party state represented retired currency from the nationalist era. More revealingly, the anticolonial inheritance left to the youth could no longer mask years of corruption and stagnation represented by staggering unemployment and a deadening lack of opportunities.

By 1989, after the government opened up the political process to multi-party elections for the first time, Algeria had become the epicenter of political reform in the Middle East and consequently a magnet for political Islamists who saw in the Algerian *glasnost* a real opportunity to create the first democratically elected Islamic republic in history. So important was Algeria's sudden transformation to contemporary history that by 1990 it was considered one of the most dynamic and salient tests for political reform in the world, because it brought out such an unusual cast of competitors (including secular feminists, moderate liberals, moderate and radical Islamists, old-school and even exiled nationalists, ethnic groups, Francophones and Arabophones), all of whom came to the same political stage with dramatic expectations and loud calls for change. Each faction eagerly challenged opponents in an effort to determine what kind of idea of civil society and which cultural mores would prevail. These options corresponded to a central question in the minds of many reformers: would Algeria be a theocratic state or a secular republic? Yet, despite the profound differences among the secular liberals and the Islamists over the constitution of the idea of Algeria, each side remained united in its opposition to the FLN's misspent hegemony.

This kind of political competition was indeed as monumental as it was exciting. Each political faction gained strength from the core issue uniting even the most vehement enemies: the call to end the old regime. Distilled, the demands of Islamists and secularists alike echoed claims that the FLN had squandered the nation's valuable resources and that the one-party secular model, with its military-backed state, had led the country down the wrong path for so many years that it would not dare attempt to reverse the nation-wide call for political liberalization.

The political liberalization that began with spirited debate and great optimism in 1988 ended suddenly for Algeria in January 1992 in the same way that Hungary's democratic reforms ended in the streets of Budapest in 1956, that the Prague Spring ended for Czecho-slovakian reformers in 1968, and that the Tiananmen Square protests ended for the Chinese students, activists, and intellectuals in 1989: with a crushing military intervention. To be sure, the military was, as it claimed, responding to the threatening declarations of the Front Islamique du Salut (FIS) leaders – especially the hard-line Salafist politician, Ali Belhadj, arrested along with Abassi Madani in May 1991 after Belhadj publicly threatened to use violence against the state. After the January 1992 coup, the FIS, which had emerged victorious from municipal elections in 1990 and from the first round of the national elections in 1991, quickly saw itself banned. Other Islamist leaders and their supporters were also jailed and hunted down, and Islamists were thereafter blocked from the legitimate political arena and declared personae non gratae. By pushing the FIS outside the political process, Algerian generals provided militant FIS supporters and other radical Islamists with their justification for forming para-military movements and for commencing a jihad against the military-controlled state. While the military argued that it took action against FIS in order to protect the country from the theocrats promising to eliminate the democratic process once in power, the FIS used the international arena to insist that the democratic process had been thwarted by an illegitimate military junta. The great irony and per-haps tragedy of the reform era is that the success of the democratic process (which yielded quite unexpected results) ultimately enabled the military to re-establish complete control. The immediate result of the calls in October 1988 for reform was unthinkable: the military killed over 500 unarmed street protestors. And, once the military came out from behind the shadows to seize power in 1992, the first phase of the struggle, the reform phase, came to an abrupt end.

For Algeria, as for France during the French Revolution, the period of political reform gave way to a middle state of the conflict, the age of terror. That middle phase of absolute terror in Algeria lasted roughly from 1992 to 1998. As a national drama with international significance, that phase made Algeria stand out as one of the most violent conflicts in contemporary world history, one that did in fact spill over its borders, reaching the US, Canada, Europe, and Southeast Asia. After the 1992 military coup, the unprecedented reforms of the previous three years disappeared behind the carnage of a new generation, if not an altogether new breed, of terrorists and counterterrorists. In this new kind of war, the perpetrators of violence were every bit as brutal as those who fought the war of national liberation had been, each side insisting that they represented the very authenticity of the nation itself. During this middle phase, both at home and abroad, Algeria was known as one of the deadliest countries in the world, with gruesome attacks of violence committed daily by an increasingly internationalizing terrorist network.

Truth be told, the Algerian military – the holders of power through most of the conflict – created the earliest conditions for the terrorism of the middle phase by staging the coup and thwarting the democratic process. It is hardly surprising, given Algeria's own revolutionary heritage and history of violent revolt, that guerrilla forces formed to try to take down the government. While these revolutionaries never had mass support within the country, many different types of terrorist groups emerged, and with vastly different agendas. Some vowed to use violence to restore the political process; others vowed to use violence to end politics altogether and to install a theocratic state; yet, most engaged in a war against the national government, or the "the near enemy," as Fawza A. Gerges has put it.[2]

The terror

This war against "the near enemy" began in earnest in 1992 with the targeting of Algerian state security personnel, but the definition of the enemy changed quickly. Radical Islamists broadened that definition to include writers, French-speakers, unveiled women, female athletes, and a host of other targets. By 1993, a new kind of cultural war began in earnest, claiming the lives of hundreds of prominent intellectuals and forcing tens of thousands of Algeria's intelligentsia into exile throughout France, Europe, and North America. This depletion of talent remains arguably one of the most important and devastating aspects of the events of the 1990s.

As with most violent political conflicts, Algeria's terrible discord during the 1990s has given rise to a range of conflicting interpretations, beginning with the debate over what to call the conflict itself. Some observers, particularly the French, have used the term "civil war" to describe an ongoing, armed conflict between militant Islamists and the state. Algerian officials and others have raised vehement objections to this definition, largely on the grounds that it cedes too much political and moral credibility to the extremists. By and large, this second group has preferred to characterize the conflict not as a civil war but as a "war on civilians" and as one between the forces of order and the terrorist organizations committed to a jihad. There are, of course, many other interpretations to consider, and because this struggle and its interpretation involve an important Muslim-majority state located at the very crossroads of Europe, Africa, and the Middle East, the debate over terminology is hardly an academic dispute: careers, reputations, lives, revolutionary dreams, and political power itself hang in the balance.

Whatever one decides to call it, because the Algerian crisis erupted during the 1990s, just as the Cold War was beginning to fade into the global turmoil of the new decade, Algeria occupied a key space in a shifting geopolitical landscape. Hence, understanding what went wrong in Algeria during those bloody years and how the Algerian government has attempted to exit the killing fields is crucial to understanding the trajectory of contemporary world history. It also has significance for other nations today, especially Iraq and Afghanistan.

A key reason for Algeria's centrality to contemporary world history comes from the fact that it was on track for becoming the first country in the Middle East and North Africa to transition successfully to democratic rule. For this reason, it stands alongside South Africa and perhaps reunified Germany as one of the most dramatic showings of reform in the post-Cold War world. After decades of totalizing, one-party rule, Algeria's political transformation transcended national boundaries. Moreover, for other military governments beset by restless Islamic movements – especially Egypt, Turkey, and Pakistan – the rise of political Islam in North Africa through the democratic process was indeed something to fear. And for those who feared the religious challenges to military regimes, democracy was seen in many ways as the Islamists' Trojan horse. In other words, according to some, Islamists would use the democratic process to subvert democracy itself. As George Joffé notes, the FIS had vowed to replace "popular sovereignty by divine sovereignty."[3] Hence, what happened in Algeria renders it a key frame of reference throughout the Middle East and wider Muslim-majority world.

In addition, because of the conflict's quick escalation, coupled with the internationalization of its terrorists' campaigns, it also became a matter of grave concern for Western governments determined to prevent Algeria's violence from spilling over European borders, into North America and beyond.[4] In this way, Algeria ironically presented many important lessons for those around the world attempting to understand complex terrorist networks well before the 9/11 attacks.

While militants escalated the jihad at home and abroad, the Algerian government was hard-pressed to find its own solution to Islamic terrorism (after it rejected efforts from the international community to intervene in the mid-1990s). As it did so, it also struggled to keep its economy afloat. Unlike other forces, moving the economy forward required a deft grasp of international norms and a willingness of political elites to work with the international community, including the International Monetary Fund (IMF) and a wide array of oil and gas companies. Defying conventional wisdom, terrorism in Algeria did not delay the integration of the Algerian economy into the global market. In fact, during the worst violence in the region, Algeria was able to invest heavily in its hydrocarbon and energy sectors and to encourage an aggressive investment on the part of major international energy firms. Algeria's economy rebounded but economic prosperity, while profiting a select few, has done little to alleviate unemployment and other social ills.

National reconciliation

As Algeria continued to enact important economic liberalization and to work with foreign energy companies to capitalize on the country's nature-given resources, toward the late 1990s it finally began to move away from the military powerbrokers and to work toward a resolution of the violent conflict between radical Islamists and the government. The first step along this path came after the election of Abdelaziz Bouteflika to the presidency in 1999, when Algeria embarked on an experimental and controversial approach to ending the terror. Bouteflika launched Algeria's third phase of contemporary history, the era of national reconciliation. At the same time, and to Bouteflika's credit, he made progress in reducing the military's control over civilian affairs.

While still intent on blocking political Islamists' access to power, Bouteflika called for an extraordinarily controversial amnesty agreement with terrorists. In exchange for laying down their arms, the terrorists' crimes would be absolved, and they would be reintegrated into civil society. Under Bouteflika's 1999 and 2005 amnesty deals, which the public supported, the terrorists neither had to apologize nor face accusers in court. Hoping to end the violence by disallowing any legal action against assailants and murderers, while simultaneously threatening to prosecute anyone who impugned the reputation of state agents by inquiring into the state's "dirty war" against Islamists, Bouteflika's government took one of the most audacious and controversial gambles in history.

As ambitious as Bouteflika's reconciliation program was, it was not enough to convince all terrorist formations to accept the government's peace offerings. In particular, the Groupe Salafiste pour la Prédication et le Combat (GSPC), formed from within the ranks of the dwindling Groupe Islamique Armé (GIA) around the same time that Bouteflika struck his deal with militants. Without an official alliance but with the blessing of al Qaeda and Osama Bin Laden, the GSPC vowed to keep up the fight against the infidel Algerian state but also to clean up the war, by ending the indiscriminate attacks on the Muslim population at large. Nevertheless, the amnesty agreements did proceed while the GSPC began to reorganize the Algerian jihad within a global framework. The GSPC was particularly successful at organizing a vast terrorist network in North America and Europe, especially in England.

Despite its global connections with al Qaeda and other groups, the GSPC might not have been able to pursue its cause of overthrowing Bouteflika's government had it not been for George W. Bush's decision to attack Iraq and Afghanistan in 2003. Prior to that, after the 9/11 attacks, the US and Algeria had sought closer relations: Algeria received military and other security assistance as a key regional partner in the US-declared "War on Terror." However, the American-led invasion and subsequent occupation of Iraq, in particular, galvanized a waning militant Islamist movement and helped to radicalize the disenfranchised Algerian youth. Aware of a possible destabilizing blowback from the Second Gulf War, Bouteflika himself argued openly against the invasion in 2003. Understanding the context and the ferocious disapproval of the American occupation of Iraq throughout the Muslim-majority world, the GSPC stated that it would join forces with al Qaeda, which was determined to attack coalition forces and Western interests.

In spring 2007, the GSPC proclaimed its formal merger with al Qaeda under a new name: Al Qaeda au Maghreb Islamique (AQMI). AQMI followed this announcement with deadly bombing attacks, including one on the prime minister's office in downtown Algiers on April 13 that killed 24 and wounded more than 222 people; another on December 12 that same year, targeting the United Nations headquarters in Algiers, killed 26 and wounded over 170 people, including ten UN staff members. AQMI attacks have continued not only in Algeria but also in Morocco and elsewhere, and its supporters have also been recruited to fight in Afghanistan and Iraq. In turn these developments in Algeria have encouraged the US and other militaries to partner with Algeria and its neighbors in the Sahel in major counter-terrorism initiatives.

With all of this in mind, the purpose of this study is to put the contemporary history of Algeria onto a broad geopolitical canvas. To do this, it is of primary importance to explain the effects of Algeria's domestic politics, including the failure of democratic liberalism and the rise of political Islam and Islamic radicalism, in both the local and global arenas. As we shall see, economic and development concerns, human rights movements, intellectual and cultural issues, domestic and foreign policy, terrorism and military power all become an important part of Algeria's contemporary history. As such, this study is intended for audiences with an interest in Algeria but also for those seeking to understand how domestic and international politics interact within a context as violent as Algeria's. It is therefore hoped that the study will yield key points of comparison for readers investigating the intersection of the post-Cold War and post-9/11 worlds in the contemporary Middle East.

Before embarking upon this analysis of contemporary Algerian history, I think it helpful to ask a series of questions that will be addressed throughout the book. These questions will frame efforts to understand what went tragically wrong in Algeria during the 1990s. For example, was Algeria's struggle for democracy part of a broader wind of change in the late 1980s and early 1990s? Was the creation of an Islamic democracy possible in 1992? If the answer is yes, it is imperative to ask if the quick negation by the military government of the results of a democratic election in which a political Islamist party would have prevailed constituted a profound step backward, not only for Algeria but also for efforts to craft a pragmatic and peaceful political Islam worldwide. Did the struggle that emerged in Algeria during the 1990s and 2000s prefigure the "War on Terror"? Or did it expose the logic of that war as faulty? Does Algeria teach us something about the relationship between religious radicalism and national struggles? Or, to put it differently, should we view the Islamic radicals of Algeria principally through a national lens, or can we see a broader pan-Islamic dimension to the course of political conflict between the military and its religious opponents? Finally, do the dynamics of the "global war on terror" seem plausible in light of the evidence from Algeria?

1 | Building a postcolonial state

On July 5, 1962, Algeria celebrated its independence from France, bringing to an end a violent eight-year war of national liberation. Algerian authorities chose July 5 for its symbolism. It was on that day in 1830 that France commenced its assault on the Ottoman Empire, the rulers who had remained in control of the territory since the 1500s. It would be on that day that Algerians would rejoice at the fact that they had finally rid themselves of the French. The war of independence had begun on November 1, 1954, and the ceasefire agreed to in Evian, France, between Algerian revolutionaries and President Charles de Gaulle's government had been in effect since March 19, 1962. Together the ceasefire and ensuing independence celebrations marked the death of "French Algeria" and the birth of a nation.

The evidence of the slow, painful death and birth in the zero-sum game of decolonization came during the spring and summer of 1962, when roughly one million French settlers fled from Algeria to France in what has remained one of the largest mass exoduses of colonial settlers in world history. Ironically, South Africa's apartheid government, whose image had been severely damaged by the Sharpeville Massacre in March 1960, schemed to convince de Gaulle to divert the movement of some of these ex-colonial refugees to the Republic of South Africa. As the South African ambassador to France R. J. Jordaan put it in a confidential briefing: "Algeria may, therefore, offer South Africa a richer field of potential immigrants, in this next year, than our history will ever again afford. The white settlers of Algeria not only include some of the best and most enterprising stock of France; they also know the realities of Africa and have no illusions about the problems of European survival on the African Continent."[1] Insisting that the "opportunity" to divert as many as 20,000 of these settlers with "high technical skills" and "considerable personal wealth" should not be lost, Ambassador Jordaan advised the creation of "[i]mmigrant selection teams" that would scout out the best and the brightest settlers willing to move to South Africa. Though this proposal came to naught, the ambassador certainly hoped to increase the European count and thus counteract the inevitable wind of change that would topple one colonial government after another across the continent for several decades.

Indeed, what distinguished the Algerian case within the European colonial world and what rendered it especially agonizing among the hard-won anticolonial struggles was the long history of settler colonialism.[2] Indeed, Algeria was unlike any other French possession. It also differed substantially from other forms of European imperialism, such as the English case in India, and more closely resembled the violence of the British experience in Kenya and the Federation of Rhodesia and Nyasaland (which, like Algeria, had a governor general).[3] But Algeria had a much larger European population. By 1954, when the Algerian revolution began on November 1, the European population in Algeria had grown to roughly one million, a far greater number than any of the British cases. These settlers in Algeria lived among eight million locals (nearly all of whom were Muslim, and roughly divided into 80 percent Arabs and 20 percent Berbers, with a small minority of Jews). Each successive French monarch and republic (all four after the French Revolution) made a firm commitment to incorporate and defend overseas Algeria, and by default its European settlers, as integral parts of France and its broader civilizing mission.

The process of "civilizing" Algeria began in 1830 with the military invasion of Ottoman lands and accelerated after Algeria's rival to French authority, the emir Abd el-Kader, finally laid down his sword in 1847, after over a decade of leading the jihad against the French forces.[4] During this conquest phase, French commanders applied such violent scorched-earth and total-war tactics against Algerians that even Alexis de Tocqueville (no friend of Islam), sent to Algeria to investigate French excesses, decried shocking human rights abuses on the floor of the French parliament in 1847.[5] Thereafter, backed by the complete instruments of state and a large military contingent with a reputation for brutality, France experimented with the nuances of settler colonialism, and by mid-century, the Algerian territory was formally divided into three French provinces. This simple fact distinguished it from every other French overseas possession. "Algeria is France," became the oft-repeated saying, which was restated incessantly by French authorities until the ceasefire was signed in March 1962.[6]

Being France and not just French brought to the fore special contradictions in "French Algeria." Most notable was the denial of the basic rights of citizenship to indigenous Algerians. Short on rights but long on special obligations, taxes, restrictions, and duties, Algerians were forced to endure brutal hardships most often at the hands of French settlers, who were in turn protected by the French administration, designed to ensure the de jure subordination of the Muslim population.[7] Hence, by the end of the nineteenth century, France had generated a vibrant and growing settler population by encouraging French peasants and entrepreneurs to migrate there in search of a better life. Naturally, that better life was often built on the backs of Algerians, whose land was systematically confiscated, whose labor was required to build the riches of this new Mediterranean paradise, and whose religion (Islam) was considered a threat to those cherished French "universal" values that spun from the European Enlightenment: progress, reason, and by the end of the nineteenth century, secularism. The European settlers, comprised mostly of French nationals but who included migrant Italians, Spanish, Maltese, and others, came be known collectively as *pieds-noirs* (or black-feet, denoting their peasant status). Industrious and fierce, the powerbrokers of the *pied-noir* community worked in tandem with the pro-settler lobby in metropolitan France during the first half of the twentieth century to ensure that Algerian Muslims would be perpetual second-class citizens, disqualified from the republican ideals that made France "French" in the minds of officialdom and its unofficial propagandists. Unable to accept the one-man, one-vote ideology that republican France had itself come to embrace over time (with French women securing the right to vote in 1945), the European system effectively segregated and discriminated against Algerian "Muslims" until 1962.[8] This pattern of abuse corresponded with similar suppositions of European superiority and native inferiority throughout the continent, from Kenya, to the Federation of Rhodesia and Nyasaland, to South Africa. In short, French oppression in Algeria, like other nations' racist colonial violence, became a way of life, part physical, part ideological, until the quasi-colonial system imploded after sustained armed resistance took definitive shape on November 1, 1954, with the FLN's first attacks on French targets in Algeria.

The FLN, the aftermath, and the state

At Algeria's birth, the Front de Libération Nationale (FLN) and its military wing, the Armée de Libération Nationale (ALN), looked to rebuild a nation whose very existence served as matter of fierce pride and as a beacon to other third-world national liberation movements (including Nelson Mandela's banned African National Congress) which were still in the thick of their own anticolonial wars. But at independence Algerians faced a daunting if not overwhelming task. Because of the ire with which its former settler population greeted Algeria's liberation, Algerians would pay an immediate price with long-term effects. The most trenchant of the French occupiers would not be ushered off the stage without a fight; resorting to sheer paramilitary terror, violent settler groups and break-away French military personnel disillusioned with de Gaulle's "retreatist" approach organized and murdered Algerians and Europeans alike throughout 1961 and 1962, in an orgy of fascistic rage. The most notorious gang of killers, the Organisation Armée Secrète (OAS), murdered thousands of innocents and failed in several assassination attempts against de Gaulle, the man whom it blamed for engineering the end of French rule.[9]

Meanwhile, during the frantic summer of 1962, boats ferried ex-colonials at a rate of some twenty to thirty thousand settlers a day back to a beleaguered and angry mainland France.[10] Totaling near one million, the unwelcome *pieds-noirs* made their way to a largely imaginary homeland, encountering closed and hostile villages and cities. The metropolitan population generally viewed these new arrivals as troublemaking refugees, responsible for defeat in a terrible colonial war and for the deaths of their sons sent to fight in the Algerian graveyard. As soon as Frantz Fanon's "wretched"

Algerians finally inherited this blood-soaked but honorable Mediterranean earth, Europeans began to set it ablaze in the spring and
summer of 1962, blowing up buildings, destroying the vast communications and transportation networks, torching libraries and
incinerating any assets – including grapevines that made fine French
wine – that could not be carried.

In addition to physically rebuilding what the settlers had destroyed on their way out, FLN leaders faced a plethora of internal
and regional political challenges. Of particular concern were the
perceived differences between the Arab and Berber populations
(accentuated by the decision to immediately arabize the nation after
independence) and a nascent conflict with Morocco over the shared
Southern Saharan border.[11] Both the Berber question and the dispute
with Morocco presented important challenges for Algerian leaders,
and both would fester for decades.

Many of the Berbers, largely from Kabylia, rejected the Algerian
state's immediate decision to adopt an "Arab" political platform
and to use Arabic as a prime tool of national unification (a decision
that incidentally mirrors the debate over the use of French to unify
the nation during the French Revolution).[12] The move to arabize the
populations (both Arab and Berber) was spectacular in many ways,
but suggested a political agenda that did not completely map onto
the linguistic and cultural realities of Algeria: both because Algerian
dialectical Arabic did not exist in a standardized written form, and
because there was a sizable Berber population that did not share
the notion of a homogenized Arab identity of the people. Linguis-
tically, there were in fact several variations of Arabic, a fact that
spawned controversies among Arabic specialists over which dialect
(if any) would be better to pursue. More simply, no common Arabic
dictionary existed prior to independence. All Arabic textbooks, and
the language itself, would have to be developed and standardized.
Hence, like the nation itself, Algerian Arabic had to be created and
tooled for specific purposes, but its most immediate purpose was
to replace French as the language of instruction in primary and
secondary schools.

This preference for an invented language that connected to a
broader pan-Arab ideology incensed the Berbers, who made up an

estimated 20 to 25 percent of the population. Berber cultural activists argued that this group had as good a claim as any to being the indigenous population, for after all the Berber people predated, and indeed resisted, the Arab conquest of the seventh century. Reacting against the claims of Algerian postcolonial leaders (many of whom were in fact Kabyle) that national unification required subsuming regional and linguistic diversity into an overarching Algerian identity, which became de facto Arab, pro-Berber politicians rejected the totalizing vision of the nation presented by the FLN, as well as its one-party ideology. As a result, Berber political leaders immediately challenged the emerging postcolonial belief that a single state required forging a single people and a single party. For their part, FLN leaders in 1962 viewed the Berbers' ethnic activists as subversive forces capable of fracturing a fragile postcolonial nation-state, both politically and culturally. As a result, the FLN repressed ethnic activists and arrested Berber leaders. The most noted case was that of Hocine Aït Ahmed, arrested and sentenced to death in 1963 for founding a rival Kabylia-based opposition party known as the Front des Forces Socialistes (FFS), that challenged Ben Bella and the FLN's right to speak of and for all Algerians.[13] In short, arguing that national unification trumped ethnic politics, the FLN persevered with its efforts to forge an authentic Algeria that was part real, part wishful thinking.

Another immediate challenge for the Algerian state came in the form of a border dispute with Morocco often referred to as the "Sands War." The antagonism had its origins in the nineteenth century. However, during and after decolonization (Morocco received independence from France in 1956), the ruling Istiqlal Party and the monarchy of Mohammed V insisted that Morocco's claims on the southern and western part of the Sahara predated the French occupation in 1830, and therefore this territory was rightly part of Greater Morocco. Naturally, the FLN rejected this claim, and in October 1963 Ahmed Ben Bella decided to go to war against Morocco. After brief but bloody fighting, which was followed by the combined efforts of the Arab League and the Organization of African Unity (OAU) to resolve the conflict, a ceasefire came into effect in February 1964. This agreement called for the creation of a demilitarized zone, which did little to abate the intensity of a conflict that would fester for years and which would eventually lead to other disputes between the two countries, most notably the conflict over the Spanish Sahara after Morocco claimed it in 1975.

Confronting postcolonial unknowns

Beside the ongoing politics of the Berber and Moroccan questions, the FLN moved forward aware that although they had defeated the most powerful of European NATO powers (earning them heroic cultural capital for years to come), they still faced many unknowns. For example, exactly what kind of post-revolutionary state would Algeria become? Democratic, secularist, socialist, Arab, or all of the above? How could the fledgling state provide for a population of approximately eight million, of which over two million had been forcibly moved into concentration camps by the French military during decolonization? What kind of political, defense, social, educational, and economic institutions could emerge in such conditions? And what kind of leadership would be required to safely guide this young state through the many difficult choices?

In answering these questions, it is important to recall that Algerian leaders were genuinely inspired by the idea of independence, and wished to make the most of its promises. They also had other models for what the modern postcolonial state apparatus might look like – ranging from Jawaharlal Nehru's India (1947), to Fidel Castro's Cuba (1959), Gamal Abdel Nasser's Egypt (1954), Sukarno's Indonesia (1954), and Kwame Nkrumah's Ghana (1957). Algerians often compared themselves to these other newly emerged nations, but they mostly looked inward and attempted to distill their new sense of identity from their long-fought war against the French and from the colonial and pre-colonial past. Above all, FLN leaders claimed that their party was obliged to remain in firm control in order to prevent independence from being sabotaged by a host of competing internal and external threats. To enforce such control, the FLN used the military might of the ALN (founded by Colonel Houari Boumediene) to grasp the reins of power and tilt the future into its hands.[14] Yet it would be misleading to claim that Algeria immediately after independence evidenced the character of a military state, along the lines established in Egypt by Gamal Abdel Nasser or the many other dictatorships that sprang up in African countries after independence. This is because although the Algerian military was indeed vital to the FLN's political authority, the army's real power lay in its ability to exercise control obliquely. At the same time, the FLN sought to foster a unified national identity and to suppress ethnic (especially Berber) and religious challengers that could undermine this goal.

Despite innumerable physical, political, and cultural hardships, Algerians began to make steady progress and set out on an ambitious political course.

In 1962 Algeria became a member of the United Nations, and Ben Bella flew to New York City to attend the induction ceremonies in October of that year. True to Algeria's ideological convictions that had sustained it throughout decolonization and which brought it to the Bandung Conference in 1955 (when the term "Third World" was coined by nationalists in a collective effort to redefine and unify those states emerging from colonial rule), Algeria announced that it would continue its affiliation with the Non-Aligned Movement, which in turn reaffirmed Algeria's commitment to what Robert Malley and others have called "Third Worldism."[15]

This so-called ideological neutralism was in truth hardly neutral, and led to frequent diplomatic gaffes. Ben Bella's fateful blunders in turn revealed the immediate perils of trying to forge postcolonial foreign policy in the middle of the Cold War. Facing about 70 percent unemployment in Algeria and the tsunami of destruction left in the wake of the French withdrawal, Ben Bella traveled directly from New York to Washington, DC for a meeting with President John F. Kennedy (who, as junior senator, had become in July 1957 the first American politician to discuss Algerian independence).[16] During his visit with Kennedy, Ben Bella requested foreign aid from the US. As an earlier supporter of Algerian rights, Kennedy's government would have obliged had it not been for Ben Bella's next move.

To the dismay of US diplomats, the day after Ben Bella's White House audience he flew directly to Havana for a two-day meeting with Fidel Castro. This was perhaps logical, given that the first of Cuba's many forays into African politics came in the form of military aid in January 1962 to Algeria for its war against the French – assistance to which Kennedy had not been privy.[17] However, the visit was viewed as both brash and naïve in Washington, and not just as a case of poor timing and bad judgment. As it happened, the day Ben Bella landed in Havana was the very day that the CIA informed National Security Advisor McGeorge Bundy of the U-2 reconnaissance photographs detailing the existence of the Soviet missiles in Cuba. Eager to placate fellow third-worlders, Ben Bella also endorsed Castro's claim to the American naval base at Guantánamo. On October 22, President Kennedy went on live television to inform citizens that the US was on the brink of a nuclear war with the Soviets in Cuba (who had over 40,000 Soviet soldiers and 20 nuclear warheads already on the island). Unsurprisingly, that same week the US State Department informed the Agency for International Development that it was suspending all economic assistance to Algeria. Hence, Ben Bella's first efforts at real international diplomacy had ended in abject failure and ended up unnecessarily turning the US against Algeria, thereby isolating it from the financial aid necessary for reconstruction and pushing it more strongly into the socialist bloc, despite its declarations of non-alignment.

Internally, by April 1963, Ben Bella had decided to consolidate his control over the government. In doing so, he moved Algeria definitively in the direction of a single-party state ruled exclusively by the FLN. In September he was elected president for a first five-year term. With this he now controlled all reins of power, as commander in chief of the armed forces, secretary general of the FLN, and president of the republic. Ben Bella's Algeria exercised the heavy hand of state control, and he expelled political opponents, arrested others, and used the Algerian police to crush political dissent.

Houari Boumediene and the planned state

Discontentment soon reached new heights when one of Ben Bella's inside supporters, Houari Boumediene, successfully carried out Algeria's first postcolonial coup d'état in 1965. In perhaps one of the greatest ironies, this coup occurred while Gillo Pontecorvo was shooting his famous *Battle of Algiers* on location. Hence, just as Pontecorvo sought to immortalize Algerian guerrilla fighters and create a fictionalized depiction of the French commander responsible for crushing the FLN in Algiers, Colonel Mathieu (a composite of General Jacques Massu and Colonel Bigeard), Boumediene's men quietly took control over all of the major sites of power. Ben Bella's deep suspicion of others, his own authoritarian approach, and his inability to convert the FLN into a mass party meant that when Boumediene struck, Ben Bella had virtually no support.[18] In other words, an important page had already turned on independent Algeria even before it could be captured by the Italian director in the film that would become the very synonym of the French–Algerian war for millions of viewers.

Boumediene, who ruled from June 19, 1965, to his premature death from a rare disease on December 27, 1978, has remained a controversial political figure in Algerian history, and analyses of his actions fall largely into two camps: supporters and detractors. Boumediene's supporters argue that only his strong and uncompromising (albeit authoritarian) political leadership could have pulled Algeria from the economic chaos into which Ben Bella's quixotic tactics had plunged the country after independence. Pointing to a swift national turn-around, his supporters thus contend that Boumediene rapidly accelerated Algeria's rate of growth, especially in key economic sectors, including major construction projects, education, health care, and other basic societal needs. He was able to do this by seizing even more power and by pushing Algeria onto a strongly state-centered socialist path, in which the nationalization of industries and economic activity as well as of religious programs came into play. Supporters, especially secularists, argue that it was only through this rigid control that massive industrial progress was achieved, and that Boumediene's control over the nation's mosques and religious institutions kept the Islamists under control.

Boumediene's detractors, on the other hand, have insisted that his autocratic and dictatorial politics undermined Algerian society and ultimately led the country directly into the political meltdown of the 1990s.[19] They also point out that Boumediene ended the free press, increased censorship, mercilessly persecuted his political opponents by jailing and even torturing them, and forced many others into prolonged periods of exile.[20] Along this line, his critics suggest that such brutal tactics ended any pretense of democratic reform in Algeria for decades, and therefore opened the country up to mercurial internal challengers that separated Algeria from the seeming stability of its North African neighbors in the 1990s.

Boumediene, the economy, and society

In terms of basic economic and sociocultural questions, most commentators consider Algeria's rapid transformation after the 1965 coup astonishing. Considering the uphill battle that Algerians faced, many of Boumediene's achievements are impressive. The most critical years of dramatic growth were from 1968 to the mid-1970s. At the core of Boumediene's strategy were two successive four-year plans (1970–73 and 1973–77) that focused primarily on industrial growth. During these years, Boumediene's Algeria enjoyed unprecedented economic development in specific areas, such as heavy industries, construction, mining, and hydrocarbons. At the same time, the agricultural sector deteriorated to the point that it would soon become Algeria's Achilles' heel. Boumediene's neglect of agriculture is explained by his ideological commitment to a planned industrial-based economy.

To make matters worse, the phenomenon of urbanization, which had begun before decolonization but accelerated during that era, completely and literally transformed the Algerian landscape. Between 1930 and 1960, the urban population rose from 500,000 to over 2 million.[21] During decolonization an estimated 2 million peasants (out of 8.5 million) were forcibly removed from villages and placed in what the French euphemistically called "regrouping camps." And these large concentration camps, located at the edge of urban centers, eventually became permanent sites of relocation for millions who would never return to their rural ancestral villages and thus accelerated losses to the agricultural sector.

To accommodate the social turmoil caused by French-induced urbanization, Algerian leaders needed a bold plan. President Boumediene believed that industry and not agriculture was the way for Algeria to enter into a new era of economic self-reliance, but his economic social planning effectively implemented the near-total destruction of agriculture in a country that during the Ottoman and colonial eras, had been one of the most fertile regions in the world. He collectivized the agricultural sectors and replaced most of the experienced farmers with unskilled and ill-equipped workers. Coinciding as it did with a staggering rise in the population (fueled by sudden urbanization), the depletion of Algeria's agricultural resources created catastrophic conditions: chronic food shortages, higher prices for staple goods, a growing reliance on imported foodstuffs, and a thriving black market.

Insufficient non-industrial investment by the postcolonial state throughout the 1960s and 1970s meant that critical elements of Algerian society were constantly underfunded. This included not only agriculture but also other vital sectors such as fishing, water, transportation, and housing. The neglect of these critical elements created "intractable problems in all social fields" and was partly responsible for the immense "cross-Mediterranean labor migration." Added to the demographic impact of urbanization and the population explosion, Algeria quickly fell behind in meeting basic needs, such as housing. Indeed, by 1982 an FLN document estimated that the government was already behind on no fewer than 2 million housing units.[22] Ironically, whereas in most segments of public life the state maintained a firm grip, in the public health sector it lost control over doctors and over the dispersion of medical resources. The FLN increasingly let doctors move into private practice and relocate from rural areas to the urban centers. And, consistent with the emphasis on infrastructure, Boumediene concentrated on building medical facilities in larger urban centers, which meant that doctors, like much of the population, were drawn away from villages and smaller communities.

The key to Boumediene's program was the decision to invest heavily in the county's oil and gas industries. Algeria's reliance on its chief export, oil, was a relatively new phenomenon.[23] After an initial period of cooperation, which saw the expansion of French companies, the Algerian government created its own nationalized oil company, Sonatrach, in December 1963. In 1963, Algeria also nationalized Air Algérie, the airline, among other industries. Under Ben Bella's leadership, Belaïd Abdessalam founded Sonatrach and ran it until 1965, after which he served as minister of industry and energy, from 1965 to 1978. First with Ben Bella then with Boumediene, Abdessalam helped set in motion the plans to overcome the colonial legacy by building a vibrant industrial base and to tackle the bigger social socio-economic problems before the oil, gas, and other natural reserves ran out.[24]

With these pressures in mind, the thrust of Ben Bella's agenda was to renegotiate hydrocarbons agreements with France and other relevant countries, and restructure investments in Algeria's favor. After seizing power, Boumediene pursued a similar strategy: one of his most enduring actions was to align Algeria with the Organization of Petroleum Exporting Countries (OPEC, created in 1960), which would use oil to recast the traditional North–South Cold War power relations. OPEC members had encouraged Algeria to join them after independence, but previous commitments to relationships with those French companies that pumped oil and gas out of the ground (which Algeria would refine) stood in the way. This changed when Sid Ahmed Ghozali, the then director of Sonatrach, brought Algeria into OPEC in July 1969.

The decision to join OPEC was accompanied with the gradual nationalization of the oil and gas sectors, a process that relieved the non-Algerian energy companies of their assets in 1971. The nationalization of oil and gas was part of a larger nationalist agenda that placed a premium on securing a state monopoly over all segments of the economy and the polity. For example, between May and June 1968, 45 foreign firms, employing more than 7,500 industrial workers, were nationalized; by 1969, only 20 of the roughly 750 French companies in existence during the colonial period were still controlled by their original owners.[25] In that year, the Sinclair Oil Company's assets were nationalized and British and American oil companies were absorbed by the growing Algerian state.

As Algeria continued to extend state control over the energy sectors throughout the 1970s, oil and gas revenues gradually became the mainstay of the regime. An imperfect example of a "rentier state," which generally derives its wealth either from commodities such as oil and gas sold in the global marketplace, or from foreign loans, the Algerian case was particular. This is because, although it was "vulnerable to external shocks," its energy production gave it more "staying power in the 1990s than many expected." Moreover,

Algeria's rents in the 1990s only provided it with a $350 per capita income from oil and gas, unlike its OPEC partner, Saudi Arabia, which claimed approximately $5,000 per capita. That meant that Algeria could not depend solely on its energy sector. [26]

With more demands being placed on the state and with more educated citizens expecting to find employment, the burdens on the state soon outweighed its own rent-produced resources. Part of the problem was generated by the Boumediene-era technocrats' unyielding ideological commitment to keep foreign investors out of the newly created monopoly. This "go-it-alone" policy was Sonatrach's guiding principle throughout the 1970s and 1980s.[27] Unfortunately, it translated into serious problems because Algeria had neither the skills nor the resources to fully exploit the oil and gas reserves, and, equally important, it could not properly maintain the equipment it did have. As a result, exploration and development continued to decline well into the Chadli Benjedid era (1979–92).

With such important natural reserves, oil and gas production quickly became the driving force of the Algerian economy and therefore vital for the government's own stability. Energy became more important after American and British "downstream" interests in Algerian industries were nationalized in May 1968, after Algeria joined OPEC in July 1969, and after the French interests were nationalized in February 1971. Oil became more political after the Arab–Israeli war of 1973, which triggered Algeria's decision to accept the ban on oil exports to nations that supported Israel. The government's reliance on the energy sector, however, came as a mixed blessing, and by the 1980s hydrocarbons accounted for roughly 95 percent of total exports and 60 percent of all government spending.[28]

Algeria played an increasingly active role in OPEC, and exercised greater influence on the international stage. Evidence of this can be seen in Boumediene's April 1974 address to the United Nations General Assembly, in which he laid out the tenets of what he called the "new economic world order" – decades before George Bush coined a rather different "new world order" during the First Gulf War. The basic themes Boumediene sounded out at the UN were the same he had applied to his own national agenda, which could be called advanced industrial secularism and which translated into greater control of national resources, industrialization and economic growth, nationalization and distribution of wealth, commitment to building projects and education, and a determination to have the wealthier nations extend greater debt relief to the developing ones. Boumediene delivered this speech not only as the president of Algeria, but also as the sitting president of the Non-Aligned Movement.[29] Moreover, as greater evidence of Algeria's stature in the world community, in 1974 Abdelaziz Bouteflika was appointed president of the UN General Assembly.

Before his death, Boumediene was able to leave a lasting imprint on the country and by the mid-1970s had moved Algeria into a strong state-centered socialist model. His continued advocacy of socialism in the third world eventually led the French intelligence services in 1975 to ask their American counterparts in the CIA to assess the effects of assassinating Boumediene, in order to prevent Algeria from ascending in world politics. The CIA's fear was that Boumediene's influence on the world stage was leading to an expansion of the socialist model throughout the developing world. However, after assessing the situation in Algeria and elsewhere, the CIA determined that it was already too late, because Boumediene had already firmly planted the pillars of the Algerian socialist state: any political replacement would merely continue on the same course.[30]

The following year, aware of possible threats from the outside, Boumediene's 1976 National Charter, adopted by a national referendum in June, put official emphasis on the Algerian socialist model in the realm of industrialization, restated the bond between the FLN party and the state, and reconfirmed Algeria's commitment to the hydrocarbon sector. The National Charter was followed by the November referendum on a new constitution, also adopted overwhelmingly by Algerians. The 1976 constitution secured Islam's place as the official religion, the republican model as the mode of government, and basic rights of freedom of expression; it also guaranteed women's status as citizens, with equal rights and responsibilities under the republic.

The 1976 constitution would soon find itself challenged in several areas. While Algeria's rising status in the third world, leadership role in the Non-Aligned Movement, new constitution, and position in OPEC, all placed the country favorably at the center of world politics, these factors did little to avert the impending crisis at home. In fact, the wealth generated by oil and gas production only masked the mounting social and economic problems left unresolved by Boumediene's political agendas. In particular, Boumediene's greatest shortcoming was to see industrialization as the panacea for Algeria's troubles.

In addition to ideological issues, the unresolved social concerns presented the state with perpetual challenges. In particular, Algeria continually confronted the strains of urbanization.[31] The demographic trend, which quickly increased the size of urban centers, would continue, and along with it came a significant rise in the birthrate in Algeria. By the mid-eighties the population numbered approximately 23 million, up from approximately 8 million at independence in 1962. Growing at a rate unmatched by the state's infrastructure and agricultural resources, the rising population continued to put pressure on the economy. With chronic unemployment, many Algerians began to look for work outside the country. For most, this meant looking for work in France (as they had been encouraged to do by France since the First World War, in increasing numbers).[32]

Chadli Bendjedid and liberalization

The commonly accepted argument, and I think the correct one, about contemporary Algerian history is that if Algeria had developed a stronger industrial base, and not used its hydrocarbon revenues to prop up a failing socialist industrial experiment during the Boumediene era, it might have been better able to weather the storm brought by the 1986 oil crisis. As it was, the idealism of the Boumediene era began to unravel quickly under the rule of his successor, Colonel Chadli Bendjedid, who was acting defense minister at the time when he took over as president in January 1979. Chadli found himself confronting mounting social and economic strains, particularly those caused by Boumediene's inability to create new jobs within the Algerian economy, and by a growing conservative religious movement.

In June 1986 the world oil markets crashed, and Chadli was at a loss for a solution. Algeria's economy went into a tailspin from which it would take over a decade to begin to recover. Algeria was particularly hard hit, because, prior to the 1986 oil crisis, the festering socio-economic problems had largely been concealed by fast-pace rises in oil and gas profits and by increasing reliance on foreign loans. Then, overnight, the ceiling fell on the world's oil prices, bringing the price of oil to below $10 per barrel and with it Algeria's economy to a grinding halt. The sudden decline in oil prices reduced Algeria's profits from exports of hydrocarbons to $7.3 billion, down from the highpoint of $14.2 billion in 1981.[33] With over 60 percent of total government revenues and 95 percent of all export revenue coming from the hydrocarbon industry, the FLN's ruling elite could no longer hide the sheer magnitude of the problems facing the country.[34] In the face of a rapidly growing and massively discontented population, the 1986 oil crisis crippled the old regime, leaving it to hobble uncomprehendingly into the violent confrontations of October 1988.

As we have seen, the population had already risen from roughly 8 million at independence in 1962 to approximately 23 million by the mid-late 1980s (it would soar to over 33 million by 2008). With this surge in the population came increasing pressures on the economy, including unprecedented demands for housing, education, and relevant social services such as unemployment relief and medical care.

Algeria's one resource, its hydrocarbon industry, was confronting its own self-generated problems. After the 1986 oil crisis, reinvesting in energy became more complex because of the other pressing social and economic strains on the country. In 1986, Chadli's energy minister, Nordine Aït-Laoussine, openly admitted that the FLN's policies had harmed the energy sector (and by implication any state plans) and that it was time to rethink Algeria's relationship with foreign companies. As he said, "we recognize that we lack the financial means and we do not have the sort of technical and human resources required to fulfill our ambitious plan."[35] A clarion call for increased cooperation between Algeria and foreign partners, Aït-Laoussine's statement and subsequent proposals represented an important sea change for Algeria's approach to energy policy. The minister pushed for and got a new hydrocarbon law in 1986 that reduced taxes on foreign companies, and made it easier for foreign companies to recuperate expenses on gas finds; previously, any gas finds were automatically appropriated by the Algerian state without compensation.[36] But more change was still needed to encourage significant foreign partnership in Algerian oil and gas exploration and processing.

In order to deal with the economic troubles caused by the inefficient socialist industrial model, Chadli began to liberalize the economy. Like Mikhail Gorbachev would do just a few years later within the Soviet Union, Chadli attempted to reform the state-engineered economy in an effort to keep the overall political system and ideology intact. Nevertheless, since only 27 percent of Algeria's industrial workforce was in the private sector, Chadli faced enormous challenges.[37] Jobs continued to lag far behind the soaring population, and housing shortages had become a permanent fixture of Algerian society.

The rise of political Islam

Meanwhile, a growing and restless Islamic activist movement continued to press for its own agenda. It antecedents went back centuries, and materialized during the era of French colonial rule in the form of the Association of Muslim Algerian Oulemas (a group of respected religious leaders with diverse academic and political views of the role of Islam founded by Abdelhamid Ben Badis in 1931). Algerian Islamists had long distrusted Western-inspired secularism and liberal parliamentarism: the French parliament had, after all, stripped Algerian Muslims of their civil rights and imposed extraordinary civil obligations on them. This democratic discrimination led directly to the revolution in 1954, as well as to an understandable, though often pathological, urge to keep foreign influences out of the nation after independence. For many advocates of political Islam, the Algerian state had failed to free Muslims from Western influence, and this secular state within the Muslim world remained a symbol of the West's persistent negative influence. Hence, inspired by the perceived success of the 1979 revolution in Iran, by the teachings of Hassan Al Banna and Sayyid Qutib (both considered martyrs and instrumental leaders of the Muslim Brotherhood in Egypt), as well as by Algerian religious thinkers such as Abdelhamid Ben Badis and later Malek Bennabi, Algerian Islamists developed a clearly articulated critique of both European colonialism and postcolonial secularism.[38]

By the 1970s, Islamists had grown tired of being kept at arm's length by the secular state and were beginning to organize within the universities and underground. By the late 1970s and early 1980s, they were mobilizing against specific aspects of secular society and began to argue for the implementation of shari'a (Islamic law). In 1979, year of the Iranian Revolution, Mustapha Bouyali (born in 1940 and veteran of the war of independence) marshaled followers behind a movement bent on convincing the government (perceived to be weakened following Boumediene's death) to adopt a pro-Islamist agenda. After meeting opposition from the FLN and after his brother was killed by Algerian authorities in April 1982, Bouyali led a militant movement known as the Algerian Islamic Armed Movement from 1982 to 1987 in direct and sustained attacks against security forces. Bouyali was eventually killed during a confrontation with authorities in February 1987.

Militant challenges aside, in 1984 political Islamists claimed a major victory when the National Popular Assembly approved the controversial Family Code. This represented a major concession to the Islamists, and a catastrophic blow for women's rights. It essentially denied women the full rights of citizenship guaranteed them by the 1976 constitution. Under this law, Muslim women were forbidden from marrying non-Muslim men (though the reverse was not true), and other aspects of the Family Code effectively rendered women minors. For example, it required male supervision for women while traveling and affected divorce and inheritance law. The regressive Family Code in turn encouraged Islamists to lobby more forcefully still for the nation-wide application of shari'a law.

On another front, while women's rights activists resented the 1984 family law, the 1976 Charter (which reasserted the primacy of Arabic and passed under Boumediene's administration) alienated Algerian Berbers and Francophones. At once cultural and linguistic, the Berber question highlighted the debate over Tamazight, the principal Berber language, and unhappiness with the Arabophone policies. This came to a head in March 1980, after one of Algeria's great Berber poets and writers, Mouloud Mammeri, was prohibited from delivering his planned speech about the Berbers and their language at the University of Tizi-Ouzou. Incensed Berber students took over the campus, and the Algerian state responded with over-whelming violence. The riots and the state response, known as the Berber Spring, brought the cultural intolerance of the Algerian state into full view and raised grave questions about the future of minority rights.

By the 1980s, first with the Berber Spring and then with the 1984 Family Code, the post-revolutionary ideal of Algeria as a tolerant, secular society began to weaken. On the one hand, nationalist hard-liners from within the FLN prevented an open discussion of the Berber question; on the other hand, Islamists grew emboldened by their success with the Family Code.[39] Defensive and conserva-tive instincts thus acted in unison to undermine the progressive foundations of postcolonial civil society. As the Cold War wound down and the world oil-driven economy suddenly melted down in 1986 with the collapse of the world oil market and the OPEC crisis, Algeria's over-reliance on the energy sector added to the domestic chaos and initiated a free-fall that led directly to the political crises of the early 1990s.

2 | The road to reform

In October 1988, Algeria's ongoing political, social, and economic malaise overwhelmed the state after youthful demonstrators took to the streets in nearly two weeks of massive but spontaneous public outcries against President Chadli Bendjedid's unpopular regime. The October riots were the largest popular protests in Algeria since 1962, and they had a devastating effect. With hundreds of thousands of protesters on the move in the country's major urban centers, the government found itself outflanked by citizens clamoring for immediate, dramatic change. Suddenly, within a period of weeks – after years of corruption, political stagnation, and failed economic policies – Algeria's political elite found itself unable to stave off popular rejection of the postcolonial status quo. Unaccustomed to such public opposition, the FLN and the postcolonial state stumbled into the future with no clear idea of what it held. However, it would be an understatement to say that no one could have predicted that within three years the FLN would be defeated by political Islamists in the country's first open national elections.

The crisis of 1988

To be sure, President Chadli had himself anticipated some sort of imminent fiscal crisis, and this fear had triggered his earlier calls for economic liberalization. Yet neither he nor the FLN leaders had fully appreciated the depth of the public rage against the regime. As a result, when people began to take to the streets in October, the government resorted to the one and only force it could use to restore order: the military. Ultimately, however, it was this fateful decision that ended the FLN's political legitimacy in Algeria. October 1988 thus marks the definitive and historic turning point, one with clear similarities to events in other troubled states the world over at the end of the Cold War.

Yet, the Algerian protesters anticipated by a year the worldwide rejection of autocratic and socialist states. Until the 1980s, the FLN, like other rulers of one-party states, had managed to keep the population at bay through systematic censorship, state-sponsored oppression, and a security apparatus that employed outright (though seldom talked about in Algeria) brutality, including torture.[1] Moreover, while the government's reaction to the October events seemed to mimic other states' reactions to popular manifestations in China, South Africa, and elsewhere, the Algerian political elite unwittingly created a climate that ensured its own swift demise by asking the military led by General Khaled Nezzar (minister of defense and veteran of the war of liberation) to keep the peace. This decision to resort to the military was not inconsistent with the prevailing logic guiding other threatened governments at the end of the Cold War; nor was it out of step with the history of over-dependence on the military in Algeria. Nevertheless, unlike the 1989 protests in China (which were decisively put down by a far superior military and state) or in Eastern Europe (which successfully toppled the old socialist regimes), it essentially meant crossing a political Rubicon without knowing how to swim. As a result, neither the Algerian state nor the military would ever be able to reverse the gravitational pull of absolute power or fully regain the public trust.

To be sure, there had been previous disturbances in Algeria when the police had met rioters with arrests and even heavy violence (as in the case of Kabylia in 1980), but nothing had occurred on the scale of the October 1988 riots, and nothing had produced such tragic results. After some two weeks of rioting, Algerians counted over 500 deaths and thousands of wounded civilians. The street killings of unarmed civilians eroded what little sympathy remained for the old guard's probity, and merely amplified the undaunted, unstoppable cries for change.[2]

In reality, in the years leading up to the 1988 riots, the Algerian state was not in a position to help its citizens escape from the net effect of decades of mismanagement and failed socialist planning, nor was the military willing to make any concessions that might compromise its considerable political power. The state's technocrats and political elites had by then already mortgaged the nation's economic system, and saw no way out of the profound chaos into which the government's economic and social policies had plunged the country.[3] Hence when the labor and youth movements began to surge in October, the Algerian state's cumulative socio-economic and political failures could no longer be hidden from the public, especially after the full consequences of the 1986 collapse of the world oil market hit Algeria two years later. Unable to assist a growing and desperate population on virtually any level, the state was forced to enact dramatic cutbacks in daily provision, compounding the austerity measures imposed in 1986 and fully effective in 1988. Government support for basic goods simply disappeared. Food prices soared, a black market flourished, the already chronic housing shortage grew worse, and unemployment overwhelmed an already battered population. With over 60 percent of the country's nearly 30 million people now below the age of 20, with official unemployment numbers climbing to around 30 percent, and with a generalized perception that government officials continued to fleece the state's coffers, the October demonstrators were in no mood for compromise.[4]

Beginning largely as a labor strike in Algiers, the unrest quickly spread to other major urban centers and engulfed civil society. As riots spread, the dynamics of mobilization shifted. Labor and economic concerns rapidly gave way to a spirit of sweeping reform. At the same time, political Islamist movements, which had been waiting for such an opportunity, quickly understood that substantial ground could be gained if groups with radically different objectives and orientations challenged the state from all sides simultaneously.

Observing the degree to which public opposition sided with them against the old regime, the Islamists quickly gauged their response and mobilized their greatest asset: the Algerian masses. But while they were consistently critical of the FLN, they were far from unanimous in other respects. Some leaders proposed a cautious approach; others favored a swift assault on the weakened state. After years of paying the price for directly challenging the state under the direction of Islamic leaders, Algerian Islamists had good reason to assess the state's strength before confronting it publicly. They did not want to suffer the same fate as their precursors. Nevertheless, the conditions favored political Islamists moving quickly into the breach created largely by the labor and youth protestors. Ironically, not even the leading Islamists could have anticipated their movement's political successes as they organized around the protests initiated by the youth and labor movements. Within a matter of days, Islamists understood that they could use the momentum created originally by street protesters – many of whom pursued antithetical political objectives – and benefit from a full-blown, multi-pronged campaign against the Algerian state.

Starting on October 7, Islamists arranged a peaceful march in central Algiers, drawing over 6,000 supporters led mainly by veteran Islamists Ahmed Sahnoun and Abassi Madani. Sahnoun (born in 1907) was by then one of Algeria's most respected Islamists, with ties to Abdelhamid Ibn Badis, and a member of the Association of Algerian Oulemas. Madani (born in 1931), like Sahnoun, had been active in the FLN during decolonization and had remained a strong opponent of secularism after independence. Madani's opposition to Boumediene's policies led to his decision to go into exile during the 1970s. Amnestied by the state, he returned to teach at the University of Algiers. Following the state's crackdown on Islamists at the University in 1982, Madani signed a statement with Sahnoun and Abdellitif Soltani (born in 1904) criticizing the state's persecution of Islamists and its secularist ideology. All three were placed under house arrest in 1982. Madani had made it clear that he rejected the growing freedoms of women in society, and called for greater restrictions to be placed on them. Soltani died in 1984, the same year that Sahnoun and Madani were released. Harboring no illusions about the state, Algeria's Islamists were nevertheless shocked when the military opened fire and killed approximately 50 unarmed marchers in October 1988.[5] Because the Islamists were the first among the groups of protesters to be killed, they won broad sympathy from the general population outraged by the state's excessive use of force. Up to that point, the older generation of Islamists had been arguing for caution, for measuring their strength before they openly announced their plans; but now the slaughter of religious protesters galvanized a wide array of political Islamists, and helped mold them into a more unified and aggressive front. As this process unfolded throughout the month, the stature of the Islamists increased, partly because they now evidenced a desire to act alongside others against the state, and to hold it accountable for its recent massacre of civilians.

After considerable internal debate about what the Islamists' next move ought to be, the much younger Ali Belhadj (born in 1956) – a former Arabic teacher and fiery imam at a mosque in the Bab el-Oued section of the capital's Casbah, imprisoned between 1983 and 1987 for his Islamic activism – succeeded in organizing a larger show of force in the streets of Algiers on October 10. With an estimated 20,000 men marching with him and despite the objections of more moderate imams, including Madani, Belhadj led his followers directly into a confrontation during which another 30 Islamists were killed by General Nezzar's men.

As an overall result of the fortnight's unrest, an estimated 500 demonstrators (many though not all of whom were Islamists) had been killed, and thousands were injured and arrested. Asked later about the incidents and the military's use of overwhelming force, General Nezzar made no apologies and later described the shootings as accidental, with untrained men firing randomly at the crowds sometimes "in the air," sometimes "at the ground."[6] As "accidental" as these killings were in the eyes of their perpetrators, there was nothing accidental about the marchers' activities; they clearly signaled a rejection of the FLN's authority, and consequently several party offices were ransacked and destroyed, as were many other random shops. With a curfew imposed and a state of siege declared, the government sought an immediate solution.

Co-opting the Islamists

Unintended or not, first the killing of protesters and then the immediate attempts to dialogue with leading Islamists altered both the reality and public perception of state and Islamist power. What began as a series of marches rooted in youth and labor movements became, in the eyes of Chadli, an opportunity to subvert the political momentum of the unrest by channeling it into the hands of the leaders of political Islam, whom he thought he could both cultivate and control. Playing this game without fully understanding which cards were in the deck (and how much the general population had come to despise the regime), Chadli invited several principal Islamist leaders to meet with him in person.[7]

Chadli believed that he could salvage the regime by bringing the Islamists on board as a partner. Whether or not he believed in sharing power with them remains open to interpretation – especially since political Islam was still a force being shaped in a context in which the FLN had yet to yield to political rivals, let alone brook opposition. That said, Chadli could not predict the future, and his decision to dialogue with Islamists in October was at the very least a political risk. At the same time, it must be remembered that he had already made important concessions to religious leaders throughout his presidency, as evidenced by the controversial 1984 Family Code. By negotiating with them in the midst of the crisis and granting even more concessions, he hoped to quell the street disturbances.

Chadli misjudged the situation. His decision to dialogue with Islamists pushed them more directly into the spotlight. The move also eclipsed the substantial labor, youth, and women's movements present on the streets in October, forces that shared a common desire to maintain the secular orientation of the state and a common rejection of the ideology of conservative Islam. Perhaps most important, Chadli's decision made it appear as if the political Islamists had been the prime movers behind the spontaneous October protests, and gave Islamists the high ground just as the FLN began to sink without any viable lifeline.

The short career of the Algerian *glasnost*

On October 10, Chadli announced his intention to hold a nationwide referendum on the 1976 constitution, as a preamble to the creation of a new constitution that established broad and expansive freedoms. More state power would be concentrated in the hands of the Algerian parliament, a move intended to decentralize power. About two weeks later, Chadli unveiled a vast plan to liberalize the state's political institutions. This proposal called for the formation of political opposition groups and represented North Africa's first version of *glasnost*, comparable to the reforms that would spread throughout Eastern Europe in the following year. Chadli's proposals clearly undermined the FLN's unequivocal authority, and by the time the party realized the extent of public impatience with its rule, it was too weak to defend itself. Hence, within weeks of the October riots, the apparatus of the postcolonial state (with the exception of the armed forces) had begun to crumble.

In many ways, Algeria's exit from the Cold War era resembled the same kind of disorienting push for change that Eastern Europe, China, the Balkans, and countries from the former Soviet Union felt. Stagnant economic conditions, difficult transitions to free-market capitalism, calls for the swift adoption of liberal, multi-party, democratic rule were all common concerns that heavily regulated socialist systems faced at the end of the 1980s. At the same time, Algeria's unique position in North Africa and the Arab world distinguished it from other states in the Middle East because the Algerian state, unlike many of its neighbors, was by 1988 no longer able to sustain its anti-democratic political system. This was not the case in Egypt, Libya, Morocco, or Tunisia. Nor could Algeria's prevarication hide the realities of its socio-economic chaos. The street demonstrations had made this impossible. Hence, in contrast to China, whose state apparatus quickly cracked down on the dissidents of the Tiananmen Square movement in April 1989, in full view of the international media, Algeria's predicament resembled the developments in the former Soviet Union in that the ruling party, at least in theory, immediately collapsed. And, for the next three years, as the military elite worked behind the scenes to re-establish the postcolonial status quo at the expense of the political elite, it seemed on the surface that liberalization would yield a true balance of power and ensure a permanent place for democratic governance.

Part of the problem for Chadli and the FLN in 1988 was that both failed to appreciate how the calls for economic liberalization would transform the political arena. Another problem was that the government did not have a tidy strategy for dealing with the Islamist challenges, nor did it enjoy the full support of the military as it planned its next steps. Moreover, as one prominent scholar of Algeria, John Entelis, has put it, there was also "a conflict among elites in power," in which "one segment was using the Islamists as a way by which to challenge the position of hardliners in the military."[8] From this angle, the FLN's goal would have been to weaken the military's power by introducing elections.

Like Egypt, Libya, Tunisia, Morocco, Turkey, and other predominately Muslim countries such as Pakistan, Algeria had long struggled to corral political Islam and to keep the state apparatus firmly in control of religious reformers.[9] At the same time, by 1988 and 1989, Algeria's Islamists believed that they could enter into and benefit from a democratic framework. This, in itself, represented a massive development within the region. In going the route of democratic mobilization, Algeria's Islamists were important regional and international trendsetters, and their decision to embrace the democratic process caught the attention of the entire Muslim-majority world. That Algerian Islamists entered the political process with enthusiasm also sent important messages to Western observers, who watched developments in Algeria with great attention.

Before political Islamists and the Algerian state deadlocked in what would become one of the world's most violent and relentless conflicts of the 1990s, and before the First Gulf War disrupted the democratic process, the Algerian *glasnost* would go forward with unimaginable alacrity. Internally, the sudden political thaw generated a sense of optimism among the Algerian intelligentsia and a genuine belief that the transformation of civil society could finally proceed. Indeed, it was a time when the conditions for the possibility of a more pluralistic system had emerged, as evidenced by the fact that state censors had given way to the pressures of serious critical and oppositional writing, and calls for unprecedented press freedoms. Unfortunately, as was the case for Czech intellectuals such as Václav Havel during the Prague Spring in 1968, these new freedoms would also trigger harsh punishments for those who came forward to identify themselves as critics of the regime.[10] The same held true for aggressive Islamists bent on replacing the republic with a theocracy, who wrongly believed that the democratic opening had created a protected space from which they could safely preach their anti-democratic platform. Nevertheless, as the Cold War's ice began to break away and release the country from the FLN's frozen nationalist ideology, hundreds of Algerian journalists and intellectuals, as well as religious figures, engaged this new era with optimistic enthusiasm.

But few did so naïvely: it was understood that Algerian society could not be transformed without the government's willingness to respect human rights. As Anouar Benmalek, a journalist writing for the Algiers newspaper *Algérie-Actualité*, put it in an open letter to President Chadli on November 3, 1989:

> To live as a republic requires at the minimum a contract of confidence between the state and citizens. Torture is an extreme rupture of this contract. Know that one can be tortured for thinking differently; know that those responsible for this torture will continue to carry out their business, either at the old jobs or at new ones. This is what keeps all of us hostages in the grip of barbarism.[11]

The fact that the practice of torture could be criticized so openly, in a major newspaper, demonstrates that for a brief period the state lost its totalizing powers of censorship. But it also indicates that Algerians maintained no illusions about the difficulty of establishing a human rights agenda and of erasing torture from the state's political lexicon – despite the state's official denials and its own constitution forbidding it.[12] For the first time in a generation, writers inside Algeria were openly accusing the state of malfeasance. This public criticism is perhaps the best evidence of the profound changes in Algerian political realities in 1988, and of how powerless the state was, momentarily, to quash criticism. The state's sudden and complete loss of credibility seemed to ensure that such open criticism could not be suppressed.

As a result, liberal and secular-leaning intellectuals as a group experienced a brief respite from censorship. This in itself was encouraging. Under President Boumediene's secular political program, Algerian Islamists also existed, but their actions were extremely constrained, so the sudden liberalization under Chadli afforded Islamists an opportunity to develop plans for the implementation of political Islam.[13] The principal umbrella organization that eventually melded many strains of political Islam in Algeria into one concerted bloc was the Front Islamique du Salut (FIS). The FIS came into existence as a formal Algerian party on March 9, 1989, when it introduced itself with an ambitious 15-point plan of action. On the one hand, its program resembled that of other new political parties that intended to "end the monopoly of a one-party State."[14] On the other hand, the FIS made it clear from the beginning that it had an ambition to reform many aspects of civil society. Most contentious by far was the eleventh point of the action program that stated its goal of making sure that the nation's leader would institute shari'a law for the entire Muslim population.[15]

The FIS's desire to institute shari'a was by no means a novel idea for Islamic activists, but it represented a direct challenge to Algeria's secularist tradition and to the future of political and cultural diversity within the country. Within the broader Muslim world, the room opened up for a legalized Islamist party that sought a massive overhaul of the public space also represented immense possibilities and threats. Algeria was the first state in the contemporary Middle East to allow the creation of an openly Islamist party whose chief objective was installation of an Islamic republic and the application of shari'a. As a result, what happened in Algeria would have tremendous significance for the entire region, and was closely watched by Western governments.

As Islamists organized around the FIS into a united front, they eclipsed rivals. Overseen by a council comprised of 14 members and led by Abassi Madani (named president of the FIS in early 1989) and Ali Belhadj (regarded by many as the second in command and seen as a much more polarizing figure), the FIS did not go unchallenged, however. Mahfoud Nahnah, for example, argued for an alternative Islamist vision but was quickly "brushed aside," as the noted political scientist William Quandt has said.[16] Nahnah's movement more closely resembled Egypt's Muslim Brotherhood's model of activism, and at first he was able to sit with FIS leaders at the meetings with Islamists called by Chadli during the October riots. In contrast to the FIS, Nahnah argued that Islamists must be willing to co-exist with secular parties. In December 1990 he formed the Harakat al Mujtamma al Islami Party (Hamas Party). Inspired by Hamas in the Occupied Territories, Nahnah wanted to ensure a culture of dialogue and create an alternative to the totalizing world-view of the FIS, one that would offer a bridge to a vibrant multi-party system.

Well organized but not widely followed, however, Nahnah's group (perhaps because it was less polemical) would remain outpaced by the better-organized and far larger FIS movement.

Most historians agree that the principal cause for the meteoric rise of the FIS had as much to do with the population's revulsion toward the FLN, due to decades of corruption and mismanagement, as it did with the religious ideology of the FIS.[17] Moreover, after the October riots, the collusion between the military and the FLN sealed the fate of the FLN, which the public largely viewed as responsible for the regime's brutality.

The secularists within the government held out the hope that once citizens finally had the opportunity to vote freely for their own party and for their own convictions, they would be reluctant to cede those rights to ideologues, even devout ones. Furthermore, the diversity of Islamist parties and the considerable range within the FIS movement itself suggested that political Islam in Algeria was dynamic and adaptable to political realities, and, once confronted with the issues of governance, could become a positive democratic force in a pluralistic society. In a word, the FIS's harsher electoral rhetoric would have most likely given way to far more pragmatic concerns in order to stay in power.[18]

Faced with the prospect of becoming the world's first popularly elected Islamic republic, Algeria's governing officials dreaded the possibility of an Islamist victory. For them, it was necessary to ensure the vibrant democratic elements of civil society once the FLN was removed through the ballot box. At the same time, the secular democrats drastically underestimated the staying power of the Algerian military and overestimated their own capacity to generate sustained civil debates about the future of the polity. Nevertheless, from 1988 to late 1991, secular politicians also enjoyed momentary successes and looked forward to overseeing lasting political reforms.

President Chadli found himself increasingly isolated from the nationalists within his own party who finally understood that one-party rule was over. On the other hand, the president's decision to overhaul the nation's political structure and offer Algeria a chance at liberal reform was endorsed by the FLN, and in November 1988 the FLN formally ratified its decision to have Chadli stand as the party's candidate for president in the scheduled elections. In December 1988, Chadli was elected for a third term (a feature subsequently banned by the 1996 constitution, but reinstated amid great controversy in October 2008, to allow President Bouteflika to stand for a third term), and in February 1989 Algeria's new liberal constitution was welcomed by a national referendum that received over 73 percent of the popular vote. The 1989 constitution guaranteed open democratic elections and removed the state's previous commitments to socialism and non-alignment, the political mainstays of the Boumediene era.[19] In addition, for the first time the constitution separated the FLN and the state, ending their nearly 30 years of marriage.

Evidence of the desire for a seismic reconstitution of the political field found expression in the form of a dozen new parties, which were quickly legalized. One of the most important was a Kabylia-based party known as the Front des Forces Socialistes (FFS), led by Hocine Aït Ahmed (a hero from the war of independence who returned to Algeria, after years of exile, in December 1989).[20] Ahmed Ben Bella returned to Algeria in September 1990 for first time since his release from prison by President Chadli to form the Mouvement pour la Démocratie en Algérie (MDA). Another important party was the Berber-backed Rassemblement pour la Culture et la Démocratie (RCD), founded by Dr. Saïd Saadi. RCD campaigned on a secularist platform, and insisted on the separation of Islam and the state. The RCD's second in command, Khalida Toumi, was perhaps Algeria's most outspoken feminist politician and had been one of the most vocal opponents of the 1984 Family Code, arabization, and political Islamism.[21] Meanwhile the FLN's leader, Abdelhamid Mehri, aimed to reinvent the old party in order to sell it to a skeptical public. The FLN came up far short, and could not counterweight FIS momentum.

The various political parties to emerge during Algeria's *glasnost* represented the range of historical and political tendencies within the country in 1989 and 1990. This went from religious conservatives to secular liberals, but the diversity also highlighted a growing divide within the country over the very secular values that had guided Algerian politics for three decades. For those who favored the secular model, Islam represented a direct challenge to gender equality and to political tolerance; for many who favored the religious paradigm, secularism represented cultural decadence and a backdoor entrance of Western ideologies. At the same time, increasing divisions between Arabic-speakers, Francophones, and Berbers re-emerged, making it clear that linguistic, ethnic, and cultural identity would remain key parts of the debate over diversity in civic life.

As local elections scheduled for June 1990 drew near, the lines separating political schisms in Algeria widened. FIS supporters called for the end of Algeria's historic bilingual (Arabic and French) practices, arguing that Arabic was more authentic and thus truer to the identity of Algeria's Muslim heritage. In this vein, the FIS insisted that the continued use of French kept Algeria in the so-called infidel's ideological camp and subservient to the West.[22] At the same time, the FIS called for the immediate application of shari'a by the president. It used the rhetoric of the FLN's founding declarations, which officially identified Islam as the state religion since independence. Islamists remained concerned about the role the armed forces would play, knowing that the military elite remained fervent defenders of secularism.

Assessing the Islamists' success and the First Gulf War

Pragmatically, at the local and provincial levels, Algeria was divided into two electoral categories. There were 48 separate *wilayas* (provinces), each of which had representative assemblies called Assemblées Populaires de Wilaya (APW); and there were 1,539 municipal councils referred to as Assemblées Populaires Communales (APC). Prior to the elections, the majority of pundits predicted that the FLN would dominate at both the provincial and municipal levels, and that its main rival, the FIS, would come in a close second.

Reality told a different story. When the local elections were held on June 12, 1990, with approximately 65 percent voter turnout, the FIS trounced the FLN, winning 54 percent of votes cast. The FLN obtained only 28 percent. The FIS showed strongest amongst urban voters, and scored mostly heavily in the urbanized northern part of the country.[23] And, capping the FLN's humiliation, the FIS gained control of the wilayas, taking 32 in total.[24] Suddenly, FIS politicians were in firm control of both local and provincial governments, and had a firm popular mandate as they moved toward the first round of the nation's scheduled parliamentary elections.

FIS leaders were emboldened by the dramatic victory. Ali Belhadj, far younger and more charismatic than most FIS leaders, immediately hardened his rhetoric. A kind of Saint-Just of the FIS movement, Belhadj made frequent allusions to the re-establishment of the Caliphate, to the worldwide Muslim community (*ummah*), and to the pernicious nature of the state security forces. His tone became more menacing and began to challenge the democratic process itself. As he wrote in the Arabic newspaper *El-Mounuid*, "Democracy is one of the numerous nefarious intellectual innovations that obsess the conscience of people."[25] Since Islam accomplished many of the humane goals of democratic thought, without introducing the fallacy of human freedom that came from the Enlightenment and from thinkers such as Rousseau, he argued, Islam was the divine answer to politics and its rules were clearly spelled out in the Qur'an. Those who refused to accept these rules were enemies of Islam and would have to accept their fate.

At the same time, after winning the local elections, many local and regional FIS leaders quickly began to institute the program of moral reform called for by hard-liners. These reforms prohibited the sale of alcohol, required women to wear the hijab, and separated boys and girls in school. The national government viewed such efforts to enforce a creeping shari'a by separating the sexes as a direct affront to the state's statutory requirements for co-education, and, consequently, the tensions between national and local governments sharpened. However, still reeling from the magnitude of their defeat and the political mandate handed to the FIS by local elections, FLN leaders saw no clear way of recovering lost ground.

The unforeseen Islamist victories generated considerable unease within the military. Reluctant to show their hand after the October riots, army generals now saw the democratic experiment as a threat, and began to plot their course of action. They would allow elections to go forward, but only on condition that the central government consent to the military's new stake in power. Chadli's administration, breaking with tradition, named General Nezzar minister of defense.

The decision to separate the presidency from this all-important position for the first time since independence, and cede it directly to a military commander, would have extensive ramifications for the next decade and would lead directly to the erosion of civilian governance.[26] Closer to the levers of power, the military permitted the scheduling of national elections for June 1991.

As Algerian politicians set their sights on acquiring seats in the National Popular Assembly, Saddam Hussein's designs on Kuwait moved into full view. In mid-July 1990, Tariq Aziz, the Iraqi foreign minister, publicly accused Kuwait of stealing Iraqi oil from the Rumalia fields. Three days later, US Secretary of Defense Richard Cheney declared that the US would support Kuwait if it were threatened by Iraq. Hussein stationed over 100,000 troops on the Kuwaiti border, and on August 2, 1990, Iraq invaded Kuwait. A few days later, the Saudi royal family requested support from President George Bush.

Saddam Hussein cloaked himself as an Islamic warrior, despite all evidence to the contrary. Algerian politicians clearly understood the implications of the debate over Iraq's invasion of Kuwait and the US response to it. At the same time, US President Bush argued that the First Gulf War presaged a "new world order." In fact, Bush's position caused "blowback" in countries like Algeria because it intensified a serious clash between the secularists and both their military and Islamist opponents.[27] Jockeying for the political high ground, Islamists and government alike advanced their cause to the electorate by vowing that they would be the first to support Hussein. In the event, both sides had time to contemplate the situation when the First Gulf War forced the government to delay the parliamentary elections. As the prominent British scholar Hugh Roberts has argued, the decision to postpone elections for the National Popular Assembly due to the conflict in the Persian Gulf completely "transformed" Algerian political debates. Prior to the beginning of the war, Islamism had been largely confined to supporters of the FIS (albeit represented by a large following) and marginal parties. However, after the invasion of Kuwait on August 2, 1990 and the subsequent US response, Islamists' internal divisions and battles were momentarily set aside in favor of "anti-Western (and especially anti-French) sentiments." This in

turn "radicalized the international outlook of a younger generation."
Hence, Hussein had put FIS leaders in the rather awkward position
of having to look beyond their loathing of him and the Ba'th Party's
well-known persecution of Islamists. Biting their tongues, the FIS
recast their position on Hussein in terms that presented him as an
Arab brother being bullied by the West, calculating that this position
would chime better with the sentiments of Muslim masses. Revealing
itself as the most "populist" of Algeria's Islamist movements and in
that sense more "shallow" in terms of "intellectual and doctrinal
content," the FIS party was clearly beginning to be driven by the
instincts of mass politics.[28]

Understanding how other Arabs throughout the Middle East
and North Africa would react, Hussein "played the Islamic card" by
casting his military defense against the coalition forces as a jihad.
After this, a decidedly pro-Hussein movement swept through the
Middle East and North Africa. By no means fond of Hussein but
also not immune from the public's sympathy for him, FIS leaders
were forced to contemplate jettisoning their strongest ideological
convictions and supporting Hussein's rather curious jihad against
the American-led forces gathering in Saudi Arabia. At first Madani
held to a balanced view, one that condemned both sides, and before
the coalition forces attacked, both Madani and Belhadj (who also
previously condemned both Hussein and the coalition) went to Iraq
on several occasions attempting to mediate, as did Ahmed Ben Bella.
Once the hostilities began, however, the FIS joined the public outcry
against the US-backed attack on Baghdad, and against France, which
had joined the coalition forces.[29]

All of Algeria's politicians understood the potential domestic
dividends for coming to Hussein's aid. The government led by President Chadli and Prime Minister Mouloud Hamrouche also understood the domestic pay-offs of coming to Hussein's defense. Acting
swiftly, the Algerian state thus became the first in the Middle East
to denounce the American-led invasion. At the same time, the First
Gulf War forced the FIS to take an especially pragmatic view that
put its "constituency before its international links, and its popular
character before its Islamist doctrines."[30] By early 1991, FIS leaders
were openly calling for the Algerian government to create "training

camps" from which Algerian fighters would go to support Hussein's men in battle.[31] Wanting to take advantage of the perceived internal divisions that Hussein had exposed within the FIS, the government called for national elections to be held as early as possible. The first round of elections was quickly reset for June 27, 1991, and the second round set for July 18.

As all the parties geared up for the first round of national elections, the state tried to strengthen its hand by nearly doubling the number of constituencies, which in effect increased the power of rural areas (where the FIS had not done as well during local and provincial elections). The National Assembly also changed the election law to eliminate from the second round all but the two parties receiving the most votes during the first round. Believing these moves crafted by Prime Minister Hamrouche were designed to limit the influence of the FIS (which they clearly were, as well as to scupper the old-guard FLN), FIS leaders replied with a call for a crippling general strike. In addition, by this time, Ali Belhadj openly advocated violence against the state.

The strikes began in April, and the situation became volatile. A larger strike began on May 25. The situation grew intense, and officials were split on how best to react to the Islamists' show of force in the streets. Hamrouche was in favor of letting the strikes run their course, provided the FIS did not resort to violence and refrained from efforts to seize government buildings.[32] In the end, the generals convinced President Chadli to declare a state of siege on June 5, 1991 (which brought into effect a curfew and legal repression), and to postpone the upcoming elections. In protest, Hamrouche resigned and Sid Ahmed Ghozali was appointed prime minister on June 6. Ghozali tried to instill calm, promising elections by the end of the year. However, General Nezzar and other officers again pressed for harsher treatment of the FIS, which had called the strike, arguing its leaders were a danger to state security. Ghozali met with both Belhadj and Madani soon after taking over as prime minister, in order to reassure FIS supporters. By June 25, the violence had intensified. The military and the police decided to intervene in order to protect the key "symbols of the Republic."[33]

"The Nezzar plan": radicalizing the Islamists

Within weeks of declaring a state of siege, the government moved against the FIS, though the plan was in fact hatched well before when, following the FIS victory in local elections, the chief of Sécurité Militaire (SM), General Mohammed Betchine, was removed from his post. In September 1990, SM was renamed Département du Renseignement et de la Sécurité (DRS) and given a far more propagandistic orientation. A subsection known as Direction du Contre-Espionnage et de la Securité (DCE), commanded by General Smaïl Larmi within the DRS, was created specifically to operate against Islamists and to infiltrate Islamist networks.[34] The DRS has been commanded by General Mohamed Mediene since its creation in 1990, and the DRS and DCE's principal objective during the first few years was to undermine the FIS. In addition, as General Nezzar points out in the action plan included in the appendix of his memoirs, the military sought to provoke and discredit the FIS in order to make it appear anti-democratic.[35]

This move to undermine and radicalize the Islamists within Algeria indicated that the military had changed course. It had given up on the political process entirely after it realized the Islamists were going to carry favor with the general electorate and dominate both rounds of the national elections. Consequently, on June 30, Ali Belhadj and Abassi Madani were arrested after Belhadj threatened to start a jihad against the government in plain view of the media. Both were charged with plotting to overthrow the government and inciting violence, among several other counts. On July 15, 1992, a military court convicted Madani and Belhadj to 12 years in jail.[36] Thousands of FIS followers, including members of the FIS executive council and activists, were arrested and sent to large concentration camps in the Sahara Desert. Allegations of torture reappeared. Others were simply disappeared by Algerian security forces.[37]

In theory, the government's actions were intended to weaken the FIS's commanding political position and to flush out moderate political Islamists willing to replace the arrested leaders. In reality, the military and DRS deliberately arrested the more moderate political Islamists and encouraged more radical Islamists (especially those belonging to the El-hidjra Oua At-takfir, a radical group with

Afghan connections) to attack unveiled women in order to discredit the Islamist cause.[38] This decision amounted to a tactical blunder, because it further alienated political Islamists of all stripes and gave credence to calls for armed revolt issued by radicals. Naturally, many of the radicals released by Nezzar moved quickly into the emerging terrorist cells intent on taking down the state.

Sensing peril if the party took Nezzar's bait and moved to the radical fringe, FIS leaders tried to prevent the disintegration of the movement by organizing the Batna Conference in August. This called for the reorganization of FIS leaders in the ruling council (Majlis al-Shúrú) and the nomination of Abdelkader Hachani to serve as interim FIS president (with Belhadj and Madani continuing to serve as leaders in abstention while in detention). Of paramount concern at Batna was the re-emergence of rival Islamic parties, such as Mahfoud Nahnah's Al-Irchad wal Ishal (Hamas) and Ahmed Djaballah's Movement of the Islamic Renaissance (al-Nahda) that hoped to press forward with their own moderate Islamist agendas as the elections proceeded. Both parties' names originally contained the word "Islam", but after the crackdown on the FIS, the government passed a law forbidding specific references to religion in party names. Hence, Hamas became the Mouvement de la Société pour la Paix (MSP), and Nahda became Ennahda. Both Hamas and Nahda remained committed to an Islamic world-view, but both accepted a "gradualist" approach and shied away from the more aggressive tone of the FIS. Furthermore, in contrast to the FIS's open hostility to the question of women's rights, Hamas and Nahda had "active women's sections," and Nahda openly condemned violence against women while it sought to expand women's rights.[39]

As the first round of the December national elections neared, all sides jockeyed for position, including the FLN. The arrests of FIS leaders temporarily derailed the party, but it quickly set about organizing their districts. Clearly backfiring, the government's political purges galvanized FIS followers and increased its chances of success.

The FIS enjoyed especially strong support from younger voters. Since the majority of the population was under 30, this advantage yielded huge dividends, as voters broke on generational lines. Older voters were less likely to support the FIS, with the exception of the over-60s.[40] In contrast, the FIS attracted younger voters less invested in the FLN's mythic anti-colonial past. Since decolonization's struggles were long over, the youth wanted change, not a rehearsal of nationalist rhetoric.[41] And, despite the arrest of Madani and Belhadj, the FIS continued to poll well before the elections, especially in heavily populated urban centers where high unemployment and inadequate public services continued to fuel young people's deep resentment against a regime steeped in history but short on real solutions to its woes.

As for the other opposition parties, the RCD pitched itself (as did Aït Ahmed's movement) as the respectable middle way between the bankruptcy of the FLN and the intolerance of the Islamists. RCD leaders Saïd Saadi and Khalida Toumi made impassioned appeals for a democratic and tolerant Algeria. In addition to the issue of minority rights (most importantly the Berbers'), RCD campaigned as the chief spokesman for secularism and the principal advocate for women's rights. Undeterred by the FIS's violent rhetoric – to the contrary – Toumi (a former math teacher) had even confronted Ali Belhadj and Abassi Madani live on a televised debate and accused them of using Islam to keep women in the dark ages.[42] Such outspokenness earned her and the RCD respect among secularists and women's rights supporters, but also eventually a fatwa calling for her death, and she was forced to go underground in 1993.

The December 1991 elections and the coup d'état

Moving toward the elections, Abdelkader Hachani understood that the military would intervene forcefully if his party advocated achieving power via anything other than the democratic process. The FIS made every effort to assure the government and foreign observers that its followers would adhere to democratic principles and recommit to the electoral process, on condition that jailed FIS leaders be freed and the state of siege lifted. Though Prime Minister Ghozali and President Chadli refused to release Belhadj and Madani, the FIS, which had promised to boycott the elections, announced on December 14 that it would proceed with national elections.[43]

On December 26, the FIS defied the odds and carried off a

crushing victory against the FLN and other rival parties. Of the 231 contested seats in the national assembly (out of a total of 430), FIS captured 188. In contrast the FFS won 26, the FLN picked up 15, and independents claimed what was left. With 47.5 percent of the voters casting ballots for the FIS, the FIS clobbered its opponents and shocked everyone, especially the political elite, who complained of voter irregularities and election fraud. Because the new election laws in place allowed only the two most successful parties to advance to the second round, the FLN was abruptly shut completely out of Algeria's political future.

The unexpected FIS success at the polls in December caused the generals and political elite to panic. Ghozali argued that allowing the election results to stand would be catastrophic. Fearing the end of Algeria's secularist traditions and of its own power as the victorious FIS moved to clinch their advantage during the second round of elections, the military acted. Led by Chief of Staff Adbalmakek Guenaïza and Generals Nezzar and Belkheir, the military first forced Chadli to tender his resignation during a televised press conference on January 11, 1992. In this address, Chadli announced the dissolution of parliament. After the President of the Constitutional Council refused to accept the position of interim president, the military announced the creation of the High Council for Security, whose first action was to nullify the results of the December election and to propose the creation of a permanent five-person ruling body known as the Haut Comité d'Etat (HCE). The HCE authorized the arrest of FIS leader Abdelkader Hachani on January 24, declared a state of emergency on February 9, and banned the FIS on March 4.

Algeria's attempt to see through the region's first democratic reform ended in catastrophe. Unable to provide an alternative to the FIS, the FLN could not save itself. Other rival parties, secular and moderate Islamist alike, also proved incapable of withstanding the religious winds of change that arose from the ashes of the old regime. Understanding that the failures of the postcolonial state had given birth to an ambitious political Islamist movement, bent on rewriting the state's commitment to secularism and challenging the status quo that had given the military its unbridled position as the protector of the state, the generals stepped into the breach. This move in turn started perpetual conflict between Islamists (who had achieved what no one thought possible) and the state (now revealed to have been controlled by the military all along). With the democratic process now in tatters, Algerians looked uneasily into the future. Few, if any, could have predicted the sudden and bloody slide into terror that rendered Algeria one of the most violent national dramas of the 1990s, but most came to regret that the democratic experiment had led directly into a cul-de-sac where the dynamics of terror and state repression would dominate everyday life for the next decade without reprieve.

3 | The kingmakers: generals and presidents in a time of terror

The 1992 military coup d'état set in motion a powerful series of events that would plague Algeria for over a decade. Once those controlling the government made the decision to overturn the election, they also made it clear that they would stay in power at all costs. In doing so, they argued that they had acted to safeguard Algeria's republican institutions from political and radical Islamists, who, regardless of their different public personas and platforms, shared the common objective of turning Algeria into a zealous theocratic state. It was, in their minds, better to be Turkey than Iran.

The Turkish secular-military model was, however, by no means easy to replicate in Algeria. Once the military seized control of the government in January, it became impossible for Algerian civil society to break free of the generals' grip. There was perhaps one brief moment when the separation of powers looked possible, but this was short-lived, and it would take several years for the next window of opportunity to open. That first opportunity came at the hands of the military itself, when the generals called on war hero Mohamed Boudiaf in February to head the Haut Comité d'Etat (HCE) in an effort to restore the government's lost legitimacy. But Boudiaf's assassination on June 29 cast a long shadow of doubt over the military (which was blamed by many for orchestrating his murder) and Algeria's future. It would take over a decade before a civilian government would re-emerge and provide real evidence that it could distance itself from the military's powerbrokers. However, during the first few years after the military coup, a considerable disequilibrium plagued the nation, one that precluded the re-establishment of civilian leadership.

In clear contrast to Turkey, where political Islamists eventually entered the corridors of power in Ankara in 2002, the actions of the military government after 1992 ensured that Algeria's Islamists would remain perpetual political outcasts, barred from the impregnable fortress of state power. With the ruling generals taking the position that any accommodation with Islamists was unthinkable, several remaining FIS leaders were forced to flee abroad and set up a government in exile. Many FIS supporters too joined ranks with radical Islamists in an effort to bring down the military government and reinstate the FIS. However, after 1992 security forces and militant Islamists descended into the logic of a total war, and for the next decade, national security concerns dominated domestic affairs. Meanwhile, political Islamists (the FIS in particular), denied the rewards of the democratic process, were split over whether to proceed to armed revolt or pursue an open dialogue with the government in an attempt to re-enter the political arena. At the same time, it is important to remember that the Algerian electorate, which had voted overwhelmingly for the FIS, did not rise in a revolutionary collective to overthrow the junta. Given Algeria's clear revolutionary tradition, the absence of a mass revolt prompts other questions. In this spirit, the present chapter will explain the fate of the military junta from 1992 to 1995 and examine how it maintained power in a progressively deteriorating situation.

The military gamble

The HCE was originally controlled by five men: Mohamed Boudiaf (who was named president), Ali Haroun (minister of justice), Tidjani Haddam (a former minister of religious affairs), Khaled Nezzar (minister of defense), and Ali Kafi (the general secretary of veteran affairs). The HCE ruled collectively over Algeria from 1992 to 1993, after which the retired army general, Liamine Zeroual, emerged to accept the presidency by appointment in 1994.

Upon returning to Algeria, Mohamed Boudiaf was widely admired as a hero of the war against the French. He had spent 27 years in exile in Morocco, and in February 1992 (at the age of 72), Boudiaf was called by the Algerian military to lead the HCE as its president. Considered a political outsider and reformer, Boudiaf was until that time known as someone unconnected to the military and therefore not infected by its corrupting influence. In addition, he possessed unique credibility as a notorious opponent of the FLN's Stalinist tactics after 1962. Independent, honest, and determined to set Algeria on the right path, Boudiaf accepted the task given to him by the military and returned to Algeria. He came home in a time of need out of a real desire to refashion civil society, to move the nation through a time of turmoil, and to find some sort of a compromise with political Islam. The HCE was, for him, simply a means to an end, and he clearly meant for it to be a short-lived stopgap institution.

Having negated the Islamists' electoral victories, the government gambled on the belief that the population would soon come to its side, and that the Islamists' political base would erode once the FIS's leaders and followers were behind bars. As it pressed its case, the junta assured the skeptical public that the HCE would be a purely transitional body, which would relinquish power once the Islamists renounced threats of violence and stability was restored. The military establishment thus set out immediately to bleach Algeria of its political Islamists and to silence both secular and religious opponents who dared criticize a state "under siege." This repression involved the use of force, propaganda, and coercion, which together were sufficient to keep the regime in power, but not to go unchallenged, either inside or outside the country.

The democratic forces that rejected the military's seizure of power, including intellectuals and activists who questioned the validity of a government that had violated popular sovereignty, also came under attack and were persecuted for their activities. Calculating that Islamists represented the most immediate threat to security but keenly aware that the free press could undermine its power, the newly enthroned HCE erected a repressive bureaucracy endowed with the power to silence challengers. The security actions against Islamists led to the creation of massive concentration camps in the Sahara Desert, where thousands of suspected Islamists were detained without due process and under a variety of politically motivated charges. Thousands would simply be "disappeared" by the military, a hideous tactic of counter-insurgency warfare invented and perfected by the French military during decolonization. Algeria became well-known at home and abroad as one of the most questioned and watched states in the world. As part of their *modus operandi*, the military and security forces undertook elaborate schemes to create whole cadres of double agents and agents provocateurs who infiltrated a variety of Islamist movements (the Groupe Islamique Armé or GIA in particular) in order to discredit and subvert them, and thereby strengthen the power of the state. In short, while the military seized the reins of power, it also laid out the conditions for the "dirty war" that was to characterize Algeria throughout the 1990s.[1]

Even before the dirty war began, the HCE wasted no time in destroying the FIS hierarchy and political base. During January 1992, Abdelkader Hachani and Rabah Kebir (the main FIS spokesmen) were arrested on charges that they were organizing armed revolt. The eminent historian of Algeria, John Ruedy, estimates that by February 1992, between 50 and 150 political Islamists were killed by the government, between 200 and 700 wounded in security attacks, and several thousand placed in prison camps in the Sahara. Having declared a state of emergency to be in effect from February 9, the HCE controlled all the important levers of power, and even replaced FIS leaders voted into office at local level after the 1990 municipal elections. As a result, in March 1992, approximately one half of the FIS politicians elected in 1990 were replaced with those appointed by the HCE's government. Simultaneously, the HCE greatly reduced press freedoms and began to censor and arrest journalists critical of the regime.[2]

To his credit, Boudiaf understood that the military had exceeded its authority, and, contradicting the view of many of the generals behind his ascension to the presidency, he initiated dialogues with Islamists and other democratic forces disenfranchised by the coup. Nevertheless, Boudiaf made it clear that he would be tough, that he would pursue those who threatened the security of the state, and that he would discipline and call out abusive security personnel and corrupt officials. Boudiaf could make such bold promises because his popularity, stature, and position endowed him with sufficient clout to push for meaningful political reform as he re-established order.

In a February 1992 interview with a French television journalist, Boudiaf noted that above all he wanted to restore the legitimacy of the government by respecting "debate" and "democracy."[3] In his view, although he had not been elected, he could make such claims as president because he was motivated purely by the desire to find a peaceful solution to the current crisis. He insisted that ensuring a return to democratic debate meant that citizens had to be able to freely express themselves and "discuss without fear." At the same time, he knew that economic stability was paramount for political success, so he affirmed that the nation was already "on the path of liberalization" and that it would be "open to foreign investors." A month later, in another interview with French television reporters, Boudiaf vehemently defended the army and its response to the FIS: the army "wanted to avoid ... bloodshed."[4] It was, after all, a "republican army" committed solely to the restoration of order. To be sure, he acknowledged that there had been excesses, as in October 1988, but he insisted that the military's response had been conditioned by the chaos in the streets.

The revolution that did not happen

One of the critical factors working against the FIS in early 1992 was that the Front did not have sufficient time to react to the cancellation of the elections and the creation of the HCE.[5] The Algerian authorities and armed forces ("*le pouvoir*," as it is often called), simply moved against the FIS too quickly for effective resistance to be organized, and by the time its leaders understood the magnitude of the forces arrayed against political Islam, they were already outflanked, in prison, or on the run. Yet, curiously, although the situation was ripe for revolution on a mass scale, such a revolution never materialized. This prompts the question of why did Algeria not go the way of Iran, with revolutionary masses taking the state?

Part of the answer has to do with the fact that while the expression of political support through the voting process was relatively easy, to reclaim the state via direct and violent confrontation with the military demanded of supporters an altogether different level of political commitment. Hence, while FIS leaders in exile such as Anwar Haddam did insist that armed resistance against the illegitimate regime was a legitimate course of political action and in accordance with Islamic principles, the average FIS supporter who was happy to turn out at the polls simply refused to risk his or her life.[6] The government's quick arrests of FIS supporters, as well as its widespread use of torture and extrajudicial killings, likely created an even greater separation (mostly out of fear) of the FIS leadership from its constituency. Another reason why average FIS supporters may not have opted for the revolutionary road, is that they had supported the FIS as democrats. For many, the move from democratic expression to jihad required an extraordinary shift in purpose, and would have run counter to the goal of bringing Islam into a democratic framework as an expression of popular sovereignty. In fact, as one leading historian notes, the majority of recruits to the guerrilla forces preparing to engage the state through violence came from the ranks of those who had never bought into the idea that the ballot box "was a way to support an Islamic state."[7] In other words, supporters of Islamic activism remained political first and foremost; whereas the radical Islamists, particularly those Salafists who had opposed the integration of Islam into the political arena from the beginning, were far more likely to take up arms against the state.

For its part, the state used blunt force to crush armed resistance and what remained of Islamic activism. In doing so, it pushed many young men into the arms of guerrilla groupings. Younger men – especially the so-called *hittistes*, young and mostly urban unemployed men, who lined the streets with their backs against the walls – were increasingly drawn to the jihadi cause, less because of ideology than because it was a means to make a living in a new kind of economy of terror.[8] Some *hittistes* who joined the armed struggle simply wanted revenge for their perceived or real social mistreatment, while others felt a more pious obligation to do something about "an impious state headed by atheists – Communists who were in addition French-speaking."[9] In either case, much of their rage was class-based, as most lived on the social margins with few opportunities and little to no help from the state.

Understanding that there was still widespread support for political Islam, and that the government needed to make efforts to restore trust in the Algerian polity, Boudiaf attempted to curb government corruption. Certain civilian and military leaders were particularly alarmed by his stated decision to prosecute corrupt officers and FLN party officials. This tactic generated hazards for Boudiaf, because the generals had benefited from a special relationship to the government for decades. Boudiaf, however, presented himself as a populist president, outside the old power structure of the FLN (which he publicly criticized), eager to end corruption, and committed to national reconciliation.

In an attempt to re-engage secular political parties and thereby jump-start the political process, Boudiaf created the Rassemblement Patriotique National (RPN) during the spring of 1992. Through this cooperative of various secular political parties, which showed signs of early success, he hoped to convince the population that Algeria was on the path to civilian leadership, a path that would offset the influence of the FLN, which was still intact as the largest party in 1992.[10] At the same time, he tried to reassure the population that the National Consultative Council (comprised of 60 members) that replaced Parliament in April 22 was more than a de facto rump parliament. In short, given the circumstances in which he had accepted power, Boudiaf attempted to bridge the gap between the population and the government and to convince those in power to respect a space within civil society for political debates.

The generals who brought Boudiaf to power in Algeria dramatically underestimated his resolve to quickly move the nation back onto the path of political and economic liberalization. His calls for unity and his promises to restore trust by tackling the problems of the military mafia and corruption resonated with the population. At the same time, he, like the military powerbrokers, remained determined to stamp out the FIS,[11] operating on the thesis that once the Islamic activists were out of the way, the government would carefully reconstruct the political arena to ensure that they could not be voted back into office. And yet, Boudiaf insisted that the HCE intended to cede power to its democratic progeny.[12] That said, Boudiaf's optimism, anti-authoritarianism, and ambition to create a broad consensus-based movement, unsettled the military elite (largely Francophone and secular), who had enjoyed great privileges during the FLN era and rejected any compromise with the FIS.

Belaïd Abdessalam, repression, and the question of legitimacy

Boudiaf never saw through his plans to unify the nation. On June 29, one of the guards assigned to protect him, Boumarafi Lembarak, shot the president in the back while he was speaking on national television. Lembarak confessed to the crime, stating that he had murdered Boudiaf because of religious convictions. However, many (including Bouteflika's current minister of culture and communications, Khalida Toumi) suspected that the assassination was part of a military conspiracy orchestrated by the very men that Boudiaf had rattled with his unification policies and plan to expose corrupt officers.[13]

Boudiaf's assassination traumatized the nation and pushed it to the brink of total chaos. Though the military pinned the crime on a radical Islamist, many Algerians no longer trusted the armed forces, and regarded the murder as an inside job. Unable to convince the population otherwise, the Algerian interior minister, Larbi Belkhair, resigned from office acknowledging his failure to prevent the president's assassination.

Boudiaf's murder could not have come at a worse time for Algeria's economy. Tumbling oil prices, combined with massive external debt and a stagnating GDP, hastened Algeria's economic collapse. Foreign investors' financial fears were now accompanied by anxiety over political instability, and these problems, together with high unemployment, a shortage of housing and basic food staples, and a downward turn in all economic sectors placed the state in a dangerously fragile position. The HCE scrambled to restore confidence in the government and in the economy, and, on July 3, named Ali Kafi to replace Boudiaf as president. Redha Malek, leader of the National Consultative Council, filled the HCE's vacant fifth seat. On July 19, the HCE named Belaïd Abdessalam prime minister.

Responsible for forming the government, Abdessalam was simply the wrong choice for this critical position. Coming as he did at the nadir of postcolonial Algerian history, this old-school official and throwback from the Boumediene era could not shake the nationalist mindset of the past. He concentrated power in his own hands, holding for himself the posts of minister of finance and head of state. Unable to see a way forward, on August 10, he declared Algeria to be in a war economy and blocked efforts (advised by the international community) to devalue the dinar, as well as other important recommendations for economic and political liberalization.

Under Abdessalam, legislative decree N. 93-03, known as the "anti-terrorist law," sponsored the creation of special courts to try terrorist suspects but offered only vague definitions of terrorism, leaving it up to authorities to determine what or who constituted a threat to state security.[14] The decree granted authorities broad powers over the press, giving the government the right to suspend any publication or newspaper for up to six months. Despite these measures, Abdessalam could not prevent the spread of violence against the regime.

In 1992 Algerian authorities began to encounter significant resistance from armed Islamic groups. By November, the security situation had deteriorated to such an extent that the police and military were drawing casualties almost daily, and European intelligence services and senior US analysts offered dire predictions that the government would collapse within 18 months.[15] In fact, foreign intelligence services remained wary of the possibility of full Islamic revolution in Algeria. For example, one US diplomat called 1992 a "watershed" moment with regional and international implications, reaching as far as the Soviet republics in Central Asia; a European analyst put it this way: "Whatever happens in Algeria will profoundly influence the course of political development in the Middle East ... The potential magnitude is even greater than what happened in Iran." The bombing of Algiers International Airport on August 26, which killed nine and injured 100 people, represented a shocking change in tactics for the guerrilla forces, because it was the first terrorist attack on the civilian population since independence. The government arrested more men, and over 200 security force members were killed in 1992. And even greater repression by General Mohamed Larmi's anti-terrorism unit followed.

With draconian measures implemented in the domestic sphere by the military, the state moved to eliminate possible foreign sponsors of terrorism. Believing that the Islamic threat was at least partially foreign-born, the HCE broke off diplomatic relations with Iran in November 1992, amid allegations that the Iranian government was supplying assistance to the guerrilla forces. The next month, on December 5, authorities imposed a curfew between 10 p.m. and 6 a.m. Then, in the worst single attack against security personnel to date, on December 14, five police were killed. This terrorist strike confirmed for many that a new war was beginning and that indeed the HCE was engaged in a fight for its very survival.

As the guerrilla forces arrayed against the government steadily increased their attacks, including a failed assassination attempt against General Nezzar on February 13, 1993, the HCE focused on the dual program of restoring the Algerian economy and implementing an effective counter-insurgency program. Ensuring success on both fronts was vital, because by "1993 the regime was placed in check."[16]

One of the first radical groups to emerge with the goal of placing the government in check was the Mouvement Islamique Armé (MIA). Formed in 1991 by Abdelkader Chebouti and other followers of the martyred Mustapha Bouyali – the Islamic activist who organized a militant movement in the 1980s and was killed by Algerian forces in February 1987 – the MIA was determined to relaunch a full scale "guerrilla war."[17] Unlike the Afghan veterans, the MIA did not at first endorse the attacking of state officials, but after the coup in 1992, it became one of the most important principal movements determined to overthrow the regime and committed to the restoration of the FIS through violent means. Abdelkader Chebouti was selected as the MIA's national emir in 1992, yet despite his leadership, the MIA was not entirely unified and found it difficult to consolidate authority over so many emerging and diverse militant groups.

The primary reason for the MIA's difficulty in establishing command over the guerrilla forces in Algeria had to do with the rise of other important terrorist groups, known collectively as the Groupes Islamiques Armés or Jammat Islamiyya Mousalaha (GIAs). There is considerable disagreement over the composition of the GIAs. Some scholars and commentators suggest that the GIAs acted more as a singular organization, without nuance, and that they formed a more or less united front with a common agenda. In this interpretation, during the early years they are seen as the GIA, in the singular. As Lawrence Wright explains it, "[a]ccording to the logic of the GIA, democracy and Islam were incompatible; therefore anyone who had a voting card was against Islam and deserved to be killed."[18] Believing that the Islamic state was a religious mandate and that they were carrying out jihad as true believers, the GIA maintained a far more militant and subversive agenda. Hence, because GIA guerrillas were not trying to restore the results of the democratic process, GIA methods and tactics were severe and far more totalizing. Eventually, the GIA made it clear that there was to be no neutrality, and all enemies would be killed.

It is important to point out that the FIS leader-in-exile in the US, Anwar Haddam, among many others, disputes the claim that the GIA initially existed as singular entity and contends that it was really various sets of GIAs acting as diverse groups with different agendas.[19] He cites the fact that several key FIS leaders quit the FIS early on after the coup in order to lead the armed resistance against the military state. According to him, both explicit and tacit support from FIS leaders for individual strains of the GIAs were logistically necessary to ensure the recovery of the state from the military interlopers. And, at least from 1993 to 1995, Haddam insists that the GIAs he and other FIS leaders-in-exile supported were created with the sole purpose of restoring lost elections through revolutionary action.

The HCE also had to compete for political legitimacy against the FIS leaders who managed to make it into exile. The most prominent were Rabah Kebir, Anwar Haddam, and Abdelbaki Sahraoui. Kebir moved to Germany, Haddam to the US, and Sahraoui fled to Paris, where he was assassinated. Haddam was at first granted special status in the US, and was originally seen by the Clinton administration as an exiled opposition leader. Eventually, however, following his controversial support for segments within the GIA, he was held without charge by US authorities from 1996 to 2000, when Attorney General Janet Reno ordered his release. The FIS leaders stated that they were forming a government in exile and that the HCE constituted an illegitimate political body. However successful the FIS in exile were at drawing sympathy from the international community and their respective host societies, bitter acrimony soon surfaced between these leaders, especially Kebir and Haddam, each of whom claimed to represent the FIS party.

Challenges also came from international and national human rights organizations. Led internationally by Amnesty International and domestically by the Ligue Algérienne de Défense des Droits de l'Homme (LADDH), human rights groups cited evidence that the Algerian state had committed heinous crimes against its citizens and pressed for immediate accountability. LADDH, directed by Algeria's best-known human rights attorney, Abdennour Ali Yahia, specifically charged that the government had systematically engaged in massive human rights abuses; Ali Yahia frequently acted as defense counsel for arrested Islamists.

Algeria's democratic forces pressured the HCE to make good on its promise to relinquish power. Aït Ahmed's FFS, which had come second, behind the FIS, in the bid to capture parliamentary seats, called on the HCE to reopen the political process; the RCD party led by Saïd Saadi and Khalida Toumi demanded the HCE yield power to democratically elected officials. In fact, Toumi (appointed minister of culture and the official spokesperson for Abdelaziz Bouteflika's government in 2002) insisted that while the FIS must be suppressed, the political process needed to begin again. Moreover, she openly blamed Boudiaf's assassination on the military mafia in power. As she said in an interview with Elisabeth Schemla in 1995: "The assassins of Mohamed Boudiaf are still in power. President Zeroual knows them quite well. Justice has never been served. As long as the truth has not been told, the crisis of confidence between the Algerians and their leaders will persist."[20]

Between eradication and dialogue

By August 1993, the generals responsible for bringing Prime Minister Abdessalam into office realized he had become a liability. Abdessalam's commitment to past ideology and his defensive nationalist mindset no longer accorded with the demands of the 1990s. Consequently, Redha Malek came into the prime minister's office, offering a return to the liberalizing policies begun by Ghozali along with an unflinching desire to eradicate militant Islamists. With Ali Kafi as the president of the HCE and Malek serving as prime minister, Algeria moved in several directions simultaneously. Regarding Islamists, "eradicator" policies called for increasing military personnel and the defense budget. Despite the pledge to restore the democratic process by December 1993, officials insisted that the HCE was still necessary to organize the fight against terrorism and to lay the groundwork for democracy.[21] And yet most opposition parties maintained that if the government were to have political legitimacy, it had to broker deals with the FLN, the FFS, and the FIS.

The effort to co-opt the FIS ended even before it began. Hardliners refused to re-legalize the party, while FLN and FFS leaders made their participation in negotiations contingent on the inclusion of the FIS (understanding that without the FIS present the public would reject the outcome). Similarly, the effort to confer with the dominant secularist parties stagnated, and the government's inability to create sustainable political discussions provoked debate within the military leadership over whether the state should pursue a harsh or conciliatory approach vis-à-vis Islamists. This conflict has been described as a "tussle within the regime ... between the *éradicateurs* and the *conciliateurs*."[22] This "tussle" continued to frustrate efforts to move beyond the framework of a provisional government. The differences were not overcome for several years, but a clear effort was made when 52-year-old General Liamine Zeroual (defense minister from 1993 to January 1994) was selected as the next president of the HCE on January 30, 1994.

Liamine Zeroual: from general to president

Zeroual jump-started the process of entente-building within days of accepting charge of the HCE, and this effort would remain the central aspect of his leadership as head of state until he resigned from the presidency in April 1999 (a year early). Though a former general, Zeroual viewed himself primarily as a civilian agent of change, and promised a political solution to the Algerian crisis. However, throughout much of his leadership, Zeroual was hampered by the fact that two conflicting forces within his government competed for dominance. On the one hand, nearly all of his cabinet members were civilians, in favor of conciliation; on the other, most of his inner circle were generals and hard-line eradicators. This tension within government made it difficult for him to attempt any sort of rapprochement with Islamists.[23] The eradicators argued that the FIS would neither compromise nor renounce violence, and that the FIS were not helpless to prevent the escalation of terrorism against the regime.[24] Nevertheless, from the beginning Zeroual worked behind the scenes on private negotiations with Islamists, but these negotiations bore no tangible fruit.

Frustrated by these failures throughout 1994, Zeroual turned to pressing economic concerns. Under the strain of domestic financial dislocations and a globalizing financial system, Zeroual and Prime Minister Redha Malek undertook negotiations with the IMF and other financial backers in an effort to stabilize Algeria's economy. Ironically, even economic discussions hinged on the government's ability to arrive at some sort of conciliation with excluded Islamists and with other pro-democracy parties. Foreign financial institutions and the states that backed them called for Zeroual's government to reinitiate dialogue with all parties as a precondition of loans. With this pressure in mind, Zeroual moved to isolate those within his government who refused to compromise on negotiating with Islamists. Prime Minister Redha Malek and Interior Minister Selim Sadi were both forced to step down. Ultimately, although Zeroual was able to secure international financial assistance, he could not broker a deal with the Islamists and others and, as a result, on October 31, 1994, he addressed the nation with the news that dialogue had failed. He would now escalate the conflict with militant Islamists.

Although Zeroual's initiatives came to naught, a month later the main representatives of the FIS, the FLN, and the FFS met in Rome under the auspices of the Sant'Egidio religious community (a lay Catholic order known for mediating conflicts) to begin to work out a framework for national dialogue. This preliminary meeting was followed up in January 1995 (shortly after the hijacking of the Air France plane by the GIA – see Chapter Six) with a meeting of the leaders of Algeria's seven main opposition parties along with exiled FIS leaders, Rabah Kebir and Anwar Haddam, and the human rights leader, Ali Yahia. The political leaders were Abdelhamid Mehri (FLN), Hocine Aït Ahmed and Ahmed Djeddai (FFS), Rabah Kebir and Anwar Haddam (FIS), Louisa Hanoune (Workers Party), Ahmed Ben Bella and Khaled Bensmain (MDA), Ahmed Djaballah (Islamic Renaissance Movement/al-Hahda), and Ahmed Ben Mouhammed (Contemporary Muslim Algeria Movement, JMCA). As a collective, this pro-reconciliation group created the Sant'Egidio Platform, which represented a bold agenda for the reconstitution of Algerian civil and political life. The principal components of the platform, signed on January 13, 1995, called for a repeal of the ban on the FIS, a rejection of violence as a means to stay in power for the existing government, a separation of powers (executive, legislative, and judiciary), and respect for a multi-party system, among other things, including the recognition of Berber cultural identity. As the preconditions for negotiation, the platform demanded the release of FIS prisoners and an end to torture and capital punishment for political crimes, as well as to extrajudicial killings.[25] In addition, the platform called for a return to constitutionalism and a return to popular sovereignty.

The participants at the Sant'Egidio meeting extended an invitation to Zeroual, who rejected the offer and the platform out of hand. On many levels, the Sant'Egidio conference was an embarrassment to Zeroual, whose own attempts to find a solution looked all the more impotent in light of the rallying of Algeria's diverse parties behind the Sant'Egidio initiative. To add to Zeroual's problems, Sant'Egidio caught the public's attention in Algeria and Europe. After reports that Abassi Madani and Ali Belhadj had both endorsed the platform for national reconciliation and dialogue from prison, even more attention shifted away from Zeroual. On a very pragmatic level, Zeroual's rejection of the Sant'Egidio agreement showed a spectacular "lack of political imagination," as William Quart has phrased it. Rejected because it undercut the government's authority and because Sant'Egidio was initiated by parties in an extralegal predicament, the platform was in truth very similar to Zeroual's own strategy. Not wanting to be upstaged, even when international human rights organizations and other foreign leaders were urging the Algerian government to join in, Zeroual ignored the proposed platform while simultaneously working clandestinely to persuade FIS leaders to renounce violence. For example, Belhadj was reported to be close to reaching such an agreement with the government, until negotiations collapsed in mid-1995. But, in truth Belhadj had lost control over the actions of radical Islamists, especially members of the GIA, many of whom rejected the very notion of political Islamists and/or were frustrated with the government's treatment of Islamists.[26]

Political Islamists were not alone in believing that Algeria's eradicators were obsessed with destroying the Islamist movement well before guerrilla fighters started to sow carnage in 1993. As Abdennour Ali-Yahia argues in *Algérie: Raisons et déraison d'une guerre* (1996), the eradicators who dissolved parliament, ended the electoral process, and targeted Islamists with naked aggression had acted out a pathological urge to uproot political Islam from Algeria. This impulse grew stronger as the state's loss of control over Islam increased. According to him, after independence, Islam, which was "profoundly rooted in Algerian society," became an instrument of state propaganda; it was, in his words, "realized in a political arena for the political system, as a means of propaganda."[27] However, the emergence of the FIS, and other moderate parties such as Hamas and Nahda in the late 1980s and early 1990s, challenged a status quo that had embraced Islam as a cultural force but not a political one. And because Islamists had insisted that reclaiming the legitimacy of Islam implied notions of religious and political authenticity, the Islamist movement subverted the statist paradigm. Islamists had done this by using the political arena opened up by the state against the state's own narrow conception of Islam that limited it to the service of state propaganda.

The 1995 presidential elections

The question for Zeroual and the HCE was, how long could the political process be postponed and when could it be reignited without the possibility of the FIS being able to reconstitute itself? Zeroual still had a use for the FIS and its imprisoned leaders; the military's interest in the FIS was confined to enlisting its support to end the violence. However, since the violence of jihadi movements had clearly surpassed FIS control, Zeroual made a conscious choice to "give *carte blanche* to the military to eliminate the armed groups," and to give up on talks with FIS leaders.[28]

As the conflict with radical Islamists intensified, Zeroual knew that the credibility of the HCE's claims to be a transitional body had been exhausted. As a result, Zeroual announced that elections would be held in November 1995. Under considerable international pressure for the return to the ballot box but with firm control over the press and the levers of real power, Zeroual moved forward but with conditions: the FIS would be excluded from the process, and rigorous limits were placed on those seeking office. These restrictions narrowed the field of candidates and parties. Four candidates could compete for the presidency: Zeroual, Mahfoud Nahnah (Hamas), Saïd Saadi (RDC), and Noureddine Boukrouh, who ran on an Islamist platform but had few followers. For many the results of the elections were predictable. Zeroual won the election (which the government allowed international observers to oversee) with approximately 61 percent of the vote. Nahnah was placed second with a healthy showing of 25 percent, Saadi recorded 9 percent, and Boukrouh drew 4 percent.[29]

Politically, the elections represented a step in the direction of re-establishment of trust between the population and the government. Since FIS leaders had called for a boycott and this appeal had gone largely unheard, political Islamists understood that the population had largely decided to move forward without them. However, there was never really doubt that Zeroual would carry the elections, considering that the main Islamist party (as well as many other opposition-party candidates) were excluded. In this sense, the elections did little to dispel the belief that the military and the government were one.[30] And, while the outcome of the election was unsurprising, political and radical Islamists were infuriated that the population went along with these fraudulent elections. Meanwhile Djamal Zitouni, the man who claimed to be the national emir of the GIA, was so frustrated that people had voted at all by voting for Zeraoul that he issued a fatwa against the entire population.

Having moved through the first of what would be a series of limited presidential elections in post-1992 Algeria, Zeroual used the opportunity to redesign the constitution and to make other changes. On this count, the new constitution limited the executive to two five-year terms (which Abdelaziz Bouteflika reversed in October 2008). Zeroual's constitution also created a bicameral legislature divided into upper and lower houses. The People's National Assembly members would be elected to five-year terms, and the Council of the Nation (the lower house) would draw its members from local sites (cities, villages, and wilayas). To ensure a balance of power and prevent the possibility of one party scoring landslide victories in either house, the 1996 constitution created a system of proportional representation. Most importantly, however, it expanded the scope of the executive and gave the president the power to overturn any legislation that came out of parliament. Another important clause of the constitution forbade parties to openly identify with linguistic, ethnic, or religious practices and from advocating open hostility to the identity and security of the nation.[31]

In November 1996, the proposed constitutional revisions were put to a nation-wide referendum. According to the government, 80 percent of the population supported the new constitution. Once the constitution was ratified, Zeroual began the process of opening up national elections for the People's National Assembly and the Council of the Nation, which would have 380 seats.

The new constitution's prohibitions on religious and nationalist affiliations forced existing parties to change their names in order to remove the references to Islam. For example, Hamas became the Mouvement de la Société pour la Paix (MSP) and Nahda became Ennahda. The FLN, for its own part, underwent a political facelift by reconstituting itself as the Rassemblement National Démocratique (RND). Understood to be the "regime's party," the RND emerged victorious in the June 1997 elections, recording 156 of 380 seats and 32 percent of the vote. The MSP (formerly Hamas) captured 62 seats, the FFS drew 20, and the RCD gained 19. Despite the fact that the FIS and other Islamist parties were disenfranchised from the political process, Algeria experienced a relatively free election by regional standards.[32] Moreover, Algeria moved toward progressive reforms as the three main winners of the election gained the right to send ministers into Zeroual's cabinet, despite wide-scale accusations of voter fraud by those parties that either boycotted the elections or that were not allowed to join. These allegations were confirmed by the United Nations' monitors present during the elections. Ahmed Ouyahia, who had succeeded Mokdad Safi as prime minster (April 1994 to December 1995), was reappointed in that post, where he remained until Bouteflika's election in December 1999. A member of the RND (the restituted FLN), Ouyahia had tried to restore calm to Algeria and to organize a coalition government as terrorist attacks intensified at an alarming rate.

During the local and provincial elections held on October 23, 1997, the RND exceeded expectations and secured over half of the seats, 155 out of 380. Hamas captured 69, and the RND's predecessor, the FLN, 64.[33] The overwhelming victory for the RND (viewed by opponents as the party of the armed forces) generated more accusations of voter fraud, and sparked massive street protests. These protests did in fact carry weight, because a good many seats that were first recorded as RND victories were reallocated to other parties after appeal.[34] Nevertheless, Zeroual's government continued to rebuild the political process and engaged in efforts to bring about a ceasefire with the Armée Islamique du Salut (AIS), which some FIS leaders claimed represented the FIS's militant wing. Ironically, however, it was precisely this effort to broker a deal with the AIS that led, in part, to the escalation of violence in Algeria toward the end of 1997 and beginning of 1998. In fact, after the AIS announced the ceasefire on September 21, 1997, the rival groups forming the GIAs escalated their campaign of terror: systematic massacres were carried out in the Relizane province (to the northwest) in December 1997 and January 1998. Over 1,000 people were estimated killed in different massacres throughout the province in one month. In one village, nearly 120 people had their throats cut, and in village after village, innocent people were caught in a web of violence that the government could not end.[35]

Though the military disputes claims that it was involved in human rights abuses during the terrible years after the coup, former Algerian officers and members of the security branches have come forward with allegations of army involvement in terrorism against civilians. Perhaps the most important whistleblower was Habib Souaïdia, who published *La sale guerre* (2001) as an indictment of the Algerian military.[36] According to him, ultimate responsibility for the military violence against civilians and for human rights violations committed by the military in the 1990s rested with General Khaled Nezzar. As Adam Schatz points out, Nezzar replied to these charges by filing a defamation suit in France in 2001 against Souaïdia.[37] At the same time, relatives of the "disappeared" brought a suit against Nezzar in France. Nezzar eventually lost to the victims of the disappeared, and his suit against Souaïdia was dismissed in 2002. Despite these setbacks, he has remained steadfast in declaring his innocence, as well as that of his colleagues.

Regardless of such denials from key Algerian generals, other former security agents, army officers, and officers have continued to come forward with charges against the regime, including Abelkader Tigha, Mohammed Samraoui, and journalists like Sid Ahmed Semiane.[38] Each of these three has produced extensive dossiers documenting the state's manipulation of radical Islamists, and has alleged criminal wrongdoing on the part of the Algerian military during the 1990s.

All of these declarations, which came to light after Zeroual's decision to step down, caused the next president to fundamentally reconsider the power relations in Algeria. By 1998 and 1999, it was already clear that a new direction for the nation was necessary and a way out of the terror had to be found. Despite the military's objections, the government would inevitably have to negotiate with Islamic militants in order to secure the peace. Walking between the military leaders who refused to dialogue with radical Islamists, and militant Islamists who were now ready to lay down weapons on condition that they be allowed to re-enter civil society with impunity, required extraordinary nerves. It also required a leader who understood that the page had to be turned on the violence if the nation were to go forward. Just what would be the price for turning the page was still unclear, and, when it turned, it is fair to say that it was unsatisfactory for nearly everyone.

Ironically, while the military had its clear preferences for who the next leader might be, it had no idea of how its own relationship to power would change over the course of the next few years. Nevertheless, changes had to be made, and one of the most important of those changes would come from the very man that the military believed would be able to maintain the status quo. The army was caught by surprise when change finally came, just as were political reformers who had hoped that any future change would mean the re-establishment of political norms. As the government attempted to restore confidence in the political system and in its ability to provide security to a beleaguered population, it was plain to all that it would have to restore at least the semblance of a democratic process, and try to convince the Algerian people that the HCE and the post-coup leaders were no longer necessary. To move to this next stage and beyond the period of absolute terror, which culminated in the extermination of entire villages, the government would have to stabilize, terrorism would have to be contained, and economic viability would have to be restored. The question on everyone's mind was: who was capable of integrating each of these key points into a national platform?

4 | The Bouteflika era: civil society, peace, and sidelining generals

For the better part of the 1990s, the military called the shots in Algeria, making the "kings" who ruled only with its consent. It is a matter of continued dispute whether the nation has yet broken free of the generals' dominance; however, the election and re-elections of Abdelaziz Bouteflika (1999, 2004, and 2009) did significantly alter the military's relationship with the state, and within his first five-year term he had taken measures to inoculate the government against excessive military control. At the same time, Bouteflika fell prey to his own excesses, and, while taking steps to remove key military leaders in order to revive civilian leadership, he initiated a major constitutional overhaul that allowed him to run for a third term and thereby extend his own unyielding control. This controversial move ultimately undermined his credibility as a political reformer keen on jump-starting the democratic process.

As the process of reclaiming the space of civilian leadership unfolded under Bouteflika, it became clear that the public – which had been excluded from practically all aspects of governance after it brought the FIS into local office – would have to be entrusted with the right to elect its leaders, however limited that choice actually remained. Perhaps more important, as elements of popular sovereignty were restored, the public would be expected both psychologically and personally to share the burdens of peacemaking. Specifically, these burdens would come in the form of two important amnesty agreements enacted in two separate national referendums. Only this final step, which brought the public back into partnership with the state in an effort to end the scourge of terrorism, Bouteflika insisted, could create the conditions of a relatively stable polity.

The process of restoring civilian control started on September 11, 1998, when Zeroual shocked the Algerian establishment (and indeed most postcolonial African leaders, who in general have clung to power indefinitely) and announced that he would step down from the presidency before the end of his term. Unable to stop the violence and regain the public trust and the confidence of the international community, Zeroual was vulnerable and isolated.[1] By the time of his resignation, he had alienated most of his "eradicator" supporters by his willingness to dialogue with radical Islamists; and, paradoxically, Islamic activists reviled him because they considered his "conciliator" efforts lackluster, if not outright mendacious. The appalling massacres of 1997 and 1998 had marred his last two years in office and destroyed his credibility in the eyes of the international community, Algerian citizens, and his own inner circle. Perhaps most important, many generals viewed his rapprochement with Islamists as a failure that bore few rewards and many risks.

Despite the many criticisms of Zeroual, it is important to point out that there was a peaceful transfer of power. He formally resigned from the presidency on October 18 without great fanfare, and Prime Minister Ouyahia's departure followed on December 14. Algeria's next prime minister, Smail Hamdani (December 1998–December 1999), oversaw the process of setting the stage for the presidential elections, scheduled to take place in February but delayed until April 1999.

There was initially great excitement about the upcoming presidential election. It was to be the first opportunity to elect a president not directly related to the HCE and the 1992 coup. Nearly 50 people announced their candidature, 12 of whom gathered the requisite number of petition signatures required by the constitution, and seven of whom met the Constitutional Council's criteria to run for high office. Those left standing were Hocine Aït Ahmed (FFS); Mouloud Hamrouche and Mokdad Sifi (both former prime ministers); Youssef Khateb (a former colonel in the army of liberation); Ahmed Djaballah (a moderate Islamist); Ahmed Taleb Ibrahimi (a well-respected politician with a reputation going back to the war against the French, who had also served as foreign minister and minister of national education, and was a founder of the moderate Islamist Wafa party), and Bouteflika (minister of foreign affairs for 16 years who spent many years outside the country, but who had been convicted in 1983 of embezzling state funds from the coffers of Algerian embassies). All but Aït Ahmed ran as independents. Moufoud Nahnan, Sid-Ahmed Ghozali, Louisa Hanoune, and Noureddine Boukrouh were excluded from running on the grounds that they failed to gather enough signatures on their petitions.

Unlike his political rivals, Bouteflika had the clear backing of the military. Born in 1937, Bouteflika had been a member of the FLN during the war against the French and emerged from it as a close associate of Boumediene. Despite his career as a civilian diplomat, the army considered him an ally because of his resolve to fight terrorism and because it had become clear that they needed to recede, at least publicly. In addition, Bouteflika was known as a careful and tactical politician, who had played a major role in Boumediene's government in which the military remained a powerful force. His experience in international diplomacy would be vital to the government as it sought to restore confidence in Algeria. With this in mind, the military unofficially supported Bouteflika because he was considered to be their strongest supporter and because of his reputation in foreign affairs. Ironically, Bouteflika would leverage the trust bestowed on him by the military to sow a quiet revolution by initiating the slow process of removing key officers from power.

During the campaign, which lasted from the end of March to mid-April 1999, Bouteflika and his seven opponents made their cases to the Algerian electorate. However, Bouteflika enjoyed enormous advantages: he had more access to media coverage, and more resources at his disposal. Moreover, during the election there were significant irregularities, and on April 14, as the main polls opened, Bouteflika's opponents requested a special meeting with Zeroual. When Zeroual refused to meet with them, they issued a collective statement announcing that all six were withdrawing and would be asking their supporters to boycott the election. Despite these actions, the election went forward. With just over 60 percent of the population voting, Bouteflika recorded nearly 74 percent of the vote. It was an imperfect beginning to a new era of civilian leadership, and the last-minute calls for a boycott cast a shadow on the legitimacy of the political process.

Pax Bouteflika: the law on civil concord

Undeterred, Bouteflika was sworn into office on April 27, 1999. He had campaigned on a simple promise that was anything but easy to fulfill: he would bring peace to Algeria. Algerians had endured seven years of a brutal conflict between security forces and radical Islamists that had all but destroyed civil society; the military had managed to stay in power, but at tremendous cost, and with tactics that corroded its reputation both domestically and internationally. The principal radical Islamist groups were dwindling and losing their resolve, but new recruits continued to join the jihadi cause. Foreign powers were also growing more vocal in their fears about the spread of Algerian terrorism overseas through vast terrorist networks in Europe and North America. All of these factors presented Bouteflika with a unique political climate in which he could outline his agenda.

With the support of key generals, especially General Larbi Bekheir (who had been instrumental in the 1992 coup that forced President Chadli to resign, and who some have accused of being behind the assassination of President Boudiaf), Bouteflika staked his career on his ability to put into effect legislation that would grant amnesty to combatants on all sides. As the legislation materialized, it was baptized the Law on Civil Concord (*concorde civile*). The law would guarantee Islamists immunity on condition that they lay down their arms and renounce terrorism. For Bouteflika the law was more than symbolic; it was vital for the economy and for peace. But in order for it to be accepted by militant Islamists, Bouteflika had to challenge conventional wisdom and stand up to the eradicator generals who refused dialogue with political Islamists such as Rabah Kebir, Abassi Madani, and Abdelkader Mezrag. In July, after consulting with former FIS officials, he announced that he would appeal to the public through a national referendum. By calling on the public, he could bypass the military.

According to Bouteflika, the referendum was necessary and required public consent because it was the Algerian people who had suffered the most during the past seven years. Success or failure would lie in the hands of citizens who would be asked to play an active peacemaking role, by giving the government authority to grant radical Islamists immunity from prosecution. The public's benevolence would simultaneously reintegrate fugitives and outcasts back into society, by offering former terrorists a new social contract that included help in creating businesses. The comprehensive peace would clear the way for the nation-state to re-emerge from the carnage. As Bouteflika put it in a nationally televised speech on July 4, 1999:

> This is out of my conviction that Algeria has moved from revolutionary legitimacy to popular legitimacy. I am referring the matter to the people of Algeria to support our march for civil concord or reject it. The people make the final decision.
>
> ... I have dropped from my political glossary the words clemency, repentance, and surrender. The state is strong now. The strong one is capable of forgiving. It [the state] is opening its arms, its horizons and all its capabilities to open a new chapter for those who lost their way and want to come back, which is legitimate, into society.
>
> I do not think that we need a winner and a loser. Every drop of blood shed in Algeria every day is an Algerian drop of blood. I am calling upon you today honestly and sincerely in the name of the constitution, to which I continue to cling, and in the name of the republic's law, I call upon you to support me in achieving what we now call civil concord. I am sure that, as you did your best in defending the country, you will do your best in closing ranks and creating an objective atmosphere for national reconciliation. I am an advocate of national reconciliation. However, at the same time, I am an advocate of what I term civil concord.[2]

Bouteflika warned, however, that he would be relentless in the pursuit of terrorists who refused to accept his olive branch.

Many of the military commanders who had fought for years against Islamic terrorists opposed Bouteflika's magnanimous approach. Knowing this, it was all the more important for him – as a newly elected president, still unsure about his ability to thwart a putsch – to muster broad public support that could mitigate criticism from within the ruling elite and protect him from the real possibility of a forced removal. He could take these steps because the general public was eager to move beyond the logic of a military solution, and the amnesty law was palatable partially because it would grant impunity to between 5,000 and 6,000 militants (primarily members of the AIS), as a first step toward ending the violence.

In its application, the law was intended to amnesty those who had fought in what most considered the FIS's military wing (the AIS). It was the result of a deal worked out after long negotiations with AIS militants, and on June 6, the AIS announced that it would dissolve itself and accept Bouteflika's proposals. Technically, those seeking amnesty were first supposed to have their requests vetted by a formal panel. Yet in practice this condition was never implemented: AIS guerrillas would not even be required to make a public statement. Tellingly, while the law made important concessions to violent Islamists and allowed them to re-enter civil society unmolested, it said nothing about the FIS itself, which remained banned.

While unwilling to contemplate the possibility of unshackling the FIS, Bouteflika's hope in sponsoring the Law on Civil Concord was that the plan would be bold enough to end the Islamists' call to arms in Algeria. As he said in an interview with the *Washington Post* in September 1999: "Algeria will rise – I was going to say like a phoenix – from its ashes. ... The experience of the '90s, the fascism – never again."[3] But, in the face of international concerns about military excesses, Bouteflika promised to use "every means" to eliminate those rebels who refused to accept the amnesty deal, which was set to expire on January 13, 2000. Making clear that any form of violence would be used by security forces whose goal would be to liquidate any remaining resistance, he continued: "I want to say this before everybody – before the United Nations, before Amnesty International, before the world community ... We will use all means." At the same time, he restated that the FIS would not be granted the opportunity to re-enter the political process, and that the GIA would largely be excluded from amnesty as well.

Indeed, the *pax Bouteflika* was a risky venture. The state's use of amnesty was highly criticized in Algeria and by the international human rights community, and there could be no certainty of success. Peacemaking is, of course, often speculative, but Algeria's efforts were doubly so in that they represented a major departure from what is often called the "truth model" of reconciliation (most famously illustrated by South Africa's post-apartheid Truth and Reconciliation

Commission). Human rights organizations and the international community, more comfortable with this truth model, rejected Bouteflika's proposal vociferously.

On July 8, 1999, the law cleared the Algerian legislature with a healthy majority, and Bouteflika then expanded it to offer limited amnesty to some GIA fighters. The law passed with nearly 99 percent of the Algerian vote on September 16. Bouteflika's law, as John Ruedy has pointed out, identified five crimes: "1) homicide, 2) rape, 3) infliction of permanent disability, 4) collective massacres, and 5) setting off explosives at public places ..."[4] However, only those who committed collective massacres and who set off bombs in public places were originally disqualified from seeking amnesty.

In the end, over 5,000 Algerians had been granted amnesty by the time the deadline for applications arrived, in mid-January 2000. Some 5,000 convicted prisoners were also released. The 1999 law did not mention the role of the Algerian authorities, especially the state security forces. The government had no intention of opening this discussion, or yielding to calls for inquiries into crimes committed by the state while prosecuting the war on terror during the 1990s. Pragmatically, since the military still held the reins of power and Bouteflika had yet to prove himself as a formidable public force, it would have been unwise for him to open the door to investigating the army's conduct of the war, even if he wanted to in the hope of gaining broader international support.

The most virulent of terrorists rejected the amnesty outright, as did human rights, women's rights, and victim's rights groups, along with some FIS leaders. Most urgent, however, was an important cluster of terrorists, comprised of former members of the AIS and GIAs, who refused the Algerian government's offer and continued to consolidate resistance to the regime. That cluster, which would eventually regroup as the Groupe Salafiste pour la Prédication et le Combat (GSPC) had been formed by Hassan Hattab in 1998 – after the Salafists condemned the targeting of civilians by the GIAs, and after it became clear that the AIS fighters would lay down their arms in exchange for amnesty. Eager to derail Bouteflika's reconciliation agreement, the GSPC launched a jihad against the national government.

Less than a month after the referendum, Abdelkader Hachani was assassinated in an Algiers dentist's office on November 22. Hachani had been a central figure in negotiating the AIS ceasefire, but had rejected Bouteflika's 1999 amnesty agreements. Unlike Rabah Kebir and Abassi Madani, who supported the amnesty, Hachani thought that it did not go far enough. To be successful, Hachani insisted, the government had to legalize the FIS and allow it to return to politics. Only by normalizing relations with the FIS would the government have support from the Islamic community's leaders. More to the point, Hachani challenged the framework of Algeria's amnesty process and publicly urged the government to follow the South African model, which would have also implied specific compromises on the part of the state, especially regarding the FIS. Because of his outspoken objections to Bouteflika's amnesty program, Hachani was often prevented from speaking to journalists by the government.[5] Widely admired by even secular political opponents as a leading voice of reason within the Islamist movement and as someone who had shunned violence, one leader commented about Hachani's murder: "This is not just the killing of an Islamist ... it is the liquidation of a political opponent and a warning to others in the opposition." Abdelaziz Balkhadem (a former speaker of parliament, who would later become prime minister under Bouteflika) said that Hachani's death "is a tragedy for Algeria that will aggravate the crisis."[6] After Hachani's murder, Madani withdrew his support for Bouteflika's amnesty law.[7]

Assessing amnesty and controlling power

Initially, reconciliation was not as successful as Bouteflika had expected. In fact, in 2000 the number of terrorist-related deaths went up to 5,000, approximately twice the number reported the year before. In part this was due to the rapid and all-out war against those militant Islamists who refused to lay down arms in exchange for impunity. Aware that the military had questioned the wisdom of granting amnesty to its foes, Bouteflika began to take steps to insulate himself from a possible removal from power. A key factor in this regard was his decision to keep for himself the portfolio of minister of defense. This position gave Bouteflika authority to make changes within the military's power structure, which he used to replace key generals.

Throughout 2000 and early 2001, Bouteflika tried to overcome internal dissent and to ensure that his government would be able to deliver on its promises to secure peace. But peace at what cost? Women's rights groups argued that the amnesty had done women a particular disservice, because women had suffered disproportionately from Islamic terrorism. Victims of rape and other forms of violence against women therefore asked the government to prosecute those who had brutalized them.[8] At the same time, the families of the disappeared demanded that Bouteflika either find their loved ones or reveal where the bodies were, and urged him to prosecute the military and security forces responsible for state crimes. Bouteflika had little patience with either group, and publicly chided them for their refusal to let go of the past.[9]

The world community was not convinced that Bouteflika's 1999 Law on Civil Concord had paid sufficient attention to state crimes, or that it would make the country any safer. For example, on January 18, 2001, the European Parliament emitted a resolution on the law, lamenting the fact that nothing had been done regarding the thousands of disappeared.[10] The EU called on Bouteflika to cooperate with the United Nations' Working Group on enforced or involuntary disappearances. This was not the first time the EU passed a resolution on violence in Algeria. In fact it had done so in April 1995, December 1996, and September 1997, as well as more recently. But, like his predecessors, Bouteflika rejected these pleas by international organizations, especially Amnesty International, which called for greater access to the country and for greater contrition from the government. Arguing that the Islamists who refused to accept the government's terms for peace were now without conventional rights, Bouteflika gave the green light to the military to destroy all remaining militant Islamists with whatever tactics it deemed appropriate.

Bouteflika's first two years in office were exceedingly difficult. He felt particularly pressured by the military to continue cracking down on Islamists. At the same time, exiled FIS leaders including Rabah Kebir were allowed to return home, while others such as Anwar Haddam made it clear that he also wished to benefit from the generous amnesty agreements. Bouteflika made no initial promises to Haddam, who had been tried and sentenced to death *in absentia* while in exile in the US.

Having made it through the first phase of his first term, Bouteflika continued with his ambitious liberalization program, while also trying to repair the relationship between Algeria and France. Bouteflika invited French president Jacques Chirac to Algeria in 1999 (though it would take several years for Chirac to visit), and himself visited France in June 2000, as the first Algerian head of state to visit the former colonial power in more than 20 years. By 2000 Bouteflika and Chirac especially wanted to rebuild economic ties, as both countries benefited immensely from economic exchange.

In spring 2001, disturbances in Kabylia once again moved the Berber question to center-stage, after police killed a young boy in Tizi Ouzou on April 26. A few days later, following an incident of police brutality against three more Berber youths, massive riots and public disturbances spread. An estimated 500,000 demonstrators took to the streets in Kabylia, and another 100,000 followed suit in Algiers.[11] Spontaneous and angry, the protests condemned the treatment of Berbers by the government and demanded the formal recognition of their language, Tamazight. Despite the government's 1995 recognition of "Berber culture" as part of Algeria's national identity, and the decision to allow limited teaching of Tamazight, the overwhelming sense of alienation caused by the government's resolve to finalize the arabization process in 2000 caused a massive public backlash against Bouteflika's government.

The ethnic dimensions of the protests in Kabylia overlapped with other social problems that also existed throughout Algeria, most importantly unemployment and the lack of housing, but the crux of the problem, as Hugh Roberts explains, was the "brutal contempt with which the authorities treat ordinary people and the humiliation heaped upon them. Socio-economic issues such as the lack of jobs and housing – which are also widely seen as expressing the authorities' arrogant indifference towards ordinary people – were quite naturally grafted onto the protest."[12] Hence, the disturbances in Kabylia were less about Berber identity than about the failure of the government to offer true political reform, and a way out of the chronic economic malaise. In addition, the government had failed to sponsor a meaningful democratic opposition movement. What was different about Kabylia was that here the failure of democratic reforms combined with that sense of humiliation to create the impetus for a massive opposition movement that once again used the power of the streets to vent anger against the regime.

That said, Bouteflika did not brook criticism in Kabylia, and the military responded with force. At the same time, he indirectly accused the RCD (led by Saadi) of fomenting the rebellion. As a result, the RCD withdrew from the coalition government in May 2000. Just prior to that, Bouteflika had announced the formation of a commission to examine the Berber claims of violence. Nevertheless, military and security forces continued to crack down on protesters in disturbances that lasted for several months, with a final tally of over 100 deaths and over 5,000 injuries.[13]

In August 2000, Ali Benflis replaced Ahmed Benbitour as prime minister (December 1999–August 2000). Benflis had been a career FLN politician, and as prime minister he took the lead on the Kabylia issue in 2001.[14] In addition to promising that the government would prosecute Algerian police officers for using excessive force against the Berbers, he offered to meet with Kabyle leaders. In 2002, Benflis and some Kabyle leaders reached a temporary agreement. The government would prosecute roughly two dozen police officers accused of misconduct, and give financial compensation to the families of the victims. Most symbolically, Bouteflika amended the constitution in 2002 to list Tamazight as a national language. This amendment was ratified in April. However, these concessions still proved unsatisfactory, firstly because the government refused to withdraw the national police, claiming that their presence was necessary to combat terrorism. Moreover, Kabyle leaders considered that the government had failed to deal with unemployment and to make Tamazight an official national language, on a par with Arabic.[15] This anger translated into a call to boycott the 2002 parliamentary elections by Aït Ahmed's FFS and Saadi's RCD parties. From that point forward, Kabylia would remain a challenge for Bouteflika's government.

Coming at the height of Berber protests in 2001, the al Qaeda attacks on the US on September 11, 2001 changed the dynamics in

Algeria in several important respects. First, after years of strained relations between Algeria and the US, Algeria suddenly attracted new favor. A process of drawing closer to the US and France had been initiated before 9/11. In May 2001, President Bush dispatched Secretary of State Colin Powell to South Africa to assure African leaders (including South African President Thabo Mbeki) that the US was serious about aiding African nations from North to South in economic and political reforms. Then, in the first visit by an Algerian president to the White House for 16 years, Bouteflika met with Bush on July 12, 2001 – a clear contrast with President Clinton, who had been disappointed in Bouteflika and refused to meet with him.[16]

In the July meeting between Bouteflika and Bush, with massive protests still sweeping Kabylia and other cities, the leaders conversed about bilateral relations between the US and Algeria and discussed plans for resolving the long-standing dispute between Morocco and Algeria, including UN efforts to mediate the Western Sahara issue.[17] Bouteflika also met separately with Vice President Dick Cheney, and the two men discussed, among other things, developing stronger ties with the US in the oil and gas sectors. By this time, however, prominent US firms, including Conoco, Exxon Mobil, Halliburton, and Anadarko Petroleum were already operating in Algeria. Bouteflika's first visit yielded a commitment on his part to speed up political and economic reforms, and specific trade agreements that strengthened the presence of US oil and gas firms. As Bouteflika summarized the connection between economics and political reform during the July visit: "Algeria is determined to pursue such a policy and the process of reform ... in order to ensure a transition toward a dynamic market economy, which can generate jobs ... and establish the rule of law."[18]

Mutual interests in the energy sector brought Bush and Bouteflika together, but the so-called "War on Terror" cemented the marriage ideologically. Like Tony Blair, then leading a UK government that had fought against the Irish Republican Army (IRA) for decades, Bouteflika was especially pleased to have a new ally in his own war on terror. Between September 2001 and March 2003, Bouteflika repeatedly stated that Algeria had been for over a decade one of the front-line states in a war on terror that had only recently reached

American soil. Bush sympathized with this position. The "War on Terror" had finally validated in the mind of US leaders Bouteflika's assertion that laws of conventional warfare had to be suspended in the effort to crush Islamic terrorists who had refused his generous offer of peace. To press his case, Bouteflika returned to Washington in November 2001 for a four-day meeting with officials (including National Security Advisor Condoleezza Rice) and for a second meeting with President Bush.

Amid continued revelations and allegations that the Algerian military was itself also responsible for the massacres and the killing of civilians in Algeria, this sudden rehabilitation of Algeria on the world stage could not have come at a better time for Bouteflika.[19] Uneasy with the persistent terrorist violence against the regime (which continued to undermine his claim that the amnesty had quelled rebellion) and with the new accusations of wrongdoings and double-dealing by the military, Bouteflika took special care to cultivate this new relationship with the US and Western allies. It paid off, because in 2002, the US lifted its ten-year arms embargo against Algeria. Despite the common enemy, this political partnership was, however, momentarily tested by the US decision to invade Iraq in March 2003.

The US position on Algeria and the rest of Africa had shifted considerably after the 9/11 attacks, after which strategic and national security overrode the question of human rights. This shift became more pronounced after the beginning of the Second Gulf War and more specifically after the kidnapping of European tourists in Algeria's Sahara Desert in 2003 by Salafist terrorists operating under the banner of the GSPC (see Chapter Seven). These kidnappings confirmed, in the minds of US military planners, the belief that terror in the Sahel region (adjacent with the Sahara) would continue to pose a threat to international security and that the region was a haven for radical Islamists. With its permeable borders, open spaces, and a population deemed susceptible to jihadi ideology, the Sahel quickly became the "new Afghanistan" and the new front of the "War on Terror."[20] The US and Algeria both saw the Sahel as an area of vital security importance, one where US and Algerian security interests directly overlapped. The Sahel was suddenly identified as a place where transnational terrorist networks came together and where, as a consequence, an international military presence would be required.

In general terms, this new regional partnership was formed in order to combat international and domestic terrorism and to protect mutual strategic interests, such as oil and gas. The partnership grew stronger as militant Islamic opposition to the US-led war in Iraq began to intensify after 2003, and especially following the sensational kidnapping of over 32 European tourists in March 2003 in Algeria.[21] On October 25 and 26, the US Assistant Secretary of State for Near Eastern Affairs William Burns visited Algeria. Burns confirmed that the US would supply vital military support.[22] Burns's visit came almost immediately after the US government Treasury Department added the GSPC to its list of Specially Designated Global Terrorists. As part of the military assistance that was now meant to target an al Qaeda affiliate, Burns stated that the US had provided funding to train Algerian military officers and police. At the same time he indicated that the US would not provide Algeria with lethal weapons, due to concerns about the state's human rights violations, and he encouraged Bouteflika and Algerian officials to move to more open political reforms. By the time of Burns's visit, it was widely rumored that the US had begun to establish mobile military bases in the Algerian Sahara. Burns noted that this claim was not true and that, although the US and Algeria were cooperating, the US had no plans to install bases in Algeria.

Unofficially the Pentagon's "second front" in the "War on Terror," the Sahel has seen an intensification of activities.[23] As such, it represents an important step in building closer alliances with Algeria and other members of the Pan Sahel counter-terrorism collective.[24] Bouteflika has ensured close ties with the US forces, and together Algerian and American troops have targeted GSPC fighters and other international groups that both governments claim sweep through the region's open expanses. The most famous instance of cooperation was the coordinated response to the abduction of the 32 European tourists, which some scholars and journalists have alleged was orchestrated by Algerian counter-terrorism agents in order to draw the US into the region.[25]

Regardless of the controversy over the origins of the new US–Algeria friendship, the Pan Sahel Initiative has gone forward and expanded, leading to major policy changes within the US Defense Department (DoD) and State Department.[26] In exchange for co-operation with the US on matters of security, Algeria has benefited from increased military, technical, and financial assistance; meanwhile, the US has had greater military and intelligence access to the country. As US Secretary of Defense Donald Rumsfeld stated after a February 2006 visit to Algeria: "They have things they desire, and we have things we can be helpful with."[27] When asked by a reporter whether the US would require further political progress in Algeria before the US would offer more assistance, Rumsfeld declined to answer directly but replied: "The United States and Algeria have a multifaceted relationship ... It involves political and economic as well as military-to-military cooperation. And we very much value the cooperation we are receiving in counter-terrorism because it's important to both of our countries."[28] In 2005, the US opened its first CIA office in Algiers. Needless to say, the scandalous revelation that Algiers's CIA station chief, Andrew Warren, was under investigation for suspected drug-induced and videotaped date rapes carried out on the grounds of the US embassy have been a major embarrassment for President Barack Obama's administration, which took control of the government a week before ABC News broke the story on January 28, 2009.

Well before the date rape scandal tested US–Algerian relations under President Obama, an important disagreement surfaced during the lead-up to the 2003 US invasion of Iraq. In preparation for the visit of French President Jacques Chirac in March 2003, Bouteflika praised Chirac for his opposition to George Bush's war, and even suggested that the French president should be rewarded for his anti-US stance with the Nobel Peace Prize.[29] Knowing full well that broader Arab public opinion and Algerian public opinion in particular were decidedly against the invasion of Iraq, and that radical Islamists had been effective in using the US invasion to attract recruits, Bouteflika was in no position to support the US-led invasion. And yet, despite his own opposition to the war, Bouteflika then sought closer relations with the Bush administration and tried to convince US officials that radicals intended to use Algeria as a recruiting and training site to fight against coalition forces in Iraq. In the end, Bouteflika was successful at using the threat of terror to mold an unexpected alliance with the US.

The demilitarization of state power

On April 8, 2004, Bouteflika was re-elected to a second term with 85 percent of the vote, on a turnout of 58 percent (roughly 10.5 million). His principal opponent, the former prime minister Ali Benflis (FLN), won a mere 6.4 percent of the vote. Other candidates included Saad Abdallah Djaballah (for the moderate Islamist National Reform Movement), Ali Fawzi Rebaine (Abd 54 Party), Louisa Hanoune (Workers Party), and Saïd Saadi (RCD). Former Prime Ministers Mouloud Hamrouche and Ahmed Benbitour, as well as retired General Rachid Benyelles, withdrew from the race, claiming corruption, and called for a boycott. As many opposition candidates and even General Larmi complained, Bouteflika was widely regarded as autocratic and unwilling to share power. As Ali Benflis described Bouteflika during the 2004 elections: "with him, it's absolute monarchy."[30] Bush administration officials had urged Bouteflika to ensure electoral transparency; Secretary of State Colin Powell reiterated this demand during a December 2003 visit to Algiers.[31] Yielding to pressure, Bouteflika invited international election monitors to Algeria to observe the elections, and 130 came to monitor the outcome. Despite allegations of corruption and strong-arm tactics and control over the media, Bouteflika's victory reconfirmed his position and the belief that he had overcome his critics in the armed forces.

Prior to the election, and also largely in response to demands made on Algeria to show internal political reform, Bouteflika appointed several key women opposition politicians to ministerial posts as part of his coalition government, including the prominent feminist Khalida Toumi, who became minister of culture and information in May 2003. Despite death threats against her and failed assassination attempts, Toumi remained active in Algerian political circles.[32] She had been a member of the Conseil consultatif national from 1992–93, and as a RCD member, she was elected a deputy of the National Assembly from 1997–2002. Often tagged as an eradicator,

Toumi has been a vehement opponent of Islamists. She agreed to join Bouteflika's cabinet primarily because she wanted to force women's issues back into the political debate, but within the government's inner circle. In reality, she has not been able to effect meaningful change on the question of women's rights, nor has she convinced Bouteflika to revise the 1984 Family Code.

National reconciliation

In 2005, Bouteflika presented his *summa politica*: the 2005 Charter for Peace and National Reconciliation, which offered even more amnesty provisions to terrorists and agents of the state, and which he claimed was inspired by the 1995 Sant'Egidio Platform. Put to national referendum in September 2005, this charter expanded considerably on the 1999 amnesty law, and represents the hallmark of Bouteflika's political career. But why did Bouteflika find it necessary to call for a second referendum on amnesty? Put simply, the key difference between the 1999 amnesty and the 2005 amnesty is that while the former offered an implicit amnesty for the military, the latter offered an explicit amnesty for the military, state officials, and security services.

In an interview, Hugh Roberts offered a "hypothesis" about Bouteflika's decision to call for a second amnesty referendum. According to Roberts, it represented a

> quid pro quo for those Bouteflika had just pensioned off. In order to get them out of the game, he had to promise them that they won't be bothered, that they won't be inconvenienced after retirement. Bouteflika wanted the people most associated with the dirty war, particularly people like Larmi, who had after all been his adversary, in retirement. But there had to be a deal. The deal was you leave the stage, you make way for the younger generation, and you won't be prosecuted or hauled over the coals for what you did. And one could argue that's politics in the Algerian context. If one accepts that it's a useful thing that these people were pushed out. The problem is that Bouteflika has been operating in a context that he didn't himself shape. I've always tended to have slight degree of sympathy for Bouteflika because, after all, he was out of office for 20 years.[33]

In the hopes of ending terrorism for good, Bouteflika insisted that a more extensive amnesty agreement was necessary, and that his path-breaking program of national reconciliation offered the right formula. However, Bouteflika emphasized that he would not endorse a general amnesty. It was not possible, he insisted, to pardon those who had committed massacres, set off bombs in public spaces, or committed rape. Hence a general, though not universal, amnesty was necessary to turn the page on history. A key provision of the 2005 charter stipulated that families of victims would receive financial compensation for their losses (as long as they agreed not to discuss the war), and that terrorists who laid down their weapons would be allowed to return, with full rights, to civil society. The charter excluded terrorists who had set off bombs in public spaces, been involved in massacres, or committed rape, which had been named by the UN as a crime against humanity in 2005. As Bouteflika expressed it in the lead-up to the referendum in August 2005, national healing necessitated a two-step "vaccination" against the past. The first vaccine was the 1999 "civil concord," the second was "national reconciliation."[34] In fact, the Charter's wording praised the military and security forces for their conduct during the war against insurgents. When the specific details of the amnesty were finally announced on February 21, 2006, the government formally shielded the military from prosecution with a decree that went further than anyone could have imagined:

> Anyone who, by speech, writing, or any other act, uses or exploits the wounds of the National Tragedy to harm the institutions of the Democratic and Popular Republic of Algeria, to weaken the state, or to undermine the good reputation of its agents who honorably served it, or to tarnish the image of Algeria internationally, shall be punished by three to five years in prison and a fine of 250,000 to 500,000 dinars.[35]

National reconciliation went in tandem with a major reshuffle of the military. In the lead-up to the referendum, several key generals had made their opposition to the second amnesty clear, insofar as it let the Islamists off the hook. In particular, General Mohamed Larmi, who had served as the army's chief of staff for defense since

1993, took his disagreement with Bouteflika public. As their quarrel became more intense, Bouteflika forced the recalcitrant officer to retire in August 2004, replacing him with General Gaïd Salah. Bouteflika also reshuffled several other military posts. He placed Malek Nessib in charge of the navy, Malti Abdelghani in charge of the military academy of Cherchel, Laychi Ghird in charge of the Republican Guard, and Ali Benali in charge of the 5th Military Region (which surrounds Algiers).[36]

Later, on March 18, 2006, the Algerian parliament strengthened Bouteflika's hand against the military with new legislation requiring the chief of staff to retire at the age of 64, and generals to retire at 60. It further clarified that the defense minister (Bouteflika) was responsible for overseeing the military elite's careers.[37] Bouteflika's strategy of slowly removing generals from power was part of a carefully orchestrated effort to draw clear boundaries between civilian and military affairs. In 2005 alone, 37 generals retired, and roughly between mid-2004 and June 2006, Bouteflika replaced over a thousand senior and mid-level officers. As *El Watan* newspaper put it, the military "will no longer be a kingmaker."[38] However, Bouteflika replaced these officers with commanders who were clearly more loyal to him.

Despite widespread approval of the 2005 charter, and relief that the military was finally beginning to be checked by the civilian authorities, for many critics the most difficult aspect of the 2005 charter and its 2006 implementation was the government's decision not to require amnesty-seekers, including murderers, to go before the courts (unless they were charged with involvement in massacres, bombings, or rapes). The very possibility of such a liberal amnesty for all military and security personnel triggered criticism from many quarters.

National and international human rights communities campaigned heavily against the Algerian government's application of the charter. The Algerian Human Rights League president, Ali Yahia, rejected the charter outright, arguing that it would accomplish nothing since it neither legalized the FIS nor offered an admission of government wrongdoing. Cherifa Kheddar, leader of Djazairouna, a group that represents the victims of terror, complained: "We want the courts to deal with those who ordered and those who carried out violence, even if Mr. Bouteflika later pardons them."[39] For Kheddar and many Algerians like her, the brazen reappearance in their old neighborhoods of Islamists who had committed violent crimes against their neighbors, without even a formal court apology, was particularly offensive. Amnesty International agreed, and prior to the September 2005 referendum, on August 22, 2005, it published an online "public statement" under the title of "Algeria: President calls referendum to obliterate crimes of the past."[40] Amnesty International's greatest fear was simply put: "The lack of any commitment to investigate the grave abuses committed during Algeria's internal conflict raises serious concerns that proposed measures will perpetuate a climate of impunity and ultimately encourage further abuses in Algeria."

Fatima Yous, director of the Algerian human rights organization SOS Disparus, dedicated to the investigation of state-sponsored abductions (estimated at between 8,000 and 10,000), lamented Bouteflika's reconciliation program. (Her own grandson had disappeared after being taken by police in 1997.) "All we want is the truth ... We are ready to forgive, but we want our families back and we want the truth. We are not going to sue the guy who killed him. But I want to know if they killed him, why they killed him and where his bones are."[41] In response, Mustapha Farouk Ksentini, chairman of the official commission responsible for advising the government on human rights, stated in an interview: "We know that this national reconciliation will forgive a lot of criminals, but it's the price we have to pay to turn the page. ... Algeria doesn't have the means to press ahead with trials. We made a choice and said that the national interests are more important than this."

Not satisfied with this response, Mostefa Bouchachi (an Algerian human rights lawyer) rejected the recommendations of the official government commission, and stated that a trial-based amnesty "would result in a bloodbath. But at least we would like to know who did what, and why, and who is responsible. In the Algerian reconciliation, they just tell you to turn the page. We think it's a culturalization of impunity for both camps: the security forces and the Islamists." Retired general Fodli Cherif Brhim criticized the amnesty for Islamists: "These people are fanatics to the extreme ... They don't know anything about the real Islam. This is what they did: they committed horrible crimes. They put knives in the bellies of pregnant women. These people, you have to kill them ... They will never give up."

Amnesty did also have unintended consequences. Anwar Haddam, who was detained by the US for five years until 2000, and who since had remained there, made it known that he wanted to return to Algeria and benefit from the generous amnesty accords. For example, in December 2006, Haddam gave an interview to an Algerian journalist in which he stated that he wished to return to Algeria to take part in the national reconciliation. He confirmed that he had been in conversation with Prime Minister Abdelaziz Balkhadem and that he did not wish to form a political party, because, in his words, "it is futile to engage in politics when the country is in a state of emergency."[42] As for the future of the FIS, he noted: "I do not see any future for it at the moment. My priority is to help ensure the success of national reconciliation." Haddam expressed regret that Ali Belhadj had been allowed to openly deliver "fiery speeches" on behalf of the FIS, which was one of the reasons for its downfall, but he expressed a belief that his subsequent "incarceration was an opportunity for him to acquire some further education." However, he commented that Islamists had an opportunity to set the record straight in the context of the post-9/11 world. "We have been taken hostage. We must reformulate our messages to the West and review our international relations. In other words, our message should be: If all wars are being fought for the sake of preserving the Arab world as a market, you can keep this market by peaceful coexistence, instead of war."

"President for life"

On October 29, 2008, the 71-year-old president – who has been undergoing treatment in France for an unspecified illness – gave a speech that ended speculation by asking for the constitution's article 77 to be amended, an action that would allow him to stand for a third term. Bouteflika claimed that this amendment was necessary for the sake of national security and political continuity. On November 3, his cabinet approved the proposed constitutional changes. In addition to removing presidential term limits, the proposed revisions also changed the status of the prime minister, who would have the powers of head of government but who would be appointed directly by the president, rather than parliament. On November 12, the pro-Bouteflika ruling majority in parliament (both upper and lower houses) overwhelmingly ratified (by 500 out of 529 total votes) the changes to the constitution. Opposition candidates understandably read this as a major setback for political progress in Algeria. RCD leader Saïd Saadi commented: "We are living through a disguised coup d'état ... November 12 will remain a black day in history."[43] Immediately following the constitutional changes, Bouteflika replaced Balkhadem as prime minister with Ahmed Ouyahia.

Former prime minister Ahmed Benbitour also heavily criticized Bouteflika's moves and the constitutional changes, arguing that Bouteflika had lost credibility as a democrat by forcing through these constitutional changes. In his view, Algeria had returned to its authoritarian past and Bouteflika had gone the route of the old guard.

Hugh Roberts calls for a more forgiving interpretation. He argues that the rewriting of the constitution to allow for a third term has less to do with Bouteflika than it does with the corruptness of the power structure in Algeria: "The first thing to say [about the reform allowing Bouteflika to run for a third term] is that the ruling oligarchy in Algeria has never taken its constitution seriously."[44] Because the constitution has always been seen as something that can be modified, "the constitution has never had the force of laws, binding political actors. It's been the dress whose hem they take up or lower depending on how they feel." This "instrumental attitude toward the constitution" has been a constant feature of Algerian political history for years. In other words, it reflects a "long tradition of tailoring and re-tailoring the constitution to suit one's preferences." However, from the point of view of "abstract principles" it is not that "big of a deal." What is striking, though, in contrast to the issue of amnesty, this change was not ratified by the nation in the form of a referendum. And that omission alone suggests the "presidency was nervous about how much popular support" there would be for this change. In other words, as Roberts points out: "I think the fact that they didn't put it to a referendum is significant."

In the lead-up to the election, Bouteflika campaigned on many promises. For example, he promised to "totally erase the debts of farmers and livestock raisers" and provide funding for other social programs.[45] Yet, just prior to the election, Amnesty International took the opportunity to again urge Bouteflika to come clean on the state's human rights record and to rethink the use of amnesty.[46] At the same time, key opposition candidates, including RCD leader Saïd Saadi and the leader of the FFS, called for a boycott of the elections amid allegations of voter fraud and intimidation. Abassi Madani and Ali Belhadj, who was not allowed to stand as a candidate, eventually supported the boycott.

Ali Belhadj had, however, held a different view of the possibilities of Algerian politics. In October 2008, he clarified his intention to stand as a candidate in the scheduled April 2009 presidential race. Having spent years in prison, and then five more living under state sanctions that limited his activities and ability to speak to reporters, he insisted that he had earned the right to run for office again. "I am determined to be a candidate; it is my political right, guaranteed by the law, the constitution, and the international provisions adopted by Algeria."[47] Conversely, Belhadj argued that Bouteflika had no right to run for a third time. Belhadj insisted that article 77 of the 1996 constitution, which limited presidential terms to two, must be respected.

From exile in Qatar, Abassi Madani noted in a press conference that "[e]lections in Algeria are a way to consecrate a rotten reality."[48] Nevertheless, on April 9, 2009, Bouteflika was elected to a third term in an overwhelming victory. With over 12 million out of approximately 20 million Algerians going to the polls, over 90 percent cast ballots in favor of Bouteflika.[49] The labor candidate, Louisa Hanoune, came in a distant second, recording just over 4 percent of the vote. Prior to the election Hanoune had rejected calls for a boycott, and went so far as to say that those advocating it should be "damned."[50]

There is considerable skepticism about the future of Algerian politics, now that Bouteflika has been successful at gaining a third term. In moving the country away from limited terms, Bouteflika has re-created the conditions that will make it easier for citizens to opt out of the political process. It is certainly difficult to sustain calls for change after Bouteflika's election to a third term, and he has gone the way of other African leaders who refused to cede the presidency in a peaceful transfer of power.

That said, Bouteflika's legacy will no doubt be mixed, complicated by the fact that while he was able to largely end the violent conflict between radical Islamists and the state, and able to eliminate the appearance of the military's stranglehold on power, he also introduced the specter of unlimited presidential terms and in so doing undermined his own reputation as a reformer. Whether this is important to Bouteflika is a matter of conjecture. What is much less disputed is that many Algerians feel a great sense of disappointment about Bouteflika's inability to create the conditions for a peaceful transfer of power after his second term. And there is no doubt that his decision to rewrite the constitution to accommodate his own personal political ambitions will continue to generate great skepticism about the possibility for meaningful political reform in Algeria.

5 | Energy and the economy of terror

Throughout the 1990s, political and economic chaos forced Algerians to rethink the decades-old statist development paradigm. This effort formed part of a continuum that had begun even before the October 1988 riots, when key leaders sensed a powerful new force taking shape as the Cold War drew to a close: globalization. As it played out around the world, globalization ensured the end to purely nationalist frameworks for economic growth, and presented leaders and citizens alike with a host of ideological and pragmatic challenges. Like most third-world economies, during the 1980s and 1990s Algeria's was swept up by the tsunami of globalization, which, in a debtor's world, translated into huge expectations of compliance with demands set by global capitalists. That Algeria's era of globalization happened to correspond with the rise of Islamic terrorism presented policy-makers with two sets of forces – globalization and terrorism – that overlapped and intersected at key moments to form a dispiriting, but also surprising, story.

During the early days of globalization, prophets of globalization such as Milton Friedman created the ideological and economic conditions under which the world would be rearranged by capitalists who used "crisis" conditions as a pretext for dismantling state enterprises and state economies.[1] As Naomi Klein has shown, "disaster capitalists" *à la* Friedman relied on the unfettered powers of the states – whose leaders often brutalized their own populations – to install fierce capitalist models.[2] Not surprisingly, Friedman's system of disaster capitalism worked far more effectively when "authoritarian conditions" have been in place than when "democracies" exist.[3] Since Algeria was ruled by a regime with far from democratic tendencies for much of the 1990s, it offered the perfect soil for predatory disaster capitalism. Its military junta suppressed dissent and quieted political opponents, and officials had few credit options due to a generation of catastrophic economic planning. Finally, the advent of radical Islam provided the opportunity for the government to crush even democratic opponents to Algeria's crisis management during the 1990s.

Neo-conservatives such as Francis Fukuyama storied globalization as the rise of a new world economic order, triumphantly organized around global capitalism and the decline of socialist economies.[4] During the 1980s and 1990s, the disaster capitalism that imposed key elements of economic globalization in the name of "privatization, stabilization, and liberalization" found its way to Africa, Asia, and the former Soviet bloc, where it became the model for post-Cold War, post-Non-Alignment economic growth.[5] Backed by the persuasive powers of the IMF, World Bank, and other international agencies, globalization (the Trojan Horse of disaster capitalists) became the mantra par excellence for developing nations, at the behest of the major industrial powers. These powers – Europe, the US, and Japan in particular – used their control over the international banking system to enforce privatization, to dismantle many of the developing world's national banks, and, wherever possible, to liquidate the remnants of socialism. To be sure, this suited the interests of major investors in Algeria, most of whom (including France) were involved in a similar process of privatization at home. It also suited particular individuals within Algeria's ruling elite, who profited handsomely from privatization. But it led to profound dislocations within society, massive job cuts, and the loss of all kinds of social services. Nevertheless, in Algeria as elsewhere the major economic powers forced the developing world's economies into the very financial schemes and global conditions that would come apart at the seams in the fall of 2008. The results of the dismantling of state enterprises and banks in Algeria are still far from clear, but, given the catastrophic global financial meltdown of the winter 2008–09, the need to evaluate the conditions under which globalization was implemented is clear.

To be sure, globalization came into play in Algeria during the most profound political crisis in the nation's history. Violent challenges by radical Islamists increased the stakes for Algerian policy-makers, who desperately tried to keep the economy afloat while combating terrorism. Confronting rising Islamic militancy while on unstable political ground, Algerian leaders rushed headlong into a gathering storm, but during the 1990s they had few options. Yet the story that emerges from Algeria's experience with globalization, and from what I call the "economy of terror" that resulted from the decade-long struggle with toxic terrorist organizations, is unique and largely under-studied.

As this story unfolds here, it will become clear that Algeria is at once a local and a global story, one that allows us to see what globalization looks like from the perspective of a country long considered a postcolonial success story, but which found itself on troubled ground throughout the 1990s. Because Algeria is situated at the cross-roads of the Middle East, Africa, and the Mediterranean world, and is vital to Europe's energy supply, an analysis of globalization there is illustrative of the complex web that connects North Africa's economy to Europe, America, and Asia. As such, Algeria allows us to ask how international companies and foreign governments continued to invest and interact vis-à-vis a nation in the teeth of tremendous violence and disruption. It prompts other questions, such as whether Algeria can be likened to national models such as Mexico (an important and interconnected country that could not be allowed to fail), Myanmar (a military junta and human rights violator that needed to be singled out and ostracized by the international community), or even Afghanistan (a failed state that Western policy-makers wrongly thought could be ignored).

With these and other questions in mind, one of the most fascinating aspects of the Algerian economy during the decade of terror (though far from over) is the emergence of a prolonged engagement with foreign economic partners, in spite of the nation's troubles. As we shall see, this engagement in turn led to a series of contortions and compromises by Algerian leaders and foreign investors. Foreign investors were especially keen to downplay their activities in the conflict. Finally, perhaps the biggest question to emerge from the economic considerations here is: why were the resistance groups that fervently attacked the military and state powers not able to do a better job of disrupting energy production, given their determination to unsettle other areas of society? In other words, why did violence, which was also becoming an integral part of the globalization story (something clarified by the 9/11 attacks, and discussed in the next two chapters), prove unable to stop the process of economic globalization?

Privatization, energy, and the First Gulf War

The sudden need for larger infusions of cash from international sources encouraged leaders to drastically re-evaluate the national banks and to end some state subsidies in the mid- to late 1980s. As a result, in 1986 Algeria made its first real move to liberalize the banking industries, but it took several years to enact the major components. In 1989, Algeria signed its first "standby agreement" with the IMF, which brought a commitment from the IMF to help sustain Algeria as it sought to normalize its economy.[6] In 1990, officials enacted the Law of Money and Credit, which severed Algeria's central bank (Banque d'Algérie) from the minister of finance. The IMF ensured that Algeria's debts could be guaranteed, allowing Algeria to garner much-needed international financial assistance on the condition that it continue to liberalize its economy. The 1991 agreement with the IMF stipulated that the country had to liberalize its financial sectors, including prices and the value of the dinar, which was devalued in September by 22 percent.[7] As a further concession, Algeria agreed to end subsidization of key products, except for milk and bread. In exchange, IMF agreed to float Algeria a $400 million loan.[8]

It is perhaps a truism to say that Algeria's oil and gas were the ultimate lubricants for these transactions. But, at the same time, the world markets' mercurial valuations for oil and gas spawned an unstable national economy – and consequently political field – because such a disproportionate percentage of Algeria's GDP was based on the energy sector. When the economy was in the black, this imbalance was seldom criticized, but when it went into the red, Algerians talked about the need for reform. For example, during 1990, world oil prices were steadily declining until Iraq's invasion of Kuwait in August 1990. After the invasion, oil prices steadily increased, to reach just over $40 per barrel in September and October 1990. Then, even before coalition forces started Operation Desert Storm on January 16, 1991, oil prices began a precipitous decline, dipping below $20 per barrel in mid-January 1991, and descending even further by the end of the war on February 28, 1991. With oil prices once again deflated and with economic liberalization now under way in 1991, an angry electorate considered its options: the FLN was held responsible for squandering (and in many cases embezzling) its vast hydrocarbon revenues, and for remaining unable to create an alternative for the dependence on hydrocarbons.

The elections had been postponed until after the First Gulf War, but the majority of citizens were angered by the US-led coalition's humiliation of Saddam Hussein and, at home, with the government's response to political Islamists. In spite of popular feelings and the call from Islamists for greater distance from the West, Chadli remained determined to achieve economic stability and quickly resumed discussions with French energy companies. About the same time, feeling increasingly threatened at home by Islamists, Chadli implemented martial law on June 5, 1991. The next month, in contrast with the mood of the country (when many supporters of political Islamists wished for a more radical break with the colonial past), Algeria signed an agreement with the French that created a joint company (part-owned by Sonatrach) called Société Algéro-Française d'Ingénierie et de Réalisations (Safir), that was responsible for the various phases of oil and gas delivery.[9]

These reforms of the energy sector did not go uncontested, even within the ruling elite. A powerful tug of war within the government over the future direction of the country was exposed when Prime Minister Abdessalam took office in June 1992, and reversed the process of opening up Algeria's energy sector by rejecting bids by 15 foreign companies on eight separate fields.[10] The process of liberalizing the banking and economic sectors was also challenged by Abdessalam, who repealed several key elements of the Law of Money and Credit which had opened up the country to foreign investors. However understandable the impulse to minimize foreign control, analysts have viewed Abdessalam's premiership as "an abject failure" because he did not realize the profundity of the political and economic crisis.[11]

Abdessalam's defensive measures came in a context of massive economic reforms and increasing economic dependency, especially in Algeria's all-important hydrocarbon sector. Abdessalam's efforts came after the political liberalization of the late 1980s overseen by Chadli, which had spawned substantial economic reforms and translated directly into efforts to partner with foreign companies on oil and gas exploration and processing. For example, in 1991 a new hydrocarbon law went into effect that broadened research and exploration, ameliorated existing energy systems, and developed those fields located but not yet exploited.[12] The 1991 law made it considerably easier for foreign companies to invest in Algeria's oil and gas infrastructure, and gave important incentives for the government to secure both old and new energy clients. Most important, subsequent amendments to the 1991 law ended Sonatrach's monopolies.[13] These major reforms generated much foreign interest in Algerian fields, despite the sudden disruption of the political process and the emergence of political violence. Between the late 1980s and 2000, the favorable conditions attracted 27 companies from 20 countries to actively work under contract with the Algerian government.[14] During this period Sonatrach was streamlined and divided into separate, more efficient subsidiaries: exploration, discovery, refining, transportation, and international distribution.[15]

In 1992, Abdessalam's anachronistic, protectionist stance (harking back to the Boumediene era) harmed Algeria's prospects for economic growth in very specific ways. Moreover, it "reflected the kind of inter-elite political struggle over power, patronage, and privilege that has long characterized Algerian decision-making."[16] In addition to being out of step with most of his peers, Abdessalam applied very repressive tactics against his opponents and the proponents (even secular ones) of free speech and democratic freedoms. Eventually, Abdessalam was replaced by Redha Malek as prime minister in 1993 (to 1994), after which Algerian officials once again redoubled their efforts to convince foreign investors to partner with them.

The French connection

Since the French had collaborated with the US-led coalition during the First Gulf War, mainstream political Islamists viewed any continued association with French companies through the prism of bitter resentment. Radical Islamists reacted to France's alignment with coalition forces with even greater contempt, labeling it neo-colonial. In addition, an openly anti-immigrant and racist, but increasingly popular, French National Front party (led by Jean-Marie Le Pen) began to target North African Muslims in France. Ironically, Le Pen even temporarily supported the FIS, and tried to convince its leaders to adopt a platform calling for the return of French Algerians to Algeria. Visions of this xenophobic France combined with the French government's official actions during the First Gulf War to lend credence to Islamists' claims that France was "anti-Islamic."[17] Hence, France's somewhat painful decision not to support Saddam Hussein (who was ironically no friend to Islamists) gave rise to further anti-French rhetoric in Algeria, which became the mainstay of the FIS platform.[18] This resentment against France spilled over into questions about the economy, and the FIS's openly anti-French platform fed French fears of the growing Islamist movement in Algeria and unnerved French politicians and the general public alike. As Claude Cheysson, a former French foreign minister, put it in 1991: "I am crossing my fingers hoping the fundamentalists won't get into power."[19]

Given the fact that France was the largest exporter to Algeria and one of its most important creditors, the financial implications of continued disturbances in Algeria weighed heavily on the minds of French investors and policy-makers. These implications were also not lost on Islamists, who saw France as a great defender of the military status quo and therefore as an opponent of democratic reform. Thus despite the French investors' decision to reinvest in Algerian oil and gas ventures, the French government maintained an uneasy political alliance with Algerian authorities. This was especially true after the military coup in 1992 and after the replacement of the reformist premier, Ghozali.

After the 1992 coup, French–Algerian relations were marked by defensive posturing on both sides, and a curious revival of nationalist behavior. As one historian has noted, the image of Algerian leaders after 1992 was based in the "nationalist past" and thus reflected the "regime's attempt to recapture the legitimacy of the Boumediene regime."[20] French authorities tended to find Algerians' defensive posturing more problematic than helpful. At the same time, France's deep paranoia about the Islamist movement in Algeria fed fears that Algerian Islamists would radicalize the North African immigrant population (numbering around five million) in France. To be sure, fearing this, French officials overlooked the resurgence of harsh nationalistic rhetoric and supported the government's efforts to eradicate the FIS. Moreover, as France looked to play a larger role in the post-Cold War world (as evidenced by its presence in the coalition forces during the Persian Gulf War, and failed peacekeeping operations in the former Yugoslavia and Rwanda), its economic relationship to Algeria and to Africa became even more important. Added to its political interests, Algeria's hydrocarbons were of special strategic importance in the French economic relationship with Africa – even more so since French companies such as Total and GDF were positioned to capitalize on the opening-up of the oil and gas sectors.[21]

French banks also played a key role in mitigating Algerian debt and keeping the Algerian government afloat. For example, in March 1992 Crédit Lyonnais spearheaded a $2.5 billion deal to restructure Algerian debt.[22] This financial support was especially important because, between 1990 and 1995, Algeria's industrial base declined by 1.1 percent and investments by 4.7 percent, while GDP rose by only 0.1 percent.[23] Foreign borrowing became ever more important for the Haut Comité d'Etat (HCE), and Boudiaf's assassination on June 29, 1992, clarified the stakes not only for Algerians but also for world leaders, making the case that foreign financial assistance was necessary to stabilize a chaotic situation.

International actors and the move toward privatization

As Algerian leaders worked together with their global financial backers to create the conditions for compliance with international financial standards, many state-owned enterprises were required to be privatized. As this process unfolded, Algeria's economic problems worsened. In 1994, a crippling drought forced Algeria to import even more food, more than 95 percent of its cereals, up from 75 percent in 1993.[24] In April 1994, the dinar was devalued by 40 percent. And while the government reported that over 100,000 jobs were created in 1994, some 270,000 young men and women entered the workforce, contributing to a growing unemployment rate estimated at over 27 percent.

Understanding that more aid was necessary to help stabilize an already volatile regime, in May 1994 the Paris Club (the group of financial officers from the world's 19 wealthiest nations) met to re-evaluate Algeria's economic prospects. On the Paris Club's recommendations, the IMF agreed to reschedule Algeria's debt. In fact, roughly two-thirds of Algeria's foreign debt was owed to Japanese banks, which now wished to minimize their exposure, and the French were considered to have the most at stake.

Western investors' main worry was not the allegations of extensive human rights abuses, but the possibility that Islamic fundamentalists would come to power. This was especially true of the French, but was also reflected in the Clinton administration's cautious approach. For example, in 1992 the US imposed an arms embargo on Algeria that remained in place until the Bush administration removed it in December 2002. At the same time, given the political alternatives, a senior Clinton official agreed that it did not "make sense to pull the plug" on all assistance to Algeria; but "you've got to realize the economic risks in Algeria are very high."[25]

A key point of leverage that Algeria did possess was its natural gas resources. By 1995, Algeria was already Europe's third largest supplier of natural gas, but still owed it $25 billion of "outstanding foreign debt." France, Algeria's most important trading partner, was by this point providing approximately $1.1 billion a year in export credits. Meanwhile, other major global banks, including Société Générale (France), Sakura Bank (Japan), and Chase Manhattan (US) were discussing ways to mitigate the impact of Algerian debt on their own institutions.

More than other countries', France's concerns regarding the Algerian crisis played out on several fronts. Domestically, a continuation of the Algerian crisis was viewed as a threat to French immigration policies. French officials were therefore concerned that if the IMF and the international financial community did not intervene, then worsening economic conditions would drive more Algerian refugees into France.[26] At the same time, by continuing to grant credits on imports, French businesses and France itself also benefited from a growing import market in Algeria. The duality of this logic, between domestic immigration politics and the expansion of export markets to Algeria, continued to factor into France's relations with Algeria throughout the 1990s.

In November 1994, news broke that France had sold Algeria night vision equipment in addition to Mil MI 24 transport helicopters. Soon after it transpired that France had sold Algeria nine new AS 350 B Ecureuil attack helicopters. These revelations conflicted with the European Union's military embargo on Algeria; to circumvent this, the French Interior Minister Charles Pasqua's office claimed the helicopters were intended for civilian usage, while Algerian authorities stated that they were being purchased "to survey the beaches."[27]

The guiding force behind the French government's decision to break with its European partners on the issue of arms to Algeria was the fear of radical Islamic violence. While most French officials were clearly more than eager to back the military government from 1992 on, because they dreaded the prospect of even the FIS (democratically elected political Islamists) in power, it had become clear by the mid-1990s that Algeria's political Islamists had been eclipsed by radical Islamists. Open disputes among FIS leaders in exile, as well as rival insurgent forces, provided ample reason for the French to believe that Algeria would be ungovernable without the strong hand of a military dictatorship, capable of suppressing both political and radical Islamists. As the violence began to spread to France, with the 1994 Air France hijacking and the bombing campaigns initiated in 1995, French President Chirac thereafter could see "Islamism only through its violent fringe."[28] Yet, desiring to protect France's public image as a defender of human rights, French Foreign Minister Alain Juppé duplicitously noted in January 1995 that "the hope is that aid given to Algeria is in the end help which goes to the Algerian people, and not to the regime."[29]

The IMF director-general, the Frenchman Michel Camdessus, saw the need to continue to work with Algerian leaders in order to avert a full-scale civil war. Himself a veteran of the French–Algerian war who detonated mines as a second lieutenant,[30] Camdessus remained particularly concerned about Algeria's unrest. This in turn led to many IMF efforts to help the government regain solvency. As the person responsible for guiding Mexico through its currency crisis of 1994 and 1995 by arranging for a staggering $18 billion loan, Camdessus continued to press for economic reforms and austerity in Algeria. In exchange, Algerian authorities were encouraged to find simultaneous solutions to the economic and political crises. As Camdessus saw it, Algeria, like Mexico or the post-Soviet countries, as well as Argentina and Brazil, formed part of the globalizing economy of the 1990s. And the basic preconditions for IMF economic intervention were continued liberalization and transparency. With a total foreign debt climbing to $26 billion in 1994 and with rising fears of the course of terrorism, Algeria had become dependent on foreign aid and thus unable to resist demands for reform imposed from the outside.[31] Meanwhile, in an effort to draw other European countries into its schemes, France continued to lobby for more financial assistance from fellow EU partners which had been reluctant to invest in Algeria. The Europeans had good cause to fear entanglements with Algerian investments. By the mid-1990s, for example, Algeria was the largest foreign debtor of Belgian export credits, and made up 25 percent of the exposure of Italy's state-owned export credit insurance company, Sace. Algeria also owed substantial amounts to French, Chinese, and Egyptian credit institutions.

Europe and Algerian energy

The fact that Algeria came to rely on foreign loans during the 1990s did not prevent Europe from becoming increasingly dependent on Algeria for its own energy needs. Indeed, after the 1980s, Belgium drew over 50 percent of its liquid natural gas consumption from Algeria, and France drew roughly 25 percent.[32] By 2005, Italy was the largest consumer of Algerian gas, followed by Spain, France, Turkey, Portugal, and the US. However, Algeria competed with the former Soviet Union during the early 1990s to become a principal source for natural gas in Europe, and remained unable to commit the resources necessary for development and exploitation projects. For example, during the early 1990s it could only tap approximately 15 new wells a year, whereas it needed a hundred new wells drilled a year just to maintain current production levels. In addition, Sonatrach's recovery rate for oil, which measures the ability to extract available oil reserves, was a mere 25 percent, half of the world's average; some fields were only running at 7 percent capacity.[33] Unable to reach its own extraction target for oil, Sonatrach determined that natural gas should be given more prominence within the company.

The strategy of focusing more on gas production, in turn, would become an important component of the government's plan to escape from foreign debt, and within Sonatrach it clearly made sense. Europe was, after all, expected to become more reliant on foreign gas supplies. Algeria stood to gain from European demand, and was particularly well placed to do so. Algeria decided to enhance the two major sub-Mediterranean pipelines connecting its deposits to European consumers: the TransMed and the Maghreb–Europe pipelines. The TransMed, running from the massive Hassi R'Mel field in Algeria to Italy (via Tunisia and Sicily), completed in 1983, was started by Italy's Ente Nazionale Idrocarburi in the 1970s. In 1994, its capacity was doubled. The Maghreb–Europe pipeline was run collectively by Spain's Enagas, Morocco's SNPP, and Sonatrach. It was finished in 1996 and connected Algeria (via Morocco) to Spain.

Considering the spikes in violence after 1994 and 1995, the fact that Algeria could still garner international support for its financial dealings was somewhat encouraging, especially since between 1993 and 1995 Algeria's external debt as a percentage of GDP increased by nearly 30 percent, to reach 80 percent of total GDP.[34] With roughly 80 percent of GDP coming from the hydrocarbon sector, Algeria had little choice but to try to get more yield out of its existing fields and to continue exploration. That meant Algeria had to encourage foreign energy companies to invest, and to assure foreign workers that they could be adequately protected from terrorist attacks, a phenomenon that Iraq faces today.[35]

As Zeroual came to power within the HCE in February 1994, the Mobil Corp announced that it would continue its planned investment of $55 million to drill an additional five exploration wells near Touggourt, while the Spanish firm Cespa confirmed that it would invest in the development of the Rhourde Yacoub oil field.[36] With confirmation on April 10, 1994 that IMF was going to move aggressively to free up loans with a stabilization package, other major lending nations, including France and Japan, stood ready to invest in critical hydrocarbon development. Such financial cooperation was essential and complex, as export credits necessary to finish ongoing projects often impacted the viability of planned construction projects. One important example was the Europe–Maghreb pipeline, a project overseen by Bechtel (the US engineering corporation that built the Hoover Dam). The Europe–Maghreb pipeline was temporarily held up by the Coface (a major French lender and subsidiary of Natexis Banques Populaires) and other lenders, which needed guarantees from the IMF and World Bank. Importantly, the IMF agreement freed up credit and brought much-needed construction projects back on-line in the hydrocarbon sector.

With IMF backing, in early 1995 the World Bank offered Algeria a $150 million rehabilitation loan and additional loans of $300 million and $50 million, in order to carry out privatization and other reforms. In reality, these reforms caused a painful restructuring of the economy: by 1997, more than half of the smaller public companies had either closed down or been privatized.[37]

The downside of privatization

By the time Zeroual resigned as president in 1998, dozens of foreign countries were bringing the necessary technology, financial credit, and capital projects to Algeria. These investments vastly increased Algeria's ability to tap both old and new hydrocarbon resources. Indeed, much of Algeria's recent economic success was a direct result of its strategic partnerships with foreign financial institutions and energy companies, which continued to invest in Algeria despite the steady rise in terrorism. But the transformation of the Algerian economy was also a painful process for Algerian workers.

Essentially, globalization in Algeria and elsewhere meant that in order to conform to the IMF and World Bank's expectations, intense austerity measures had to be adopted. On the positive side, these measures allowed Algeria to cut its budget deficit from roughly 9 percent in 1993 to about 3 percent in 1994; but, on the negative side, huge job losses resulted. Many thousands of jobs were lost because the Algerian state had to make difficult choices and reduce its budget. For example, between 1994 and 2000, an estimated 400,000 jobs were cut from Algeria's overburdened public sector – and that number reflects the job cuts before the real push to privatize went into place in 1998.[38] Not even Sonatrach, the dynamo of the Algerian economy, was immune from large-scale cutbacks. For example, according to Sonatrach CEO and chairman, Abdelhak Bouhafs, the company had reduced its workforce from 120,000 to 34,000 by 2001 (just two years into Bouteflika's first term).[39]

Algeria's main labor union, the Union Générale des Travailleurs Algériens (UGTA), protested vehemently against IMF-imposed reforms and the reduction of the state workforce. At the same time, it was widely reported that the union supported the government's campaign against the Islamists during the 1990s, because its members considered the Islamists to be anti-socialist. This union reaction against Islamists bore tragic results. On January 28, 1997, the UGTA's 55-year-old leader, Abdelhak Benhamouda, was assassinated outside UGTA headquarters. Benhamouda had openly criticized the Islamists and supported the military, and by the time of his murder was well on his way to creating a new centrist party. As with nearly every other assassination in Algeria, however, Benhamouda's also immediately produced conspiracy theories.[40] The government immediately blamed his murder on radical Islamists, but that claim was called into question by the testimony of a friend who ran to his side as he lay dying. According to this man, his last words were: "Kamel, my friend, they have betrayed us."[41] Once again Algerians were left with an uneasy feeling. Another murder of a well-known individual that could have been carried out with a two-fold intent: to undermine Islamists in public, and to silence a major government critic, an important union chief who contested the core values of globalization in Algeria.

Terrorism, investment, and human rights

While it was clear that terrorism and violent counter-terrorism tactics were on the rise, the Algerian masses remained exceptionally vulnerable to assassination, attacks, and intimidation. At the same time, as Algeria moved in the direction of a free market economy, oil and gas companies adopted sophisticated security measures to insulate their facilities from terrorist attacks. Indeed, Algeria offered one of the great enigmas of the global marketplace during the 1990s.

Algeria spiraled into deadly violence and needed the international community's financial and technical support in order to stabilize its economy and modernize its hydrocarbon sector. Foreigners continued to invest in the country but were wary of the threat of violence against them and their companies. To secure the safety of foreign investors, the government focused its decisive actions on securing the locations that were deemed vital to Algeria's energy sectors. All the while Algeria continued to frustrate foreign business leaders. As Cameron Hume, US ambassador to Algeria from 1997 to 2000, recorded in his memoir, *Mission to Algiers*: "US companies were interested in Algeria, but it was a difficult place to do business." That was because "Algerian officials took too long to negotiate with foreign partners," and because their concern for protecting national assets often outweighed the pragmatic concern necessary to carry out plans in a timely fashion. As frustrating as it was, Ambassador Hume explained that

> [t]he right strategy for the United States was to help Algerians widen their horizons and expand their contacts to enable them to benefit from modernization and globalization. The elements of such a strategy would be to promote democratic institutions (including a free press, the parliament, and the labor unions), the rule of law (including prison visits by the International Committee of the Red Cross and suitable training for the police), a free market economy ... and cooperation on matters of regional security.[42]

Algeria had good reason to worry about safeguarding vital oil and gas sites. Since the government relied on these resources, insurgents began to target employees, installations, and the energy infrastructure. The GIAs were particularly interested in disrupting oil and gas supplies, and news reports did occasionally note the killing of foreign workers. While the terrorists threatened to disrupt the oil and gas industry, the government remained tight-lipped about terrorists' successes at sabotage. Occasionally, though, reports did get out: one in November 1997 acknowledged that the TransMed pipeline had to be closed for five days, after an explosion attributed to Islamists.[43]

Toward the end of February 1998, in a rare disclosure, Sonatrach officials announced that terrorists had bombed and destroyed 100 meters of the pipeline connecting the Hassi M'el region with the plant at Arzew (the world's largest site for the production of lique-fied natural gas).[44]

While terrorists had failed to cause a permanent disruption of oil and gas operations, terrorism, state violence, and the energy sector remained intertwined. For example, on January 22, 1998, a reporter noted that a group of Algerian exiles addressing a British parliamentary committee blamed Algerian authorities for being behind the massacres, and called for an international commission (organized by the UN) to investigate military crimes.[45] Calling for a far-reaching inquiry, including the investigation of "alleged torture chambers," this group, which included a former Algerian prime minister, insisted that France was impeding efforts to push forward on the investigation because of its "cultural and financial" ties to the Algerian regime.

According to this view, human rights were secondary to protect-ing economic interests. If the inquiry went ahead, those testifying claimed, it could trigger economic sanctions that would cost the government "billions of dollars." Likewise, French oil and gas com-panies did not want uncomfortable inquiries into state violence, because they were heavily invested in Algeria. Moreover, since the French government openly used the rhetoric of human rights and was demanding greater access for human rights groups, the govern-ment's humanitarian interests ran counter to economic interests. That kind of contradiction, so the group testifying before the British parliament argued, undermined France's integrity.

However, oil companies claimed that they were concerned about the violation of human rights in Algeria and had asked human rights organizations to investigate crimes.[46] These charges remind us that human rights violations continued to dog Bouteflika's government, and remained a good reason for many firms to beware the potential public relations fallout from doing business in Algeria. The threat of terrorism was equally high, if not higher, on the list.

Eager to put the past behind him and cognizant that his politi-cal future would largely be determined by the dual success of his platform for national reconciliation and his economic policy, Boute-flika pressed hard to allay fears at home and abroad that radical Islamists still posed a major threat to economic stability, and that government stability required a tabula rasa. In fact, his 1999 and 2005 amnesty referendums did much to convince foreign companies that it was safe to invest in Algeria.

Nevertheless, the election he won in 1999 did cause problems for Western diplomats eager to strengthen economic relations, as Boute-flika's principal rivals boycotted the election after filing allegations of fraud and intimidation. For example, because of the questions surrounding the democratic process, the Clinton administration held to its guarded view of Bouteflika, knowing that the real power in Algeria remained the military. A less cautious view emerged after George W. Bush came to power in Washington. All the same, during his first two years Bouteflika was determined to undertake the necessary economic reforms, particularly in the energy sector, to attract more foreign investment and develop closer ties to Western powers.

The Bouteflika imperative

During the two years of his first term in office, Bouteflika quickly devised a program to encourage more investment in the oil and gas industries. Aware that part of Algeria's problem in 1986 was a result of its over-reliance on its oil projection, Bouteflika and his economic team were determined to diversify Algeria's position in the world energy market. Yet Bouteflika continued to balk on the issue of political and historical transparency, and refused to cooperate with calls led by Amnesty International for international commissions to investigate human rights abuses. At the same time, he pushed for greater compliance with global standards on economic transparency and evidence of liberalization. Some of the key economic reforms were set in motion before he was elected into office: in August 1998, Algeria sold 600 state-owned hotels to the private sector, and in September the European Union signed a loan to Algeria for $40 million, that allowed the country to privatize more enterprises.[47]

Once in office, Bouteflika moved swiftly to produce more evidence of reform. With Chakib Khelil as minister of energy and mining and Ali Benflis as prime minister at his side, Bouteflika embarked on an ambitious plan to recast the way Algeria did business in the oil and gas market. As a former employee of the World Bank, Khelil pushed through major reforms that crucially reduced the time necessary to complete contracts with foreign energy companies, shortening the process from years to weeks.[48]

By early 2001, Sonatrach had made important internal changes, most noticeably a decision to increase its natural gas production. Knowing that European demand for natural gas would continue to rise and that gas was far less volatile on the world market, Sonatrach entered into several important contracts with companies from around the world, including Japanese, French, Italian, Portuguese, Indian, Malaysian, Spanish, German, Greek, Turkish, and US firms. Many of these contracts were signed as joint ventures, which allowed Sonatrach to expand both its downstream and upstream projects. Moreover, in the spirit of transparency, its CEO Bouhafs guaranteed that all awards for work would be made public.

While the IMF indicated that Algeria still had to proceed with critical reforms in the banking sector, it also acknowledged that Algeria had made important progress on other fronts. It had privatized its communications and transportation sectors, restructured the hydrocarbon divisions, and even by early 2000, there were clear indications that the decision to diversify its hydrocarbon holdings were paying off. For example, for the first three quarters of 2000, Algeria recorded a $7.52 billion trade balance and showed an increase of 72 percent in earnings from exports from the same nine-month period in 1999, bringing its total earnings from exports to $14.46 billion, and about $20 billion for 2000.[49]

Unemployment remained a major obstacle to economic recovery. In 1998, the government acknowledged it stood at 29.5 percent (in 2003 it was 28.4 percent).[50] And by 1999, it was estimated that approximately 30 percent of Algeria's unemployment rate was the result of aggressive economic reforms and privatization.[51] Nonetheless, some positive results were beginning to show when in 2000 the economy posted a 2.4 percent rate of growth. Yet, still unable to combat high unemployment rates as well as slower than ideal economic growth, in 2001 Algeria decided to follow the IMF's advice and adopt a plan to stimulate the economy. Known as the Emergency

Reconstruction Program and overseen by Prime Minister Benflis, this plan was intended to "reduce unemployment, improve infrastructures, and increase economic growth to 6 percent annually."[52] In 2004 and 2005, significant advances were made when the GDP rose by 5.3 percent, just below the target rate of 6 percent growth.

The unprecedented rise in oil prices that began shortly after the American invasion of Iraq in 2003 gave Algeria and other oil-producing states an important economic lift. With record prices posted almost daily, from the beginning of the invasion in spring 2003 through October 2008, Algeria, having just invested heavily in gas, recorded staggering profits in oil. Ironically, once profits were posted, Algeria used the opportunity to impose new taxes on foreign companies, thus returning to its defensive posture regarding the penetration of major foreign companies. In July 2005, a new hydrocarbon law introduced a windfall profit tax on international oil companies (IOCs). In October 2006, the National People's Assembly passed amendments to the law that were further clarified by the government in December 2006. These new laws targeted the profits of foreign oil companies. For example, depending on how much oil a company produced, the law called for an adjusted tax between 5 and 50 percent if the price of a barrel of oil exceeded $30. More important, the 2005 law reset Sonatrach's ownership control to 51 percent on all joint oil and gas ventures.[53] Hardest hit was the US firm Anadarko Petroleum Corporation, which by this time was the largest foreign oil company in Algeria. Other companies, including British Petroleum (BP), were also heavily impacted. While foreign oil companies viewed the recent actions as infringements of their contracts, they continued to operate in Algeria and record sizable profits.

The rise in the price of oil strengthened Algeria's economy in substantial ways. In 2004, Sonatrach's export sales rose to $31.5 billion, from which $3 billion was paid to foreign partners. In 2006, Sonatrach's profits increased to $44 billion, with $5 billion going to partners.[54] Backed by record high oil prices in June 2006, Algeria signed a deal to repay an $8 billion loan to the Paris Club.[55] In addition, with the average price of oil rising to over $50 per barrel in 2005, Sonatrach announced that it was planning to invest $32 billion between 2006 and 2010 in different oil and gas operations.[56]

In 2007, Algeria posted revenue earnings from oil and gas at $58 billion of which the new windfall profit tax accounted for $2 billion.[57] By October 2008, with the price of oil reaching nearly $150 a barrel, Algeria was able to announce that its oil revenues would exceed $80 billion for 2008, regardless of a decline in the price of oil.[58]

Hydrocarbons were not the only source of foreign investment in Algeria. In fact, many larger foreign companies, including pharmaceuticals, finance, and other firms, as well as thousands of smaller firms began to do business in Algeria during the 1990s. Exporters moved there and began to record impressive profits. Most of this interest can be attributed to the effects of globalization and to the removal of trade barriers. Some argue that the violence was in fact exacerbated by the silence of major foreign investors, whose sudden proliferation bore the marks of irresponsible corporate greed because they seldom, if ever, put pressure on the Algerian state to curb its human rights violations.[59] From this point of view, foreign business's lack of interest in the government's human rights abuses translated into de facto support for the "military dictatorship" that ruled over Algeria throughout the 1990s. In fact, according to this logic, "multinationals have rewarded the total war approach of the military and the entrenchment of the military regime, presumably to increase what they see as 'stability' and to reduce the risks on their investments."[60]

The dual economy and security inequalities

Private security firms, many comprised of former soldiers, increasingly became part of the new security economy. The ex-soldiers found employment protecting the thousands of miles of oil and gas pipeline connecting Algeria's energy sources to Europe. Major US firms such as Halliburton and Kellogg Brown and Root (now KBR) also found themselves on economic front lines of the war on terror. Algeria was, in this sense, a key part of the territory that all parties (the Algerian government, foreign companies, and dozens of other nations, including the US) saw as a vital component of the world's energy system.[61] This is precisely why terrorists threatened to kill foreign oil and gas workers.[62]

Despite the number of international and Algerian employees

working in the hydrocarbon sector and their attractiveness as targets for terrorists, these workers were considerably safer than the rest of the population – a point that has not been lost on critics of the Algerian government.[63] In fact, some have argued that the government helped foster the creation of veritable dual economies, with the oil and gas companies being physically shielded and isolated from the hostilities, while the general population went largely unprotected by security forces.[64] This difference in treatment corresponded to a physical partitioning of the country, and the creation of two distinct zones. Much of the southern part of the country, where the oil and gas fields were located, was declared off limits to citizens, and security passes were required for entrance. The northern part, where most of the population lived, had minimal protection, and as a consequence large massacres were frequent, sometimes with hundreds of people killed in a single village on a single night.

This separation of the country into two spheres yielded specific consequences and odd results. One example came in the area of transportation. Whereas most European airlines halted flights to Algiers because of the threat of terrorism after the hijacking of the Air France flight in December 1994, some airlines commenced direct flights directly into the southern energy-producing zones. Air Algérie created a Geneva–Hassi-Messaoud flight that bypassed Algiers altogether, and Sonatrach formed Tassili Airlines, which now carries people and equipment to southern oil bases. Likewise, one of General Khaled Nezzar's relatives formed Go Fast, an airline that offered a direct Paris–Hassi-Messaoud route. The airport at Hassi-Messaoud developed into a truly world-class destination: "The engineers land at the local airport in special chartered flights which do not transit Algiers. The runway is the longest in the country; it can accommodate all types of large carriers, and the air traffic is the second most important in terms of freight activity."[65]

Transnational firms and Sonatrach also benefited from a highly developed security system, where private contractors guaranteed the safety of those living in these private oases in the desert. More directly connected to the rest of the world than the underdeveloped and "infected zones" of the North, the South and its employees enjoyed the full protection of the state. So glaring was this problem that Amnesty International's General Secretary asked: "Should one conclude that the Algeria that resides twenty minutes away from the capital where the massacres and bombings follow one another is a 'useless Algeria'?" Given the fact that large contingents of troops often protected civilian oil and gas employees, sometimes at a ratio of three to one, and that foreign firms such British Petroleum and Halliburton employed private security forces that provided armed escorts, it is easy to understand the moral outrage of human rights organizations who decried the vast inequities in security throughout the country.

Algeria's dramatic upsurge of personal wealth for some brought its own problems, as evidenced by the emergence of financially related crimes. In 2007, there were 375 abductions in Algeria for which the victims' families paid over $18.7 million, according to Interior Minister Noureddine Yazid Zerhouni.[66] Of these abductions, 115 were connected to al Qaeda-based terrorism, and 260 connected to organized crime syndicates. Perhaps more disturbing, Zerhouni suggested that some of the abductions were targeting children to supply an organized organ-harvesting ring that had moved into Algeria. The for-profit abductions, on top of the threat of terror attacks in the form of suicide bombings or other forms of violence, meant that the Algerian state and individuals (citizens and foreign nationals alike), particularly those in the energy sector, began to employ private security companies to protect both people and infrastructure. To be sure, the reforms of the 1990s did create dual economies, which in turn generated new opportunities and wealth for Algerian businessmen, and this indirectly provided "backing for the regime's war efforts."[67]

The business of peace

Indeed, the government was particularly skillful at using the economy as a device to bring Islamists into civil society. Once they entered the economy as shop-owners and businessmen, they were far less likely to support political movements that would damage their interests. In this way, officials used the economy to "assimilate" those who might have otherwise continued to side with terrorist or underground forces. A new generation of "petty traders" emerged and became one of the "few economic success stories in post-colonial Algeria." As a result, the private sector's contribution to GDP rose from 25 percent in 1980 to almost 40 percent in 1995. The rapid expansion of small businesses presented an opportunity to draw Islamists closer to the government and away from the FIS and Hamas. Hence, the government willingly made important concessions, such as a reduction of price controls and access to foreign markets. Many of these new businesses, unhappy with their treatment by France, which had been the principal source of economic interaction, began partnerships with businesses elsewhere in the Middle East and Europe, such as Turkey, Saudi Arabia, Spain, and Italy. The effect of this new pro-business climate in Algeria is clear.[68] As Luis Martinez explains:

> Liberalization of the economy was for the government a political instrument for changing public opinion. Steady assimilation of the economic actors from the private sector into money-making networks hitherto reserved for the state sector helped to lure them away from the temptation to go into partnership with guerrillas ... The liberalization of trade thus facilitated the integration of the private traders, it made them respectable actors able to make the economic "take-off" possible.[69]

From the government's point of view, its ability to integrate those previously committed to the pro-Islamist movement of the early 1990s into the global and national marketplace was clearly a winning strategy. Moreover, by creating a business environment that allowed for more Algerians (albeit many pro-Islamists) to share in the collective wealth generated by a vibrant and rebounding community of businessmen, the government was also better able to weather public criticisms over the expansion of foreign investments during the 1990s. Since Algeria needed to adjust to the pressures of globalization, it was also necessary to integrate the national economy into the fabric of the world economy. Using its primary natural resources, oil and gas, which also happened to be (along with banks) the hub of globalization, Algeria was able to overcome the effects of terrorism and prove that if wells, pipelines, and processing plants could be secured, the economy would recover. That economic liberalization and globalization also cleared a pathway that local entrepreneurs used to enter the marketplace only furthered the government's efforts to normalize civil society.

Today, the looming question is whether liberalization has been a blessing or a curse. After the catastrophic collapse of free-market capitalism in the US and around the world that began at the end of 2008, it is still unclear what the effect on Algeria of the economic downturn will be; but it does not look promising. Starting in October 2008 the price of oil began to plunge, falling within two months from nearly $150 a barrel to below $40 by mid-December. While its natural gas revenues have been vital, it is clear that this sudden fall in oil prices will affect the country. Moreover, given the even more catastrophic failure of the international banking system, which began as a credit crisis, it is fair to question the wisdom of requiring nations like Algeria and those in Eastern Europe to embrace free-market reforms, when the same deregulation and liberal reforms have caused the greatest financial collapse in over 70 years.

Given the country's limited resources, Algerian politicians cannot offer a stimulus package that could mitigate the losses which are sure to affect it and the rest of the world. And while the US and Europe can begin to openly discuss the potential re-nationalization of their own banking systems, Algeria's transition back to that economic model is certainly more complicated.

Now that Algeria has joined the liberalization camp, it is clearly more exposed and vulnerable. Hence, the overriding question will be: what will happen as unemployment continues to rise, when the old structures of the socialist state no longer exist? As this question comes into focus, Algeria, like other African, Asian, and Eastern European countries, will once again find itself at the mercy of disaster capitalists who offer aid but only in exchange for an increasing slice of future assets, meaning that most citizens will once again find themselves cut out from the nation's wealth unless leaders take measures to protect the country from the Friedman-like world. Indeed, if there were ever an argument for making sure that a true democratic system was firmly in place (which would require open and free elections for all political groups), it would be that transparent democracies seem to create an effective bulwark against the fire sale of national resources and economic mainstays.

6 | A genealogy of terror: local and global jihadis

After the military coup in January 1992, Algeria became the nation par excellence for Islamists to battle out the differences between those who favored political accommodation and those who advocated violent rejectionism. That split was furthered when the military junta banned Islamic activists from the political arena; and, from the coup forward, Algerian Islamists began to tilt ever more in the direction of violent confrontation with the state. As the process of rejecting accommodation unfolded, Algeria quickly became the major battle-ground in which the logic of jihad was tested and refined in local and international arenas in the decade before 9/11. For this reason, Algeria remains especially important for understanding distinctions within Islamist camps, and how a local jihad was transformed into a global one. Algeria clearly dramatizes the tensions that emerged between the development of an Islamic radicalism intended to serve national political objectives, and a pan-Islamic radicalism that rejected conventional politics altogether.

In considering the genealogy and nuances of radical Islamist movements in Algeria, it is important to emphasize that the nullification of the election results in 1992 served as an ominous example of what happens when a government effectively disallows the participation of Islamic parties in the democratic process. Today, there are, of course, important parallels such as the Western rejection of Hamas's 2006 election victory in Palestine, as well as a notable contrast with the rise of political Islam in Turkey. Yet Algeria's story remains salient because it illustrates how increasingly radicalized Islamists (many of whom had ties to global terrorist networks) could exploit and benefit from the suspension of the democratic process, and the marginalization of legitimate Islamist parties from the democratic process.

The military government's resistance to the efforts of Islamic activists to find legitimacy within the democratic process is undoubt-edly one of the principal causes for the radicalization that occurred throughout the 1990s. Nevertheless, the rise of radical Islam in Algeria is not just about domestic affairs; increasingly, international jihadis concentrated their propaganda efforts on Algeria because of its perceived potential to spearhead a pan-Islamic revolution. This was especially true of al Qaeda's propagandists, based ironically in London, who saw Algeria as a strategic means to move beyond the national to the global jihad.[1] Yet, despite the interest of foreign jihadis in events in Algeria, Algeria's radical Islamists were equally determined to shape their own fight along purely nationalist lines, and therefore rebuked direct involvement of foreign fighters for the better part of the 1990s.

How democracy became *takfir*

Because the Algerian military decided to combat the insurgency with an "eradicator" policy, some FIS supporters and even FIS leaders joined the guerrilla movement in order to recover the Islamists' stolen elections. Moreover, once Ali Belhadj, Abassi Madani, and others were arrested in June 1991 and the FIS banned from the legitimate political field in March 1992, important FIS leaders in exile advocated a violent response to the coup. (It must also be remembered that Belhadj had already threatened to use violence against the state.) The FIS leaders supporting an armed response believed this would eventually lead to the reinstatement of the politi-cal process, and so insisted that their supporters confine themselves to attacks on state officials and security personnel. Similarly, what propelled the pro-FIS guerrillas into combat was an understandable sense that an injustice had been carried out when the FIS, as a legitimate political actor, was disenfranchised by the generals who carried out the military coup. The Islamists' call to arms and the military's refusal to rehabilitate the FIS thereafter locked the nation in a spiral of violence.

During the first years of the conflict, several radical movements emerged. The FIS did not have its own official paramilitary organ-ization, and exiled FIS leaders were split over which, if any, guer-rilla group to endorse. Meanwhile, Algerian veterans of the Afghan jihad began to return from Afghanistan and to circulate within the country even before the 1992 coup. As journalist and author Ahmed Rachid notes, between 1982 and 1992, over 35,000 Muslim radicals from 43 countries trained with al Qaeda in Afghanistan; eventually, over 100,000 would have "direct contact" with Pakistan and Afghanistan, and were influenced by the jihad.[2] The unexpected arrival of some 1,500 to 2,000 "Afghan Algerians" in the early 1990s clearly complicated the political Islamists' strategy of retaking the state by combining negotiation with the militant support of pro-FIS paramilitary groups. Part of the issue was ideological. The Algerian mujaheddin were overwhelmingly Salafist (meaning radical Islamists who support a violent jihad and see terrorism as legitimate means of achieving their goals), and opposed the FIS on grounds that it had compromised Islamic teachings by taking part in the democratic process at all. Trained as they were in insurrectionary tactics and armed combat, and unwilling to accept the arguments of the FIS, the Algerian Afghan mujaheddin were the first to begin attacking the security forces in early 1992.[3] Moreover, the mujaheddin detested the apostate state leaders and its servants, and any political accommodation with them was more than inconceivable. Within their logic, democracy was itself *takfir*, which is to say, forbidden.

The Afghan veterans who eventually formed the first sections of the Groupes Islamiques Armés (GIAs) brought with them the concept of *takfir* to Algeria, which quickly provided terrorists with ample justification for killing fellow Muslims by labeling victims as unbelievers. According to Lawrence Wright, contemporary use of *takfir* first emerged in Upper Egypt, where it paved the way for the killing of Anwar Sadat – identified as an apostate by radical Islamists for his failure to impose shari'a. From Egypt, the concept migrated to other regions of the Middle East.[4] Afghan-trained radicals escalated the violence by broadening the conflict to include Muslim civilians and by challenging even militant supporters of the FIS, who were likewise proclaimed takfir because they aimed to ensure the return of democratically elected leaders to power.

By 1993, militant movements loosely forming under the banner of the GIAs entered the struggle and transformed domestic affairs completely. As 1993 progressed, several of the GIAs guided by *takfir* began killing activists, unveiled women, French-speakers, educators, feminists, members of democratic (even Islamist) opposition groups, writers, singers, directors, academics, doctors, and intellectuals, as well as members of rival guerrilla groups. Eventually, as the GIAs began to organize behind a series of single national leaders in the mid-1990s, they began assassinating FIS officials. They also made specific and repeated threats against foreigners, which culminated in a communiqué announcing that all foreigners still in Algeria after December 1, 1993, were targets for execution. As one GIA leader, Sid Ahmed Mourad, put it in November 1993: "Our jihad consists of killing and dispersing all those who fight against God and his Prophet."[5]

It was difficult for security personnel to defend all these new soft targets, but security personnel also began to infiltrate the GIAs. At the time, there were some 70,000 foreigners registered in Algeria, and everyone was considered at risk.[6] Most endangered were those working in the oil and gas sectors, but there were many others. Before the deadline passed, several thousand foreigners left, and as attacks intensified during the first weeks, many more left. Less than three weeks after the December 1 deadline passed, 23 foreigners were murdered. One mid-December incident concerned a Bosnian and Croat construction site outside Algiers, where assassins took 18 workers hostage. After eight stated that they were Muslim and were released, the terrorists slit the throats of the remaining men.[7] After the attacks began, the government was forced to discuss the possibility of negotiating with banned FIS leaders.

Djamal Zitouni and Air France 8969

In December 1994, while under the command of Djamal Zitouni, the principals in the national GIA exported the terror campaign to France on a Paris-bound airliner, Air France flight 8969. On Christmas Eve, four gunmen (all young men in their twenties), posing as airline personnel, boarded the white Airbus A300 brandishing AK 47s, Uzis, and other assault weapons and took 171 passengers and crew hostage. Discovering a policeman on board, they shot him in the head and tossed his corpse onto the runway. The terrorists then executed a Vietnamese official and disposed of his body in similar fashion. That same day, the hijackers released the women and children (63 in total) after French authorities agreed to let the plane fly to Paris. However, the stand-off continued into the next day, with Algerian authorities refusing to let the plane depart with the remaining hostages still on board. By this time, it had become clear that the hijackers had planted explosives throughout the plane, with the intention of blowing it up over Paris. On the second day, after first warning that another victim would be killed, an airline employee was executed. Understanding that they had to do something or more hostages would be murdered, Algerian and French authorities finally agreed to let the plane depart for Paris.

The jet left Algiers early on the morning of December 26. French authorities diverted the plane to Marseilles, on the pretext that it needed refueling after nearly two days of negotiations. Shortly after it landed, French commandos of the Groupe d'Intervention de la Gendarmerie Nationale (GIGN) carried out a stunning tactical raid on the aircraft. Within seconds, GIGN forces burst through the front and rear doors of the plane. A close-range gun battle followed. Miraculously, after 22 minutes and more than 400 rounds of fire and several grenades set off, all four terrorists were killed without loss of life for the passengers or the assault team, although several passengers and GIGN men were severely wounded in the shoot-out.

The hijacking put French officials on high alert. Realizing that they had to act, French authorities developed the most aggressive anti-terrorist program in Europe. Likewise, faced with the failure of the hijacking, leaders of the GIAs vowed never to repeat the same mistakes. The lessons learned during the Air France hijacking would also aid the 9/11 terrorists, as radical Islamists used it as a case study to perfect future attacks. As one Algerian terrorist put it: "this operation is the start of a new phase which is the Martyrdom phase in which the enemy will be completely overwhelmed by the attacks."[8]

Under Djamal Zitouni's stewardship for about two years beginning in September 1994, the national GIA remained determined to extend the jihad to Europe. Several prominent political Islamist exiles opposed this extension, most notably the co-founder of the FIS, Abdelbaki Sahraoui, living in asylum in France. At the same time, in 1994 exiled FIS leaders began to fracture on the question of the

GIAs. From the US, Anwar Haddam openly championed particular GIA groups; from Germany, Rabah Kebir insisted that the FIS could not be compromised by the GIA. This split within the FIS over the GIA prompted the GIA to issue a communiqué staking out its own position on the FIS, in which the GIA announced it was founding a new "Caliphate."[9] It also named Mohammed Said as the official leader of the Caliphate, and Haddam was identified as the man responsible for "foreign affairs."[10]

Because Haddam and several other leaders (Said and Abderrazak Redjam) of the FIS had defected to the GIA, rival FIS leaders were eager to keep the GIA in check and to prevent even more defections from FIS loyalists. The anti-GIA FIS leaders responded by announcing a rival terrorist group, the Armée Islamique du Salut (AIS), in July 1994. The AIS brought together the fighters from the MIA and other groups not affiliated with the GIA under the direction of Abdelkader Chebouti (discussed in Chapter Three). The formation of the AIS changed the terms of the militant Islamist movements, because the AIS claimed to have formed a resistance organization that was "officially subordinated to the political leadership of the FIS."[11]

Presenting itself as the military wing of the banned FIS, the AIS distanced itself from the GIAs and attempted to galvanize Muslims who wanted to see a return to normality and the democratic process. The AIS stressed its connections to the FIS leaders in Algerian prisons, especially Abassi Madani and Ali Belhadj. As a result, the GIA under Djamal Zitouni began a violent campaign against AIS fighters and FIS leaders. Thus, as Luis Martinez summarized it, the creation of the GIA in 1993 and the AIS in 1994 had the effect of turning entire regions of Algeria into "battlefields."[12]

GIA's tactics under fire from al Qaeda

In 1994, as Algerian terrorism changed after groups began attacking each other and as civilians found themselves trapped between the warring factions and the Algerian security forces, Osama Bin Laden flew to Britain to meet with GIA representatives and supporters in Manchester and London. He also met with the men responsible for the publication of *Al Ansar*, the London-based GIA newsletter. Financed by Bin Laden through a go-between, *Al Ansar* openly called for jihad against France in 1995.[13] As British journalists Sean O'Neill and Daniel McGrory point out, *Al Ansar* was important for the jihad in Europe and set out to mobilize England's Muslim youth by eulogizing "atrocities carried out by mujahedeen in Algeria." One article stated that British Prime Minister John Major was a "legitimate target."[14]

Bin Laden was keen to play a leadership role in the Algerian jihadi movement, but felt deep concern about the sudden spiral of Muslim-on-Muslim violence. Although not opposed to the killing of foreigners, and an advocate of "total war," Bin Laden held conflicting views of events in Algeria. According to Lawrence Wright, in 1993 Bin Laden had sent Qari el-Said, a prominent Algerian member of al Qaeda's Council, to meet with key GIA leaders and instruct them to adopt a "total war" approach: any compromise or negotiation with the government was presented as a punishable offense to Islam. However, within a few months Bin Laden understood the impact of negative publicity that the killing of Muslims had generated within Muslim-majority countries. As a result, shortly after giving money to help finance the GIA, and sending an al Qaeda representative to Algeria to coach militants in the proper use of the *takfir* total war against Muslims in 1993, even "Bin Laden recoiled – if not from the violence itself, then from the international revulsion directed at the Islamist project. He sought to create a 'better image of the jihad.'" Eventually, after the GIA offended Bin Laden by suggesting that he had become too soft, Bin Laden became "furious and withdrew his support entirely. But his forty thousand dollars had already helped create a catastrophe."[15]

As Bin Laden's brief foray into the Algerian jihad demonstrates, there was a connection between al Qaeda and senior GIA leaders. On the doctrinal level, al Qaeda and the GIA had very similar views and agreed that the MIA's support for the FIS had compromised the MIA. According to Hugh Roberts, "When Zeroual was elected president in November 1995, that was proof [for Zitouni] that the Algerian people had left Islam. The fact that a majority of the electorate had turned out with such enthusiasm was cited by Zitouni as evidence that society as a whole had left Islam." Zitouni's doctrinal response was to condemn the entire population as apostate. However,

[i]t was the GIA that had changed its position, not al Qaeda. The doctrinal issue is that under Zitouni the GIA operates under *takfir el moudjamah*, which means you condemn the entire society of having become apostate. Ordinary people are therefore all legitimate targets of jihad. *Takfir el moudjamah* was never the outlook of al Qaeda. Al Qaeda has never had the view that in a Muslim country the entire population is a legitimate target. It's the GIA that deviated and broke away from the original doctrinal agreement with al Qaeda. And that's why Bin Laden said, "okay, we wash our hands of this."[16]

The FIS and the GIA

In a 1996 interview with Daniel Pipes and Patrick Clawson, Haddam put the need to continue the FIS struggle in Algeria this way: "The Algerian people are winning back an awareness of their own identity. We were colonized by the French for more than a hundred and thirty years. Since 1962, we have not really been independent. We had military independence, but nothing more, being dependent in economic policy, foreign policy, foreign trade, defense policy, and so forth. Now we want back our own identity, and that's our right. This is our message in all the Muslim world."[17]

While the FIS leaders agreed with Haddam that Algerians wanted their own identity, they were far from united on just how the armed response to the military government complemented their goals. And many FIS leaders, including Kebir, backed the MIA because they saw it as better organized, less violent, and more controlled. From the US Haddam publicly backed specific groups within the GIAs that were under the control of ex-FIS leaders. As he put it, "until November 1995, I did strongly support the GIA. I supported it because we had a pact. We backed the armed struggle as long as it was for the sake of freeing our people, for a return to free elections, and against acts of terrorism."[18] According to Haddam, particular segments of the groups that formed loosely around the GIA were FIS allies helping to restore democracy, and he continued to insist that it was the Algerian military, not the national GIA, that was responsible for the savage killing.[19]

All the while, pro-democratic, pro-accommodation militants and anti-democratic radical Islamists jockeyed for control over the jihad in Algeria. Political Islamists also attempted to keep their movement alive by taking the struggle into the international arena. And outside supporters of radical Islam understandably saw Algeria as a front line of a new jihadist movement. Eager to undermine the FIS's goal of returning to the political field, key Algerian al Qaeda ideologues sought to present Algeria as evidence of the failure of political Islam. For example, as al Qaeda's Ayman al-Zawahiri put it in a text published in December 2001:

> The Islamic Salvation Front (FIS) in Algeria overlooked the tenets of the creed, the facts of history and politics, the balance of power, and the laws of control. It wanted to use the ballot boxes in a bid to reach the presidential palaces and ministries, but at the gates tanks were waiting, loaded with French ammunition, their barrels pointing at those who had forgotten the rules of battle between justice and falsehood.
>
> The shots fired by officers of the "French party" brought them crashing down from their soaring illusions to the hard earth of reality. The Islamic Salvation Front men thought that the gates of power had been opened to them, but they were astonished to see themselves pushed through the gates of detention camps and prisons and into the cells of the new world order.[20]

The jihad comes to France: the Paris metro bombings

Many banned and imprisoned FIS leaders were genuinely concerned with violence in Algeria and about the possibility of the jihad spreading to France. Sheikh Abdelbaki Sahraoui, the 85-year-old co-founder of the FIS and an original member of Ben Badis's Association of the Ulama during the colonial era, had been one of the first to reject Rebah Kebir's claim that he represented the FIS in exile.[21] With considerable moral authority behind him, Sahraoui also took issue with the extension of the jihad to France. Sahraoui understood that the GIA viewed France not as a "faraway enemy" (as Fawza Gerges terms it), but as the Algerian junta's most important ally in the West, and therefore a state working against the Islamists in its own backyard; however, Sahraoui also understood that attacks on France would undermine the Islamist cause and further alienate Western powers. Since the goal of the FIS was to re-enter the political process and since Islamists were making inroads with Western powers now urging the Algerian government to negotiate with banned FIS leaders, it was logical to assume that attacks on France would cause a backlash against political Islamists. On July 11, 1995, Sahraoui and his assistant were gunned down outside a mosque in Paris's 18th arrondissement. Prior to that, Sahraoui had received several death threats from the GIA; he was in France working as an "intermediary" for the French government, attempting to mediate between Islamists and the Algerian state.[22] Anwar Haddam attributed Sahraoui's assassination to the Algerian government, which he called the "terrorist regime in power in Algiers."[23] Yet many saw the murder of Sahraoui as signaling the beginning of new GIA campaign in Europe.

That fear was realized when the GIA commenced a bombing campaign against France. On July 25, 1995, a powerful explosion ripped through the Saint Michel-Notre Dame RER station, in the heart of the famed Left Bank of Paris, during the evening commute. Seven passengers were killed, and over 80 others severely injured. A follow-up bomb wounded 17 pedestrians at the Arc de Triomphe on August 17. Two weeks later, the police disarmed a bomb on the high-speed train tracks in Lyon. A bomb partially exploded in Paris on September 3; another, targeting a Jewish school in Lyon, wounded 14 people on September 7. Then, in October, two more bombs exploded in the Paris metro, injuring over 40 people.

Some GIA members responsible for the attacks were killed by French counter-terrorism forces, but several managed to escape, including Rachid Ramda, the editor-in-chief of *Al Ansar*. Ramda fled to England, where he was held in custody until 2005, fighting extradition to France. Ramda was convicted in the French courts, and sentenced in October 2007 to ten years in prison for financing the Paris metro bombings carried out by co-conspirator Boualem Bensaid. Ramda's long extradition proceedings lasted over a decade, sparking heavy criticism from the French, who viewed Britain's legalistic, "soft" approach to dealing with militant Islamists as a paltry effort to keep the jihad at bay. London was rechristened as "Beirut-on-the-Thames."[24]

The strange case of the murder of the Trappist monks

The eight separate GIA bombing attacks on French soil between July and November 1995 put France on high alert, and eventually caused it to issue warnings to its tens of millions of foreign tourists per year. Meanwhile, in Algeria the election of Zeroual to the presidency in November 1995 underscored that the terrorists were unable to prevent the public from coming out in support of a democratic (albeit limited) process. Despite calls to boycott the elections and allegations of electoral fraud, the Algerian people did go to the polls to elect Zeroual to the presidency. However, that election stopped neither the terrorists nor the state from fighting the conflict with uncompromising violence. As John Kiser has put it: "by 1994–1995, there were at least four possible suspects for any given horror: terrorists, government forces, local defense militias ... and simple bandits."[25]

Amid the killings, the French Trappist monks of the Notre Dame de l'Atlas monastery, located in the small village of Tibhirine about 60 miles from Algiers, stood out as pacifists. The monks had heard but not heeded the October 30, 1993 GIA warning of an imminent war on foreigners, which gave non-Algerian citizens until December 1 to leave the country or face the possibility of execution. The monastery had been in operation for decades, and was part of the fabric of local Algerian society throughout the postcolonial era. Led in 1993 by prior Dom Christian de Cherge, the monks continued their missionary work of providing assistance to the local Muslim population. However, on March 28, 1996, seven monks (including de Cherge) were abducted from the monastery. By this time, an estimated 109 foreigners and 33 French citizens had been killed in Algeria.[26]

Although the GIA did not claim responsibility for nearly two months, the kidnapping of monks of French nationality was further evidence of the determination of the GIA to end French support for the Algerian government. And yet the kidnapping of missionaries (albeit foreign and of another faith) posed specific doctrinal problems, even for Algerian terrorists. For example, traditional interpretations of Qur'anic law do not allow for the harming of religious monks (hermits). As John Kiser has noted, the abductors released their theological justifications for the kidnapping in a document called "Communiqué 43" on April 26, via the London-based Saudi newspaper, *Al Hayat*. "Communiqué 43" was addressed to French President Jacques Chirac, and signed by the alias of Zitouni. Among other things, it affirmed that the monks had "never stopped trying to evangelize the Muslims and to show their religious symbols and to celebrate their religious holidays ..."[27] Because it was common knowledge that holy men could not be harmed by Muslims, the GIA communiqué claimed that those abducted had mixed with the people in an attempt "to draw them away from the divine path," and were "proselytizing." Hence, if the Algerian authorities did not release "our brother Abdelhak Layada," Zitouni warned, "we will slit their throats."

The kidnapping of the monks necessitated the direct involvement of French security authorities, including the Direction de la Sécurité du Territoire (DST) and the Direction Générale de la Sécurité Extérieure (DGSE).[28] For two months, French diplomats and intelligence services attempted to secure the release of the hostages, and the drama weighed heavily on France. The negotiations eventually broke down, and on May 21, 1996, the GIA reportedly announced that the monks had been killed. The Algerian authorities claimed that seven decapitated heads were later found, but the details have never been released by the state. Official autopsies were never undertaken, and the bodies were never found.[29]

However, the most controversial part of the story only emerged a few years later, when Abdelkader Tigha broke ranks with state authorities to reveal the Algerian security service's role in the monks' abduction. Tigha had headed a security service unit in Blida from 1993 to 1996, and was one of those directly involved in the kidnapping case. He fled Algeria in 1999 and later requested political asylum in Thailand, where he offered to work with French authorities and provide evidence about the monks' case.[30] He later moved to the Netherlands as an asylum-seeker. In 2002, French journalist Arnaud Dubus published the details of Tigha's case, which brought to light the seedy underworld of Algerian security operations.[31]

What is shocking about Tigha's account is that he openly admits that he and his colleagues within the Algerian security service were responsible for the abduction of the monks. The kidnapping, according to him, was carried out by GIA leader Zitouni but orchestrated directly by Algerian officials. This was possible because by 1996, Algerian security forces had infiltrated Zitouni's unit and were work- ing with him to accept a ceasefire. The Algerian authorities wanted the monks removed, because they had been vocal in their opposition to the Algerian state's violent methods to combat terrorism. Brit- ish scholar Martin Evans and journalist John Phillips have further clarified this strange story, outlining the following important details: Zitouni's men did kidnap the monks, after which Zitouni immedi- ately contacted DRS officials in Blida. At the same time, a rival GIA group (not working with DRS) that wanted to challenge Zitouni took control of the monks. DRS authorities ordered Zitouni to regain possession of the monks, but as he attempted do so, Zitouni was killed in a skirmish with the rival GIA faction. The rival group, led by Hocine Besiou, then murdered the monks.[32]

Tigha's case is especially important because it provided direct evidence that the Algerian security forces were in contact with Algeria's most notorious terrorists, and were themselves helping to eliminate those critical of state violence. For example, Evans and Phillips have pointed out that Tigha's accusations have also been confirmed by other DRS officials, including Mohammed Samraoui, who published an important memoir about DRS actions.[33] As Evans and Phillips write:

> Within this schema, the DRS and the GIA groups represented two extremist fringes that fed off each other and needed each other to survive. For the DRS, keen to deflect any attention away from the mafia economy, the GIA was a necessary scapegoat, keeping the status quo going by justifying Algeria's draconian system. The DRS took every opportunity for extravagant hyperbole, holding up the GIA as a diabolical menace for Algeria and the world, whilst simul- taneously infiltrating and manipulating these groups. On the other side, the GIA groups wanted to perpetuate the conflict because, in an impoverished society, it became a means to personal enrich- ment.[34]

The controversy over the monks thus brought to light the dan- gerous double game that Algerian officials played during the dirty war. Ironically, the monks were seen by both the GIA and the state as anachronistic, unwanted, and menacing simply because they wanted peace.

Londonistan, the Finsbury Park Mosque, and the world of spies

Rachid Ramda – the man accused of financing the 1995 Paris metro bombing who was detained in the UK but who fought extradition to France for ten years – fomented tension between the British and French authorities. From the French point of view, the British government was either too blind or too politically correct to recognize the true danger that militant Islamists based in London posed to Europe. For the French, the most egregious example of British indifference was the festering radical Islamic terrorist clearing house run by Sheik Abu Hamza from East London's Finsbury Park Mosque. Abu Hamza's plotting became common knowledge for British and French authorities, but British authorities, including Scotland Yard, refused to take the threat seriously. It was from this mosque, during the 1990s, that Bin Laden's associates helped Abu Hamza to recruit fighters for training camps in Afghanistan. And the man who edited *Al Ansar* from London after Ramda, Mustafa Setmarian Nasar, was suspected of setting up the terrorist cell in Spain that carried out the Madrid bombings.[35]

Unable to get British intelligence to take the threat of the Finsbury Park Mosque seriously, the French security services hatched their own plans. Given the previous GIA attacks on the country and the new information security officials possessed about the spread of terrorist networks in Europe, French authorities dreaded the possibility of a GIA attack on the 1998 World Cup in France. Hence Jean-Pierre Chevènement, the interior minister in Jacques Chirac's cabinet, gave the green light for wholesale arrests. By 1997, the French had placed a team of assassins in London to eliminate radical Islamists, and embedded Algerian informants and spies in London's Muslim immigrant community.[36] French investigators had already linked Abu Hamza to a radical cell known as the Roubaix gang, that was foiled in its plan to attack G7 leaders in France in March 1996; but what they lacked was an informant capable of getting inside the Finsbury Park Mosque and Abu Hamza's trusted inner circle.

Reda Hassaine, an exiled Algerian journalist, solved that problem for the French. In their fascinating study of Abu Hamza, British journalists O'Neill and McGrory describe in detail how the French authorities used Hassaine to gain access to the mosque's activities. Hassaine was in his thirties when he left Algiers in 1993 for France, believing that he might be assassinated by the GIA. After arriving in France, he received another GIA threat because he was planning to set up a newspaper for exiled Algerians in Paris. When he was taken into temporary police protection, French authorities asked him if he would agree to go to London as a spy under the pretense of being a GIA sympathizer. In 1994, Hassaine moved with his family to London, where he became a regular of the local mosque; he also contacted Algerian officials, and offered his services as an informant. Algerian intelligence, like its French counterpart, was acutely eager to find out more about the potential plots being hatched at the Finsbury Park Mosque after Abu Hamza took control as imam in 1997.[37]

With Chevènement's financial assistance, the French helped Hassaine found an Algerian radical Islamist newsletter that would be distributed in the British mosques. As staggering as the implications of this activity are, the very first issue of this *Journal du francophone* (printed in 1998) ran the cover story "Jihad against the United States." The fact that the French government sponsored a radical paper, even as a front, calling for a "jihad" against the US reveals a lot about the intentions of the French intelligence services. From its perspective, it was crucial to gain access to the operational planning of the jihadis in London, despite any negative side effects of funding calls for a jihad against the US. The goal in fronting such incendiary material, which included a photo of Bin Laden, was to acquire real statements from the GIA before they were made public. Moreover, by overseeing the publication of such an inflammatory newsletter, Hassaine acquired the credibility and the freedom that he needed to gain access to different parts of the mosque. The French eventually decided to phase out its relationship with Hassaine, after which he offered his services to New Scotland Yard. In 2000 his cover was blown and Hassaine managed to escape from a physical attack, but his life as an Algerian agent was over.

Hassaine was not the only North African spying on radical Islamists in London. Recently, stories of other spies that highlight the importance of the Algerian question for European intelligence services have surfaced. Perhaps the most compelling story is that of Omar Nasiri. In his memoir, *Inside the Jihad: My Life with Al Qaeda*, Nasiri provides a lucid portrait of terrorist activities in Europe and elsewhere (especially in the camps in Afghanistan), and of the European security efforts to understand the infrastructure of Islamic terrorist networks. His account also confirms that Algeria remained a paramount concern for both jihadi groups and European intelligence communities.

Nasiri's journey to the center of the jihadi spy network started from the world of Moroccan drug dealers and petty criminals. In the early 1990s, he moved to Belgium and entered a GIA cell responsible for printing and distributing *Al Ansar*. In Belgium he also became an illegal arms dealer, and eventually a spy for the French secret service (DGSE) on the GIA in Europe. The hijacking of Air France flight 8969 seemed to crystallize his distaste for Islamic terrorism, after members of his cell came into possession of an audiotape from inside the plane. While listening to this tape, which the GIA used as a training tape for future terrorist operations, Nasiri finally understood how connected the GIA groups throughout Europe were:

> It was the first time I felt how close I was to all this horror. I know I could have thought about it earlier, but I'd chosen not to. I bought the guns for Yasin because it was exciting, and because I needed the money. Often I fantasized the weapons were going off to Bosnia or Chechnya, that they were being used to fight legitimate wars against enemies of Islam. Of course, I knew most of the stuff was going to Algeria, but that didn't bother me at the beginning. I had come to feel differently as I read more, and as the GIA became more vicious.
>
> Everything was different now. The people on the plane were real to me: Arab immigrants living in Europe who loved their families and their land, and wanted to go home for the holiday. The GIA had tried to kill them all. I hadn't pulled the trigger, but maybe I had supplied the guns and the bullets. I was a killer, just like them.[38]

It becomes clear, in reading Nasiri's account, that the GIA had developed a sophisticated network throughout Europe, and that its sleeper cells had spread throughout Canada and the US during the mid-1990s. These GIA cells did everything from plan operations to coordinate the distribution of propaganda materials, including videotapes smuggled out of Algeria, via Morocco and elsewhere, that showed GIA militants butchering their victims. Nasiri's memoir also demonstrates the importance of the al Qaeda camps in Afghanistan, and underscores the fact that a lot of Algerians received training there. As for himself, he says:

> I was educated in the West, and I went to Afghanistan as a spy. I was there to fight against these terrorists, these men who slaughtered women and children in the killing fields of Algeria ... But I understood these men, even as I distanced myself from their methods. I understood their rage and their anguish as more and more of their land was stolen from them. Jerusalem, Afghanistan, Bosnia, Algeria, Chechnya – it was all the same to them. These were just the latest manifestations of a war that was going on for centuries, a perpetual war against Islam. The mujahidin were not born killers. They were born Muslims, and as Muslims it was their responsibility to defend their land.[39]

When Nasiri was sent by the French DSGE to London (overseen by a British handler) to spy on the radicals in "Londonistan," like Hassaine he gravitated to the Finsbury Park Mosque. After Hamza arrived, he displaced the traditional, non-violent Muslims and brought in a new of group of followers. "Different people came to Finsbury Park ... people who were younger and less settled in their lives. The new audience was also less educated ... I knew this because no one truly educated in Islam would have listened to Abu Hamza. He knew nothing at all. He would just wave his hook wildly and shout. He shouted constantly about jihad ... Jihad against America, Jihad against the Jews. Jihad against the infidels. Jihad against the governments of Algeria and Egypt and Yemen. Jihad, jihad, jihad."[40]

Ironically, Nasiri notes that the French and British secret services chose to focus efforts on Abu Hamza and the Finsbury Park Mosque and in doing so overlooked the far more dangerous activities of the Four Feathers Mosque, which sustained direct contacts between al Qaeda in Afghanistan and its London-based cells directed by Abu Qatada – "the spiritual leader of Islamic militants in Europe."[41] Like

Hassaine, Nasiri confirmed that the British did not have a handle on the dimensions of the Islamist threat, and were ill-prepared for it. He wrote of his British handler: "Daniel wasn't a bad guy; he just didn't seem to understand what the West was facing ... Daniel asked if Bin Laden was the leader of the jihad, and I had to explain to him that Bin Laden was himself irrelevant. Jihad is not a political movement, I explained. Jihad is not the IRA or the Bader-Meinhof gang. Jihad is an order from God. No human intermediary is necessary."[42]

Perhaps ironically, it was the very cosmopolitan character of English society and its liberal legal system that rendered it a safe haven for the world's most notorious jihadi revolutionaries during the 1990s. In fact, radicals carefully exploited the freedoms that exile in England and elsewhere in Europe had afforded them, to craft al Qaeda's propaganda and plan terrorist operations. Not coincidentally, the CIA station chiefs and intelligence officers in North Africa during the 1990s also lamented the ease with which exiled radical Islamists were granted political asylum in England, France, Germany, Sweden, and Denmark. Among those drawn to London was the Syrian-born al Qaeda intellectual and propagandist whom Brynjar Lia has astutely called "the architect of global jihad," Abu Mus'ab al-Suri.[43] However, the English paradise for radical Islamists in exile did not last forever. As al-Suri put it, by the late 1990s England had lost "its 'democratic virginity' following its marriage to the 'American cowboy.'"[44] Before this happened, al-Suri, like Hassaine and Nasiri, concluded that Algeria was critical to the success of radical Islam.[45] As he put it, Algeria was "among the most important of experiences for the jihadi movement in the second half of the twentieth century." But why was al Qaeda so invested in the conflict in Algeria?

Like other al Qaeda mujaheddin, al-Suri had formed important bonds in Afghanistan with Algerian radicals. In particular, he had become close friends with an Algerian named Qari Said. From a guest house in Peshawar, Said contacted other mujaheddin who were returning home to various Arab nations and who were eager to continue their jihads. Through Said, Bin Laden promised these men that if they broke with the established Muslim Brotherhood movements, in other words with political Islamists, al Qaeda would help support their local jihads.[46] Though eager to extend his reach over several national jihads, Bin Laden was especially concerned with Algeria. According to American journalist Steve Coll, Bin Laden's attempts to influence national jihadi movements did not go unnoticed by CIA officers, who constantly warned of the unique threat that the Afghan mujaheddin posed to governments when they returned home to North Africa.[47] It is clear now that since Algeria had the most prominent political Islamist movement (the FIS) and the most avant-garde jihadi campaign (the GIAs), al Qaeda believed success in Algeria would lead to success in other countries. At the time, the CIA attempted in vain to understand the significance of the return of Afghan veterans and was unable to come to an agreement on what it all meant.[48]

It is also clear that Bin Laden and al Qaeda leaders wanted to undermine FIS efforts to return to the democratic process. If the banned FIS leaders succeeded in re-entering the political field and in gaining even partial control over the state through negotiation and non-violent means, they would undermine al Qaeda's stake in the pan-Islamist movement. Since al Qaeda viewed Islam as a pure, divine, and totalizing force, there was no space for pluralistic debate or for compromise with secular and other non-believing politicians. Hence, al Qaeda's stance on Algeria helps reveal just how threatening the emerging democratic process within Muslim-majority countries could appear to hard-line jihadis. In this context, Afghan Algerians like Qari Said, and al Qaeda supporters in Europe, were instrumental in turning Muslims away from the FIS after the military coup. When Said returned to Algeria to found the "Afghan Algerian" group in the early 1990s, one of his first missions was to decouple the alliances made between Algerians and the FIS. Said's contribution to the jihadist cause in Algeria was to help create a cadre of Afghan Arabs that would be at the very center of the GIA when it formed.[49]

In London, Said convinced al-Suri to help set up the GIA's "media cell." During other visits between GIA men and al-Suri, the GIA convinced him to help their cause. Placed in London, al-Suri worked directly with the GIA community. Indeed, as a writer for *Al-Ansar*, the mouthpiece for the GIA in Europe, al-Suri became Bin Laden's official envoy to the GIA and a key player in the propaganda of radical Islam.[50] In fact, according to al-Suri, it was he who originally advised the GIA leader in 1993 to begin to carry out attacks against France.

At first, al-Suri was optimistic about the achievements of the GIA in Algeria, but when the national emir of the GIA, Abu Abdallah Ahmed, was killed in 1994, the nature of the jihad in Algeria changed. His successor, Djamal Zitouni, radicalized the jihad beyond recognition and pushed the violence beyond the pale of "acceptable" jihadi violence. A proud Algerian, Zitouni wanted to keep the Algerian jihad a national affair and shunned outsiders, especially al Qaeda's men.

In moving Algeria into a total war against the civilian population, Zitouni blocked the participation of foreign jihadists, including and perhaps especially al-Suri. Hence, although al-Suri did not completely abandon the GIA, his relationship with it grew increasingly strained. Al-Suri and al Qaeda leaders viewed Zitouni as someone who had compromised the global jihad with the barbarity of the killings in Algeria. As al-Suri put it, "we decided to stay firm, fight back and bridge the gap, but the deviations of the GIA broke the alliance of the jihadis." In particular, al Qaeda insisted that Zitouni's excessive violence ran the risk of blemishing the jihad in the eyes of devout and sincere Muslims. When al Qaeda made contact with Zitouni via key al Qaeda leaders, including the leader of Egypt's Islamic Jihad Group, Ayman al-Zawahiri, Zitouni rebuffed all attempts by outsiders to instruct Algerian GIA fighters on the proper tactics for carrying out jihad. In fact, according to Lia, the GIA even threatened to kill Bin Laden if al Qaeda attempted to fund any Algerian militants other than through GIA channels. Yet, despite the growing rift between the Algerian GIA and al Qaeda, al-Suri continued to work on behalf of the GIA and write for *Al-Ansar* until the GIA under Zitouni carried out purges and assassinations of GIA men with Afghan connections.[51]

After President Zeroual's government entered into negotiations with the FIS and AIS, the GIA "declared war" on these groups, causing many supporters to shift to the GIA.[52] By June of 1996, two months after the monks at the monastery at Tibhirine were murdered, al-Suri publicly broke with the GIA and withdrew his endorsement. The next month Zitouni was killed in a skirmish with Algerian authorities. Following Zitouni's death, Antar Zouabir took over as national emir of the GIA. By this time, the deep divisions within the GIA had become clear, and the violence seemed to be accelerating without limit. However, al-Suri and al Qaeda had not given up on the jihad in Algeria, and toward the end of the 1990s, a new group was beginning to emerge from the GIA that better reflected the goals and ideology of al Qaeda. That group, which al Qaeda did support, was the Groupe Salafiste pour la Prédication et le Combat, or GSPC.

7 | The future of radical Islam: from the GSPC to AQMI

Several factors account for the demise of the Algerian GIAs, but two stand out: unchecked violence against Muslim civilians, and instability and internal rivalry at the leadership level. As the conflict wore on during the 1990s, various GIAs and especially the national GIA justified all forms of brutal violence with totalizing interpretations of the Qur'an and jihad that left no room for nuances. This logic of extremes, in combination with the military's equally Manichean world-view and equally violent tactics, eventually crippled the GIAs' ability to fulfill their revolutionary aspiration of establishing the new Caliphate in Algeria. As it was, the battle that radical Islamists did wage managed to trap the civilian population inside one of the decade's most vicious warzones, one easily comparable to the horrors of Bosnia and to the other devastating ethnic conflicts that rendered the 1990s synonymous with man's inhumanity to man.

But before the GIAs evolved into a new terrorist organization, their quest for Islamic authenticity played out with fatuous brutality. Entire villages were liquidated; tens of thousands of men died with their throats slit, many indeed decapitated; women were gang-raped, taken as sex slaves for wandering jihadis, and butchered; children were slaughtered, and the unborn were literally ripped from the womb and placed in heated stoves, for their dying mothers to watch them burn; massacres became routine. For example, between 1992 and 1997, an estimated 642 separate massacres were recorded, with more than 300 occurring in 1997 alone.[1] By the end of the 1990s, most reasonable estimates put the number of people killed at over 200,000. But, in 1998, after six years of internecine violence the effects of this pornographic slaughter of innocents had compromised the cause of radical Islamists in the eyes of other global jihadists, who viewed Algerian terrorists as disorganized, overly nationalistic, and most importantly, "deviants" from doctrinaire Islam. In short, the slow fatigue of this unrelenting sadism had finally brought Algeria's radical Islamists to the cross-roads of doubt.

Hassan Hattab, the GSPC, and the global jihad

When the AIS agreed to a ceasefire and after the government began talks about possible amnesty deals with terrorists, radical Islamists in Algeria did not simply disappear: those still committed to the jihad had to adapt to the new expectations of international terrorism. In this context, the Groupe Salafiste pour la Prédication et le Combat (GSPC) emerged after 1998 as a national terrorist movement with cells spread over Europe and North America. The GSPC's rise to prominence within the country corresponded to its ability to operate outside Algeria; and, because of the strength of its international cells, by 1999 it had become Algeria's dominant terrorist organization committed to seeing through the jihad. As such it targeted the various elements of the Algerian government at home, as well as Western interests in Algeria and around the globe.

The GSPC had originally formed in 1998 as a reaction to the violent excesses of the GIAs, and because a significant number of jihadis had decided to lay down their arms when the AIS agreed to disband and accept the terms of a ceasefire with the Algerian government in October 1997. After the AIS made peace with the government and agreed to "deradicalize," many GIA guerrillas remained dedicated to overthrowing the government.[2] But the GIA as a national movement remained divided and disorganized, while its extreme violence and nationalistic stance had alienated it from supporters. In contrast, when it was created by ex-GIA field commander Hassan Hattab in 1998, the GSPC fostered links with international jihadis and highlighted the connections between local and global forces.

Born in 1967 and trained as a paratrooper in the Algerian army, Hattab left the forces in 1989. After the military coup, he became radicalized and went underground. In 1994, he became the regional GIA emir responsible for terrorism in Kabylia. Hattab understood that the GIA's brutality had turned the Algerian masses against radical Islamists, and caused highly desired sponsors of global terrorism to back away from their Algerian counterparts. At the same time, Hattab clearly understood the threat that the AIS ceasefire posed for him and the jihad. To clarify his goals, Hattab issued a communiqué that was republished in the London-based *Al-Hayat* newspaper on May 5, 1998.[3] In it he announced that his new movement would offer an alternative to both the "bloodthirsty" GIA and the "apostate" AIS.[4]

Hattab's solution was the freshly minted GSPC. Shedding the GIA's damaged name and its notorious tactics, Hattab promised a "new dawn" for the jihad in Algeria and vowed to heal the "divisions and rifts" that had plagued radical Islamists for years. Determined not to stand down, Hattab offered his own slogan: "neither dialogue nor truce with apostates." Above all, Hattab pledged to wage a clean battle, focusing attacks on state targets and also tourists.

Osama Bin Laden, now in Afghanistan after being expelled by Sudan in 1996 (the same year that the Taliban took control of Kabul), and who had issued a fatwa in 1998 calling for Muslims to kill Americans, remained determined to play a larger role in Algeria. The GSPC presented al Qaeda with new opportunities to coordinate with Salafists in Algeria and thereby convince other national terrorist movements to partner with al Qaeda. In fact, as French journalist Dominique Thomas notes, in 1996 Bin Laden initiated discussions with Hattab because he represented a Salafist faction of the GIA. According to Thomas, the creation of the GSPC can be traced to al Qaeda's Salafist jihadi clerics in London, who "relayed" information from Afghanistan.[5]

In December 1999, after Abdelaziz Bouteflika's election to the presidency, rumors began to circulate that Hattab was considering surrender.[6] In truth, Hattab and al Qaeda began to close ranks. Throughout 1999 Hattab and Bin Laden were in frequent contact.[7] The alliance between al Qaeda and the GSPC was mutually beneficial. With it al Qaeda had finally gained access to the European and North American terrorist networks that Hattab controlled; and the GSPC gained a global partner with vast expertise and a leadership safely ensconced in Afghanistan. During the first few years of its existence, which coincided with Bouteflika's first years in office, the GSPC did not openly flaunt its affiliation with al Qaeda. The majority of its attacks were limited to attacks on state security personnel and international actions.

The prominent French scholar of radical Islam, Olivier Roy, has identified this period in the development of the GSPC and other militant Islamist movements as the time of "deterritorialization." This means that "[r]elations between militants and their country of origin are weak or non-existent." Importantly, many of the militants who carried out operations for the GSPC and al Qaeda outside Algeria began their journey towards the jihad inside Europe. Along with Zacarias Moussaoui, the missing hijacker from the 9/11 attacks, Roy cites the cases of Fateh Kamel and Ahmed Ressam, Algerian GSPC members who planned to bomb the Los Angeles Airport during the Millennium celebrations in December 1999, and other examples of the migration of Algerian members of the GSPC to terrorist cells in America.[8]

From millennium bomber to state's witness: Ahmed Ressam and the GSPC in America

On December 14, 1999, as a paranoid public braced for the imminent Y2K catastrophe, a slender 32-year-old Algerian named Ahmed Ressam, traveling with a fake Canadian passport under the alias of Benni Norris, attempted to cross the Canadian border from British Columbia into the United States at Port Angeles, Washington. Sweating profusely from a bout of malaria contracted on a recent trip to Afghanistan where he had trained at the same al Qaeda camp as Zacarias Moussaoui, Ressam's suspicious behavior alerted US customs agent Diana Dean. After the trunk of his vehicle was searched and discovered to be full of bomb-making materials, Ressam attempted to flee but was apprehended by Dean and her colleagues. Ressam's case, thereafter known as Borderbomb, set off a massive manhunt for radical Islamist sleeper cells in America. Over a dozen people were eventually arrested in the US and Canada on suspicion of plotting to disrupt the Millennium celebrations.

The investigation of Ressam brought to the surface the existence of an Algerian sleeper cell based in Montreal with links to the al Qaeda network throughout the US, Europe, and Afghanistan. Before Ressam was sentenced in April 2005 in a Seattle courtroom to 22 years in a US prison, the Borderbomb case highlighted the degree to which Algerian GSPC members had been trained in the al Qaeda camps in Afghanistan and brought out details about the fascinating criminal underworld of credit card fraud and identity theft rings that Algerian jihadis in the diaspora used to finance their activities.

From the beginning of the Borderbomb investigation, as Pulitzer Prize-winning journalist Lorraine Adams notes, US officials believed that there was a connection between Ressam and Bin Laden, and FBI director Louis Freeh appeared before a US subcommittee to "boast" of his organization's ability to thwart terrorists, and insist that the case was "the template" of how FBI efforts "were supposed to work."[9] Moreover, the Borderbomb case helped cement US President Clinton's view that there was a new kind of terrorism that was a "transnational conspiracy of Muslim anti-American sentiment led by Bin Laden." Together with the August 1998 twin bombings of the US embassies in Nairobi (Kenya) and Dar es Salaam (Tanzania), and the October 12, 2000 bombing of the USS *Cole* in Yemen (which killed 17 sailors), and Bin Laden's February 1998 fatwa calling for the killing of Americans, the capture of GSPC terrorists in the US and Canada helped US intelligence officers realize that a transnational conspiracy was in the works.

In this sense, Borderbomb represented a substantial step forward in understanding the connections between global terrorist groups. As one US senior intelligence officer put it, the US was the "big bull's eye" of international groups, and the Ressam case "demonstrates that there is a global network ... that really wants to hit us where we live."[10] The links to Ottawa naturally increased fears that Canada had become a front line for Algerian terrorist cells spread around the globe. As David Harris, the man once responsible for strategic planning in the Canadian Security Intelligence Service, put it: "Canada has become, by default, a charter member of the Algerian international extremist movement."[11]

At the same time Ressam's case highlighted serious failures of the FBI and intelligence-gathering communities, as well as the general incompetence of US prison officials responsible for the protection of key state witnesses. Ironically, Ressam had been at first an ideal informant on his terrorist associates, and cooperated so well with the FBI that Vincent Cannistraro (former CIA counter-terrorism chief) said of Ressam: "He's been singing like a bird."[12] Indeed Ressam did initially provide authorities with critical information on al Qaeda's operatives, including Mohammed Atta (the mastermind of 9/11) and Zacarias Moussaoui, charged with conspiracy in connection to the 9/11 attacks. During the trial of Mokhtar Haouri (who received a 24-year prison sentence), the Algerian co-conspirator in the plot to bomb the Los Angeles Airport, Ressam confirmed that Haouri had trained in Afghanistan at a camp run by Bin Laden.[13] Ressam also initially provided testimony to the FBI on Abu Zubaydah, a high-level al Qaeda leader captured in Pakistan in March 2002, who then became an inmate at Guantánamo Bay. Ressam identified Zubaydah as the leader who ran the al Qaeda camps in Afghanistan, and the man who brought Ressam from Montreal to the jihadi camp in Afghanistan.[14] As a result of the blunders and abuse committed by guards and fellow inmates, Ressam withdrew his help. Ressam was moved out of prison in 2004 and into a witness protection program within the prison system.

When Judge John Coughenor finally sentenced Ressam, he took the opportunity to criticize the Bush administration's use of torture and argued that the Borderbomb case demonstrated that in the fight against al Qaeda, secret prisons and a disregard for the constitution did not produce the kind of cooperation that Ressam's case had – despite Ressam's decision to quit testifying. In fact, Ressam's early cooperation showed that torture was not only immoral but unnecessary. And, rather than sentencing Ressam to the 35 years of prison time that federal prosecutors sought, Judge Coughenor decided on a lighter penalty of 22 years, in an effort to achieve a balance between "severity" and the reward for having provided important details about al Qaeda, and for testifying against GSPC members in earlier trials.[15]

While Ressam was in prison, the GSPC underwent important changes. It began planning more attacks within Algeria, such as the important attack on a military base in Kabylia that killed 15 soldiers in May 2002. Meanwhile, after 9/11 Western states began to reassess the connections among the various international terrorist groups with links to al Qaeda. In 2002 and 2003, analysts remained worried about the growing influence of the GSPC in Europe and about the human rights violations committed by the Algerian regime.

For example, on September 12, 2002, the UK ambassador to Algeria, Graham Hand Stewart, informed Djamel Boukrine, a journalist with *Le Matin* in Algiers: "I can tell you one thing, Algerian terrorists have been chased out of London. Those who are still there are keeping a low profile. We are keeping an eye on them."[16] However, the ambassador did note the UK government's concerns about possible human rights violations by the Algerian government. As he put it, "the Algerian security services are brutal and do not attribute much importance to human rights." The 9/11 attacks had clarified the stakes of the game for the British authorities. He continued: "I think that the most important and positive thing is the reunification of the world against terrorism. We have understood that the terrorism that has raged in Algeria for ten years is not special or specific to this country. We have understood that after 11 September the war that Algeria is waging is also our war."

By January 2003, some 200 men, of whom "about 80 percent were Algerians," had been taken into custody on terrorist charges during the preceding 15 months.[17] After a "ricin ring" was discovered in England, Europeans became increasingly concerned about the presence of Algerian jihadists in their midst. These crackdowns did have negative effects. Legitimate refugees and exiles began to fear the presence of radicals and the suspicions of the police. The chairman of the Algerian refugee council in Britain, Dr. Mohammed Sekkoum, warned jihadists using the immigrant community as a shield: "If you are in the Algerian community you know these things. I know the names of many of these people ... These people were killers in Algeria and now they are here. I have told the immigration service about them, but the authorities told me it has nothing to do with me."[18] And, more than a year before the Madrid bombings of March 11, 2004, Spanish Prime Minister José Maria Aznar confirmed that police had arrested 16 suspects (mostly Algerian) and foiled a plot to use ricin and other plastic explosives in Madrid.[19] On July 5, 2005, Italy denounced the existence of the GSPC on Italian soil.

Within Algeria, commentators began to fear the worst about the GSPC attacks. As Algerian sociologist Mohamed Arrasi warned, al Qaeda was gaining ground in Algeria and "[t]he possibility of Al Qaeda turning Algeria and with it North Africa into a new stage in its confrontation with the West should not be ruled out."[20] Similarly, a journalist for *Al Watan*, Mohamed Al Hassani, confirmed that the "killings are a message to President Abdelaziz Bouteflika that the radicals reject his proposed reconciliation offer."

Yet, while the GSPC was clearly on the move at home and in Western Europe, Hattab began to encounter resistance to his leadership from within the group. After an internal power struggle, Hassan Hattab was replaced on October 8, 2003, by Nabil Sharawi (also known as Abu Ibrahim Mustapha), who had close links with Bin Laden.[21] Sharawi had trained in al Qaeda camps in Afghanistan and emerged from within the GIA under Djamal Zitouni, for whom he helped carry out the extermination of AIS rivals.[22] Sharawi was eager to escalate the campaign against the Algerian security services and broaden the jihad into other theatres of operation. Moreover, Sharawi disagreed with Hattab's less violent tactics and promised to renew the campaign against Bouteflika's government and its newfound US ally.

Young and enthusiastic (he was 37 when he took over the GSPC), Sharawi understood that the jihad had changed course, in part because by the time he assumed control over the movement it was clear that Bouteflika's deradicalization programs had been relatively successful at integrating former Islamists back into civil society. Moreover, after the US invasion of Iraq, it was evident that radical Islamists hoped to capitalize on a wave of anti-US resentment sweeping through the region. As Sharawi saw it, President Bush's war was inspired by a bitter desire to keep Muslims subservient to the West and to make it impossible to establish a nation where the Qur'an would dictate society's laws.[23] For these reasons, the GSPC would remain dedicated to attacking the US and Algeria's so-called apostate leaders. Sharawi did not get a chance to fulfill his promises. He was killed in 1994.

The strange ordeal of the Saharan kidnappings

Hassan Hattab had challengers beside Sharawi. The most controversial was Amar Saifi, also known as El Para (he had been a paratrooper in the Algerian army, as well as one of President Bouteflika's personal bodyguards). Saifi's sudden rise within the GSPC came after he successfully orchestrated a high-profile multi-million-dollar kidnapping of 32 European tourists (ten Austrians, 16 Germans, four Swiss, one Swede and one Dutchman) in the Sahara Desert in February–March 2003. El Para also brought jihadis from Mauritania, Mali, and Niger into his operations.[24]

After the Saharan kidnappings, which would surely become one of the strangest and most puzzling episodes in the post-9/11 "War on Terror," Saifi emerged to become one of the most wanted terrorists in the world. The US placed a $5 million bounty on him and put him alongside Osama Bin Laden on the "Specially Designated Global Terrorist" list. But there are competing interpretations of Saifi, and this controversy came to light after two investigative journalists, Salima Mellah and Jean-Baptiste Rivoire, published an article called "El Para, the Maghreb's Bin Laden" in the February 2005 issue of *Le Monde diplomatique*.[25]

Saifi's emergence as a challenger to Hattab within the GSPC coincided precisely with the arrival of a US military delegation on January 5, 2003, the day after Saifi's group attacked a military convoy and killed 43 Algerian soldiers on January 4. According to Mellah and Rivoire, the Algerian Department of Intelligence and Security immediately produced a forged video recording designed to "persuade public opinion that El Para was a lieutenant of Osama Bin Laden." Convinced of the threat, the US authorities agreed to equip the Algerian military with long-sought supplies. Presenting Saifi as a new force to be reckoned with within the GSPC, Algerian officials persuaded the Americans that Saifi would focus on US targets. And by drawing attention away from human rights violations, fear of El Para cemented the newly formed US–Algerian friendship.

Mellah and Rivoire suggest that Saifi was in fact working for the Algerian military, and that Algerian officials themselves had orchestrated the Saharan kidnappings. While this is certainly plausible, the episode remains a mystery. Lasting over several months, the 2003 kidnappings generated an international crisis. After intense negotiations, a first group of 17 hostages was released in May 2003.[26] The remaining 15 were released in August in Mali, where the kidnappers had taken them. Michaela Spitzer, a 45-year-old German tourist, died of heat stroke after five months and was buried in the Sahara. Once the second group had been moved by the terrorists into Mali, Malian President Touré promised to help end the stand-off after the German government asked Mali to negotiate their release. Meanwhile, angry about the ability of Algerian terrorists to capture German citizens vacationing abroad, German Chancellor Gerhard Schroeder vowed that German "security forces will support Algerian and Malian partners in everything that could help seize the kidnappers and put them on trial."[27] While Germany was unwilling to disclose the details of the ransom, according to some estimates the kidnappers had asked for as much as $95 million. Eventually, the Malian Tuaregs negotiated the release, but the full details were never made public. As the hostage crisis came to an end, Libya's Muammar Gaddafi Foundation, which is run by the leader's son, claimed to have been instrumental in negotiating with the GSPC to lower the amount of the ransom.[28] It was said that Mali paid 5 million Euros for the hostages, and in return, Germany agreed to provide foreign aid to Mali.

The Sahara kidnappings impacted US–Algerian relations. While President Bouteflika had remained a vocal opponent of the US invasion of Iraq, US officials now regarded Algeria as a vital ally in the "War on Terror." Rapprochement with Algeria went in tandem with the launch in November 2002 of the Pan Sahel Initiative (PSI) – the US State Department counter-terrorism partnership with Chad, Mali, Mauritania, and Niger. Moreover, as the *New York Times* reporter, Craig Smith, put it, Saifi's "presence in the region was one of the catalysts for an expanding American program to rally regional governments into a loose alliance to fight terrorism."[29] For that reason, the US military "tracked" him "from Mali across Niger and into Chad."

In March 2004, with the US and other international military forces in pursuit, Saifi and his band of men were found in Northern Chad. After a gun battle, he escaped from a US-led force but was caught on March 16, 2004 by a local rebel group known as the Mouvement pour la Démocratie et la Justice au Tchad. The MDJT, itself engaged in an armed struggle to overthrow Idriss Déby's government, began a complex set of negotiations with the US, Germany, Algeria, Nigeria, and France. Keenly aware that they were negotiating with a rebel group at war with Chad's government, all parties, especially the

US, had to be cautious and avoid alienating a PSI partner. Germany was the most eager to extradite Saifi, and had already issued an international warrant following the Sahara kidnappings. Algeria also wanted Saifi, for the killing of 43 of its soldiers.

However, what complicated matters even more was the fact that US military forces had already been scheduled to arrive in Chad to provide its soldiers with anti-terrorism training, the week after Saifi's capture. Because Saifi was to be offered to the highest bidder it seemed as if, according to one US Defense Department spokes-man, it were a "Sahara version of eBay."[30] Eager to prove that it had renounced state-sponsored terrorism and that it was now a creditable partner for the US in the "War on Terror," Libya once again acted as intermediary. Hence, Muammar Gaddafi threatened to bomb the rebels if they did not hand Saifi over. In response, the rebels first offered Saifi to the US, Germany, and France, but each country refused to take him.[31] Finally, in October 2004 and after months of negotiations orchestrated by Gaddafi, the MDJT handed Saifi over to authorities in Tripoli, who promptly extradited him to Algeria. His trial was set for June 2005, but he was never seen publicly and was sentenced *in absentia*, without further explanation from Algerian authorities, to a term of life in prison.

The US welcomed the capture of Saifi and ironically now viewed Libya, which had been considered a sponsor of terrorism since 1979, as an important partner in the "War on Terror." General Charles F. Wald, the deputy commander of the US military's European Com-mand, was so pleased with Libya's remarkable change of heart that he suggested that Libya might "even start participating in North Africa from the standpoint of a counter to the Salafist Group for Preaching and Combat."[32]

By playing his anti-Algerian terrorism card, Gaddafi had redeemed himself in the eyes of US authorities. At the same time, Saifi's kidnap-ping of European tourists (followed by his own bizarre kidnapping at the hands of Chadian terrorists) helped to convince the US Congress that North Africa and the Sahel region did in fact constitute a new front in the "War on Terror." Accordingly, Congress budgeted over $500 million over the next six years for an expansion of the Trans-Sahara Counterterrorism Initiative.[33] The capture of Saifi was itself offered as evidence of the plan's effectiveness, since US military and Special Forces troops had worked with Mali, Niger, Chad, and Algeria to "corral" Saifi. Not surprisingly, suspicion still lingers that Saifi was in fact working in the service of the Algerian military. The fact that the government sequestered Saifi after he was delivered to Algeria to stand trial, and that no one has since seen this famous prisoner, has done little to convince skeptics otherwise.

The debate about Saifi did not prevent the GSPC from reorganizing while drawing closer to al Qaeda. In fact, under its new leader, Nabil Sharawi, the GSPC continued its attacks on the Algerian government. At the same time, Hassan Hattab insisted that he remained the GSPC's leader. In January 2004, in an effort to reassert his status, he vowed to continue "a perpetual jihad" aimed at the regime and its allies, especially the US, and averred that his group had nothing to do with the massacre of innocent civilians.[34] In addition, he continued to deny that his men were considering accepting amnesty as a reward for putting down their weapons. To outdo Hattab's declarations, in February 2004, Sharawi issued his own communiqué in the name of the GSPC, expressing its "jihadist solidarity" with fellow Muslims fighting against the "Jew and crusaders," and promising to pursue the struggle against the Algerian regime: "We are not finished and the fight against the tyrant is going to continue." With regard to the US he was clear:

> Cooperation between Algeria and America has gone through several phases ranging from financial support to the exchange of intelligence and going so far as the opening of an American intelligence office in Algeria, the supplying of weapons and munitions and military equipment, among them night-time vision glasses and surveillance and espionage equipment, and participation in military operations ... America does not know laws and recognizes nothing and operates according to its interests, which are fighting any Islamic group that wants to establish an Islamic state, trying to control the world's strategic points, among them Iraq, the Arab Maghreb, the Horn of Africa, the Arabian Peninsula, etc., protecting its oil wells in the South of Algeria, which are increasingly important to them, and supporting the Jews in order to establish a greater Israel.[35]

On May 4, 2004, the GSPC distributed a videotape on its website, algerianjihad.com (access since blocked), in which Sharawi spoke of the jihad in America, Palestine, Afghanistan, and Chechnya.[36] On June 20, 2004, Sharawi was killed by Algerian forces.

The GSPC and the al Qaeda alliance

Abdelmalek Droukdal (also known as Abu Ibramim Mustafa) quickly became the GSPC's next emir. Under Droukdal, the GSPC actively sought out closer relations with al Qaeda and initiated the conversation with Abu Musab al-Zarqawi, the leader of al Qaeda in Iraq (Jama'at al-Tawid wal-Jidad). Droukdal had first reached out to al Qaeda in Iraq in order to help free Saifi in Chad.[37] Al-Zarqawi understood the benefits of a merger with the Algerians. In an extraordinary interview published by the *New York Times* on July 1, 2008, Droukdal confirmed that al-Zarqawi and his "brothers" within al Qaeda had played a "pivotal role" in his decision to join "the organization."[38] Although al-Zarqawi was killed on June 7, 2006, when two 500-pound guided bombs found his safe house in Baqubah, Iraq, the bonds forged by al-Zarqawi and Droukdal – between the GSPC and al Qaeda – continued to grow stronger for several reasons. As Droukdal put it in the 2008 interview: "We and al Qaeda are one body. It's normal that they get stronger by us and we get stronger by them. They back us up and we back them up. They supply us and we supply them with any kind of support, loyalty, advice and available support."

There were other reasons for the merger. Michael Scheuer – former lead CIA analyst for Bin Laden, best-selling author of *Imperial Hubris*, *Through Our Enemies' Eyes*, and *Marching Toward Hell*, and a major critic of Bush's decision to invade Iraq – helped to clarify two of them: "One was the extraordinary violence, the indiscriminate violence of the GIA. The second was that bin Laden wanted – in many Muslim countries – to destroy the nationalist orientation of local Islamic groups."[39]

Bin Laden and his associates had another practical motive to work with the GSPC. As Rahan Gunaranta, a leading authority on al Qaeda in Europe, also noted, Bin Laden wanted access to the large network of GSPC cells spread throughout Europe under Droukdal's control.[40]

Hence, from al Qaeda's point of view, not only would its affiliation with the GSPC increase its operational market share of terrorist networks in Europe, but it would further its own aspirations to a pan-Islamic revolution. As the alliance was being formed, Droukdal continued to make the case to al Qaeda that it would be an important ally, and emphasized that his men were fighting in Afghanistan, Chechnya, Lebanon, Somalia and Sudan.[41] And, in the 2008 interview, Droukdal confirmed that in addition to Algeria his men came from Mauritania, Libya, Morocco, Tunisia, Mali, and Nigeria.[42]

Ironically, Algerian extremists were helped tremendously by an unwitting George W. Bush, who allowed al Qaeda to draw Western powers directly into the field of combat. Following Bush's declaration of the "War on Terror" in September 2001, the US and its NATO allies began to express increasing concern about Algerian terrorists' connections to like-minded African groups. After the beginning of the Iraq conflict in March 2003, NATO and Pentagon officials argued that increasing numbers of militant fighters from North Africa were joining Islamist insurgents. Because it was known that al Qaeda was keen to direct terrorist operations throughout North Africa, Algeria factored into a fundamental reassessment of US post-Cold War military planning in Africa. Of particular concern has been the fear that the Sahel region of Africa is likely to become what some American officials have called "the new Afghanistan." The British anthropologist Jeremy Keenan, a leading authority on the Tuareg and the Sahara, has called this questionable turn toward the Sahel region as a new front in the war on terror the "banana theory of terrorism."[43]

The premise of what Keenan calls the "banana theory" (in reference to the shape of the Sahel region) holds that the Algerian and American military are accomplices in inventing *ex nihilo* a new front on the "War on Terror," and argues that both states benefited politically and financially from the invention of this front. Less controversially, Keenan insists that the identification by the US military of the Sahel as a hotspot of jihadi violence has made the region less stable. Keenan's conspiracy theory, while compelling, has attracted its fair share of skeptics and others who prefer a more cautious assessment. For example, Hugh Roberts suggests that the sudden appearance of US military assets in the Sahel, which had never seen significant terrorist activity, is a "very tempting target. In other words it could bring into existence the problem it's notionally pre-empting. I can't help but think it's quite a high-risk venture."[44]

It is particularly risky now because US concerns for this "new Afghanistan" culminated with the creation on February 6, 2007, of the Unified Combatant Command for Africa (AFRICOM), a joint Department of Defense and State Department plan that combines humanitarian and military goals. Representing the centerpiece of US and NATO planning in Africa, AFRICOM grew directly from the increasing paranoia regarding terrorism in Algeria (and North Africa) and the generalized fear that jihadists from the Sahel region will continue to supply Iraqi insurgents with a steady stream of fighters eager to defeat US and Coalition forces.

Consolidating the GSPC and denouncing reconciliation

While Droukdal consolidated his authority and strengthened the GSPC's links to al Qaeda, the ousted founder of the GSPC, Hassan Hattab, announced in 2005 that he backed Bouteflika's reconciliation program and that he would do all he could to bring the GSPC in from the fight. The GSPC immediately declared Hattab an "apostate" who had "fallen into the trap of the tyrant."[45] Hattab had betrayed the very movement he had created by accepting Bouteflika's platform, in part because while Hattab appreciated and had helped foster the global spread of GSPC cells, he did not endorse subsuming the national agenda of the GSPC into the al Qaeda framework, nor did he approve of handing over assets (the terrorist cells) spread through Europe and elsewhere that could be used to strike at the US. As Droukdal put it: "The GSPC dissociates itself from the actions of Hattab, who betrayed God and the Prophet, has strayed from the road to jihad, and sold the blood of martyrs. ... National reconciliation and general amnesty are but a treasonous mirage that the renegades are applauding. It is but another episode in the war against the jihad under the banner of the great American tyrant."

In 2005, clearly concerned about the neutralizing effects of the amnesty agreements on its men and eager to prove his al Qaeda credentials, Droukdal extended the jihad into Mauritania. Mauritania was important because it had supported the US-led invasion of Iraq in 2003 and enjoyed stable relations with the US and Israel. In May 2005, Mauritania uncovered the GSPC plot to carry out terrorist attacks during the visit of Israeli Foreign Minister Silan Shalom, and a month later the GSPC carried out a cross-border attack against Mauritanian forces, killing 15 soldiers and wounding 17. The GSPC attacked Mauritania just as the US was scheduled to begin training Mauritanian forces (and those of other Sahel region nations) in a border defense program known as "Operation Flintlock," part of the Pan Sahel Initiative. Claiming responsibility for the attack, the GSPC stated its resolve not to be confined to "internal" operations in Algeria, and to pursue the "enemies of religion" wherever they were.[46] A week later, on June 17, 2005, US officials announced that the GSPC had been placed on "Tier Zero" by the director of National Intelligence, indicating that it had global and not just regional significance, and that it was considered one of the most dangerous terrorist organizations in the world.

In August 2005, Mauritania's pro-American and pro-Israeli president, Ma'aouiya Ould Sid' Ahmed Taya, was overthrown in a military coup. Clearly disturbed by the anti-Islamist position of the now deposed leader, four days later the new government temporarily released the 21 men imprisoned by Taya for allegedly belonging to the GSPC.[47] These events sparked fear among Western authorities that Mauritania could become a regional safe haven for Islamic extremists.[48] Wishing to ensure continued American assistance, in September the government of Mauritania excluded the alleged GSPC members from future agreements.[49]

As the GSPC began to expand its activities, in July 2005 French authorities confirmed that the GSPC leader had made contact with al-Zarqawi in Iraq to urge al Qaeda forces there to kidnap French nationals.[50] On August 28, 2005, two Frenchmen, Christian Chesnot (of Radio France Internationale) and Georges Malbrunot (of *Le Figaro*) were kidnapped by the Islamic Army in Iraq, who demanded that the French government repeal the ban on the wearing of headscarves in schools.[51] After a massive intervention by Chirac's government and widespread criticism from Muslim leaders within France of the radical Islamists' tactics, Chesnot and Malbrunot were released in

December, but in the meantime Droukdal continued to threaten France and French interests in Algeria.

On September 29, 2005, Algerians voted unanimously in favor of Bouteflika's program for national reconciliation, which carried with it important provisions for terrorists willing to lay down arms. Rebuking Bouteflika, Droukdal confirmed that "jihad" would "go on." The referendum meant nothing to the GSPC. As he put it: "The vote is a waste of time ... Algeria is not in need of a charter for peace and national reconciliation, but in need of a charter for Islam."[52] However, on October 2, the Algerian newspaper *El-Khabar* reconfirmed that Hattab would help Bouteflika secure the peace by trying to convince members of the GSPC to accept amnesty. Droukdal denounced Hattab, and Hattab denounced Droukdal.

In the fall of 2005, as the internal strife between past and current GSPC leaders moved into the open, Europeans once again confronted the specter of GSPC cells in France, Britain, and Italy. Since Droukdal had made France a specific target for terrorist attacks, the then French Interior Minister Nicolas Sarkozy confirmed that France was watching the movement of French Muslims to Afghanistan and Syria, among other countries. Because al Qaeda had been able to recruit jihadists from within French borders, France was on high alert. Fears intensified after the arrest of a GSPC member in Algeria confirmed that there was a GSPC terrorist cell in France preparing an attack. "Iraq is a live-fire training ground for urban terrorism, and that's exactly what we fear," one European commentator said. France's most important anti-terrorism judge, Jean-François Richard, confirmed that French authorities had taken an Algerian named Safe Bourada (who had recently served time after being convicted as an accessory to the 1995 Paris bombings) into custody. "What worries me the most is the behavior of the GSPC," Richard admitted. After its threats on France, and given its connections to al Qaeda's leader in Iraq, an attack on France appeared "inevitable."[53]

Countries throughout Europe grew increasingly anxious about the potential for GSPC cells to form within their borders. After the 7/7 bombings in London, Britain went on high alert regarding al Qaeda and GSPC operations in Britain. According to Charles Grant, the director of the Centre for European Reform in London, the conflict in Iraq had created the conditions for a worsening of the problems: "What the war in Iraq has done is radicalize these people and make some of them prepared to support terrorism. Iraq is a great recruiting sergeant."[54]

Italian security officials expressed similar concern and confirmed that the Carabinieri had been following North African cells for years. The members of these Italian-based GSPC cells traveled to jihadi training camps in Afghanistan, Chechnya, and elsewhere, and they established contact with other radicals in Norway, France, and Britain. After surveillance confirmed a plot to attack Italy, the Carabinieri made arrests on November 15, 2005. On November 24, Spanish police followed suit and arrested ten members of the "notorious" GSPC involved in drug trafficking, fraud, and robbery. These arrests yielded information about GSPC connections to other cells in Germany, the Netherlands, Britain, Belgium, and Denmark.[55] A few weeks later, Spanish authorities arrested seven more men with links to the GSPC on December 9, 2005. Many more arrests of suspected GSPC members continued to be reported throughout Europe, and even Canadian officials reported the arrests of suspected Algerian GSPC members.

The al Qaeda merger: AQMI

Despite Abdelaziz Bouteflika's generous albeit controversial amnesty agreements, the Algerian GSPC transcended its national boundaries to become key players in the Salafist global jihadist campaign. Concern for Algerian terrorism once again spiked considerably after al Qaeda's second-in-command, Ayman al-Zawahiri, formalized the merger between al Qaeda and the GSPC on September 11, 2006. Al-Zawahiri put the merger in these terms: "This blessed union will be a bone in the throat of the American and French crusaders ... and will bring fear to the hearts of the miscreant sons of France."[56]

On December 11, 2006, the GSPC threw a bomb at two vehicles transporting employees of Brown and Root Condor – (a Halliburton company involved in construction projects in Algeria), killing the Algerian driver and wounding nine others, including a Canadian, an American, and several British citizens. The GSPC issued a statement claiming responsibility: "We carried out this raid as a gift to all Muslims who are suffering from the new Crusader campaign targeting Islam and its holy places."[57] Droukdal explained his decision to attack US interests in Algeria thus:

we found America building military bases in the south of our country and conducting military exercises, and plundering our oil and planning to get our gas. Also, opening an FBI [meaning CIA] branch in our capital city, and starting an unusual Christian conversion campaign among our youths to change their religion in order to create religious minorities among us.

Its embassy in Algeria began playing almost the same role as the American embassies in Baghdad or Kabul. It intervenes in internal policy by planning, instructing and controlling. All that just to kill the spirit of jihad and resistance among Muslims so that it can put its hand on the energy stock that we have. So did America leave us any choice with this flagrant aggression? No doubt that the answer is going to be no. Therefore, it became our right and our duty to push away with all our strength this crusade campaign and declare clearly that American interests are legitimate targets to us.[58]

Finally, on January 24, 2007, Droukdal issued his communiqué renaming the GSPC as Al Qaeda au Maghreb Islamique (AQMI), and stating that Bin Laden had personally endorsed the transformation of the GSPC into this new al Qaeda group. The adoption of al Qaeda's name was proof of the "sincerity of the ties between the mujahideen in Algeria and the rest of their brothers in Al-Qaida."[59] At the same time, Bin Laden encouraged the GSPC to carry out an attack on France, because, as he wrote in a letter republished in the Western media, "This infidel country has colonized Muslim countries for a long time," so it should be hit "where it hurts most."[60]

The corporate-like merger and final metamorphosis of the GSPC into a partner in Osama Bin Laden's organization brought not only its official name-change but also successive April, September, and December 2007 suicide bombing campaigns in Algeria. The introduction of strategic suicide bombings and the renewed attacks in 2007 and later in 2008 have called into question the future success of President Bouteflika's program for national reconciliation, and increased the anxieties of Algerian and Western policy-makers and military strategists, fearful of a resurgent radical Islamist movement in Algeria and more broadly in North Africa.

The 2006 decision by Algerian and fellow North African terrorist groups to integrate local Salafist movements into a global Salafist jihad, effectively enfranchised with the parent corporation of al Qaeda, came at the moment when other terrorist groups – most notably al Qaeda in Mesopotamia – decided to buy into the global brand name that al Qaeda offers in a competitive world where individual groups struggle to achieve greater recognition. Importantly, the global branding with al Qaeda also came at the very moment when other jihadists have, as Marc Sagemen has put it, gone "leaderless";[61] hence, rather than acting spontaneously, as is the current trend with militant groups that prefer to act without guidance from a global hierarchy, Salafists in Algeria and North Africa (like those in Iraq) have united with al Qaeda and insist that collectively they can overthrow both national governments and any foreign powers in their backyard.

Suicide bombing, as political scientist Robert Pape explains in *Dying to Win*, has a strategic logic that is not so much religious as political. Its tactical use is directly connected to the expansion of American military personnel in the Arabian Peninsula, and more recently, Iraq. Although Pape does not discuss Algeria per se, his theory holds (at least in part) because the recent adoption of suicide bombings in Algeria does correspond to a widespread animosity against the American invasion of Iraq and the growing military cooperation between the US and Algerian militaries, on top of a longstanding complaint against France. Hence, following Pape's logic, the advent of suicide bombings in Algeria should not be read as a resurgence of radical Islamic practices, but as part of the political campaign waged by al Qaeda (and its new North African partners) to try to force Western powers out of Algeria, North Africa, and beyond. As Pape writes: "Although terrorist leaders harbor other goals, history shows that the presence of foreign combat troops on prized territory is the principal recruiting tool used by terrorist leaders to mobilize suicide terrorists to kill us. Suicide terrorism is mainly a demand-driven, not a supply-limited, phenomenon."[62]

However, not everyone agrees that the introduction of suicide bombing necessarily corresponds to the presence of US troops, that it represents a greater threat to the government, or that it is a question of supply. In fact, Hugh Roberts contends there was clearly no "operational need" (except in the case of the bombing of the prime minister's office) for the recent spate of suicide bombings in Algeria. Instead, Roberts sees suicide bombings an "index of weakness," because AQMI employed the tactic mainly in order to demonstrate that the new organization was "clearly imitating al Qaeda. It's also about playing to Western media, about getting headlines, and perhaps most importantly about convincing the elements of young Algerians from which al Qaeda attempts to recruit – the desperate, frustrated, angry youth – that the organization is no longer merely the GSPC but is now al Qaeda." To be sure, "if one assumes that the GSPC had trouble getting new recruits," the name-change was a ploy to draw attention, in much the same way as marketers suggest that when a commodity loses traction the best way to spark renewed interest is to repackage the product and sell it as something new. The idea was that if the Algerian jihad appeared as "part of an international movement, that suddenly provides a reason for the frustrated youth to join." Ironically, "it's a perverse rationale, to induce the young to commit suicide as a way of getting them to join al Qaeda. It's macabre. But quite clearly there is an element of the youth that is that desperate."[63]

By February 2007, Europeans understood the threat AQMI posed. No longer just an Algerian organization, AQMI threaten to pool terrorist resources across North Africa. As Henry Crumpton, the US ambassador at large for counter-terrorism noted: "It's [AQMI] forging links with terrorist groups in Morocco, Nigeria, Mauritania, Tunisia, and elsewhere."[64] Terrorism prosecutors throughout Europe echoed concern that AQMI had been actively training terrorists throughout North Africa and within Europe. From Tunis to Milan, the connections linking AQMI associates were exposed by a number of arrests. French magistrate Jean-Louis Bruguière commented in an interview with Craig Smith: "It's the same thing we saw in Bosnia, Kosovo and above all Afghanistan. Al Qaeda's objective is to create an operational link between the groups in Iraq and the GSPC."[65] Indeed these fears were based on intelligence reports that showed that as the GSPC transitioned to al Qaeda, somewhere between 800 and 900 active GSPC jihadis could be found in the "exile network" throughout Europe, and this network had greater appeal for the "estranged young Muslims that idle at the fringes of major European cities."[66]

While Europeans grew anxious and the French anticipated AQMI strikes that would be timed with its upcoming presidential elections, Droukdal's men started their bombing campaigns inside Algeria. On February 13, 2007, AQMI set off seven synchronized bombs targeting police stations across Algeria, which killed six people. On April 11, three suicide bombers killed themselves in Casablanca during a shoot-out with Moroccan police. The next day, the worst attack in over a decade was carried out when suicide bombers carried out carefully timed attacks. One group targeted the offices of the Algerian prime minister and the minister of interior; a dozen people were killed and approximately 118 injured. Another destroyed a police station, killing 11 people while injuring over 40 others. Algerian Prime Minister Abdelaziz Balkhadem, whose office had just been destroyed, immediately spoke on national radio: "It can only be described as cowardice and betrayal, at a time when the Algerian people are asking for national reconciliation."[67] The people agreed, as thousands poured into the streets carrying flags and pictures of Bouteflika, demanding an end to the violence.

On May 8, Al-Jazeera, the Qatari-based satellite TV station, broadcast al Qaeda's video tape recording the suicide bombers' preparations for the attack on the prime minister's office. In the video, Abou Moussab Abdelouadoud (Droudkal) explained AQMI's decision to employ suicide bombers was part of the strategy to destabilize the area: "From now on, we have decided to resort to suicide attacks as a strategic option in the confrontation between us and our enemies. In order for this decision to materialize, we have instructed regional and local emirs [leaders] to open the door to volunteers who seek martyrdom and who wish to confront the enemy. We have instructed them to urge Muslims to sacrifice themselves for the sake of God. We have also instructed them to make every effort to provide the necessary devices for the martyrdom seekers, and to be meticulous in identifying and selecting targets in such a way as to achieve the aims of the jihad."[68]

Next day, the Algerian daily *Liberté* blasted Al-Jazeera for irresponsible journalism and for encouraging terrorism in Algeria by broadcasting Droukdal's message.

Rarely has a television station in the world acted as megaphone for terrorism the way Al-Jazeera is doing. ... The problem is that Al-Jazeera no longer knows the limits of credible information, appealing to spineless political opponents and unleashing a flood of hatred at our country but in particular, since the April 11 attacks, serving as an amplifier for the terrorist actions of the GSPC or AQMI with a truly perverse satisfaction ... This media hypocrisy is the trademark of a channel that refuses to talk about Algeria as it actually is. Fifteen years of terrorism are so many market shares for this channel, which trades in the deaths of our fellow citizens, who have become so many audience ratings figures. The images that are broadcast in a loop do not justify terrorism. They legitimize it.[69]

Despite widespread public outrage over the recent actions of AQMI, boosting support for Bouteflika and his national reconciliation program, further reports of AQMI plans to attack American and Israeli, as well as French, EU, and UN targets, continued to surface after the April attacks. At the same time, Algerian police made arrests of minors between ten and 17 years old, who had been lured into joining the group. However, divisions within AQMI continued to appear, with disagreements over the use of suicide bombers to kill innocent civilians. Further splits within the group formed after Hassan Hattab turned himself in to Algerian authorities on September 22, 2007. As a condition for his surrender, Hattab applied for amnesty under the terms of the National Reconciliation program. Two weeks before, the GSPC leader of the Saharan region, Abdal Khader bin Massoud, had also agreed to lay down his arms and request amnesty. Back in July Benmessaoud Abdelkader, a prominent member of the GSPC, had given himself up: this was important, because his area of command bordered the Saharan region near Mali and Niger.[70] All these men claimed that that there were deep divisions within AQMI. They urged other former GSPC members to come in from the battle and accept National Reconciliation.

Despite the growing popular repudiation of the violence and the many GPSC members seeking clemency, AQMI continued to build its networks and alliances and plan attacks. In November 2007, Ayman al-Zawahiri released an audio recording announcing that the Libyan Islamic Fighting Group had also joined al Qaeda. Al-Zawahiri called for his fighters to overthrow North African governments and specifically those of Algeria, Libya, Morocco, and Tunisia. In the 28-minute recording titled "Unity of the Ranks,"[71] al-Zawahiri declared that al Qaeda was adding Libya's group to its ranks because Gaddafi had sold out by dropping his weapons program and working directly with the United States over the past few years. Interestingly, the Libyan group merged directly with al Qaeda and not with AQMI.

Within Algeria, AQMI struck again on December 6, when suicide bombers killed 11 civilians in Batna as President Bouteflika toured the city. On December 8, AQMI suicide bombers killed 28 members of the Coast Guard in the small coastal city of Dellys, about 50 miles from Algiers. Then on December 11, another pair of coordinated suicide bombings devastated two sites in the capital, the Algerian Constitutional Council and the United Nations Algerian office: over 60 people were killed and some 180 were wounded. Following these attacks, Interior Minister Noureddine Yazid Zerhouni said during a briefing that the terrorists have "one choice: turn themselves in or die."[72]

The attack on the United Nations office (which killed 41 people) was the first major strike against the UN since the August 2003 bombing of the UN offices in the Canal Hotel in Baghdad. Al Qaeda had already made it clear that the UN was an open target, and that it would continue to strike against it throughout the world. The attack also exemplified the determination of al Qaeda to change the rules of peacekeeping, for it showed that civilians working on aid missions would no longer be considered neutral in this new kind of war. Since Bin Laden had made it clear that the UN was simply a tool used by the West to dominate Muslims, the AQMI attack solidified the links between al Qaeda and the Algerian terrorist groups and put Western nations and NGOs on high alert.

Strengthening the connections to al Qaeda had clearly given Algerian insurgents a new sense of purpose, and helped revive a waning radical Islamist movement. The multiple suicide attacks confirmed analysts' worst fears about the new breed of terrorists in Algeria. With the introduction of suicide bombings, a tactic that migrated from Iraq to Algeria largely after the GSPC converged with al Qaeda, came more reports of terrorists from across North Africa working together. As Judge Bruguière told reporters, "Al Qaeda has succeeded in creating an advance unit in a strategic region: North Africa is the door to Europe ... The methods they are employing are imported from Iraq."[73] And as journalist Michael Moss and his colleagues covering Algeria for the *International Herald Tribune* reported, "the transformation of the group from a nationalist insurgency to a force in the global jihad is a page out of Bin Laden's playbook." In joining forces, al Qaeda has helped "reinvigorate" the insurgency with "fresh recruits and a zeal for Western targets." Equally important, joining al Qaeda allowed Algerian terrorists to re-enter the ranks of other radical Islamists who had rejected indiscriminate killing of Muslim civilians during the 1990s. At the same time, the merger with al Qaeda forced the Algerian government to redouble its efforts to eliminate the insurgency. For example, in 2007, the government arrested or killed approximately 1,100 militants. And, according to one local mayor, "'[w]e don't arrest them anymore ... we just kill them.'"[74]

In 2008 AQMI violence spiked, killing an estimated 125 people in August alone. One of the largest attacks came on August 19 when a suicide bomber drove his bomb-laden vehicle into a police academy, killing 43 people, just as new police recruits were waiting in line to take a qualifying examination. At the end of September, another car bomber killed himself and three others outside of Dellys. AQMI took credit for the attack and praised Abu Al-Abbas Abd al-Rahman for carrying out his mission. As AQMI put it in a statement, "We bring [the Muslim Ummah] the glad tidings of the mujahideen's victories and their massacre of the apostate slaves of the Americans."[75]

It is not entirely clear how effective AQMI will be in the future. What is clear is that the successive name-changes represent an effort on the part of Algerian jihadis to find legitimacy after the demise of the GIAs within the arena of global terrorist networks. As one terrorist expert described the rebranding from GIA, to GSPC, to AQMI: "This corresponds to the failure of a purely national fight." When it was created, and then with Djamal Zitouni, the GIA's goal was to establish "the emirate in France." In the years 1994–1995, Zitouni refused to pledge allegiance to the internationalist movement, stating that he was the sole true fighter internationally. The adoption of the term "Salafist" by the GSPC was capital in the evolution of the Algerian terrorist movement. This progression was finalized with the creation of AQMI. However, adoption of al Qaeda could also signal the weakening of local support for Islamic terrorism in Algeria. Hence, while it may be more appealing for young recruits to belong to a global jihadi movement, terrorist movements in Algeria might be a declining phenomenon. To be sure, AQMI will continue to carry out spectacular attacks when it can, but the likelihood of it ever accomplishing its mission of overthrowing the state is slim. In other words, the successive name-changes, as one terrorism expert put it, are evidence of the decline in the Algerian population's support for radical Islam: "It's a natural, logical, and necessary evolution because these terrorist groups have failed in their fight, because they have not known how to attract people to them."[76]

The Algerian state's confrontation with radical Islamists has long been a paramount regional and international concern. During the past few years, continued violence has clarified the degree to which global terrorist networks have partnered with the principal local groups. The determination of Algerian terrorists to keep their struggle viable through an alliance with al Qaeda is perhaps the best evidence that the Algerian state's deradicalization campaigns and successive amnesty agreements were effective in neutralizing the radical opposition movements. It remains to be seen if the state can finally eliminate the root causes of terrorism and restore confidence in the political process. If it does not address these fundamental questions, the government will most likely be condemned to wage a constant anti-terrorist campaign for years to come.

8 | Killing the messengers: Algeria's Rushdie syndrome

On Valentine's Day 1989, the day before the Soviets withdrew from Afghanistan and four months before he died as Iran's Supreme Leader, Ayatollah Ruhollah Khomeini issued history's most infamous fatwa, or death sentence. To entice devoted followers to carry out his wishes, Khomeini offered a bounty of $5.2 million on the novelist Salman Rushdie's head. About a week later, in an act he later publicly regretted, Rushdie apologized for offending Islam. Subsequently, his Italian and Norwegian translators were critically wounded in knife attacks, and his Japanese translator, Hitoshi Igarashi (a literature professor), was murdered in 1991. Although the current government of Iran claims it no longer endorses the fatwa, to this day an Iranian foundation offers a reward of $2.8 million for anyone able to kill Rushdie.[1]

Rushdie's capital sin, according to Khomeini, was of the pen, specifically in his fourth novel, *The Satanic Verses*. Though Khomeini boasted that he never read it, *The Satanic Verses* came to his attention shortly after it was published in 1988. During that first year of the novel's turbulent life, a violent storm had already begun to brew within the Islamic world. Conservative Muslims and small groups of anti-Rushdie protesters, offended by his imaginative depiction of the Prophet Mohammed, ignited public outrage against Rushdie as they spilled out into the streets across the world, calling for immediate punishment. For example, in Islamabad, on February 12, 1989, five people died in riots against the book. *The Satanic Verses* was banned in several countries with large Muslim populations, including India, and burned in mass demonstrations against the book in England and elsewhere. Its publishers (London-based Viking Books), as well as anyone associated with the publication of the book, were condemned by the fatwa. Khomeini's call for the assassination of a British citizen of Indian descent, which was broadcast on Iranian state radio and officially endorsed by the government, caused the British government to sever diplomatic relations with Iran.

In so many ways, the Khomeini fatwa against Salman Rushdie changed the world, especially for writers, intellectuals and artists, for the worse. It led to noticeable spikes of intolerance, and it changed the West's relationship with many Muslim-majority countries. Perhaps worst of all, the Rushdie Affair, as it was later named, led to a virulent epidemic of copycat fatwas by minor radical Islamic clerics and other local jihadi emirs throughout the Middle East, Asia, and Africa, permanently changing the tenor of cultural debates within Muslim-majority nations. In short, quite intentionally Khomeini set in motion a new kind of identity politics that would accompany the birth of the post-Cold War world.[2]

The contagion of intolerance

The extraordinary fatwa against Rushdie, which he would thereafter call Khomeini's "unfunny Valentine," could not have come at a worse time for Algeria. Algeria's experiment with democratic reform began exactly the same year Rushdie published *The Satanic Verses*. Because Khomeini's fatwa represented an unprecedented departure for Islamic tradition (both Shiite and Sunni), it created a cultural ripple effect that went well beyond England and Iran, spreading to majority Sunni Muslim countries like Algeria and most recently to Iraq. It is important to stress that, as flashy as Khomeini's fatwa was, it marked a shift from traditional interpretations of Islamic law. As the noted Islam scholar Gilles Kepel reminds us, under Islamic jurisprudence a fatwa of this nature (calling for the execution of someone who has committed "blasphemy" against Islam) may only be carried out against a Muslim and within the realm where a Muslim prince resides. Ordering the assassination of a person living under a Christian sovereign, in a place where shari'a did not apply, was entirely outside the norm of Islamic jurisprudence and represented an incalculable departure, even for radical Islamists, from traditional interpretations of the Qur'an and other core Islamic texts.[3]

As a showman, Khomeini knew exactly what he was doing. According to Kepel, "at one stroke, the ayatollah had placed the entire world under his jurisdiction." The fatwa upstaged the Soviet withdrawal from Afghanistan, and cast the spotlight on the ayatollah. Moreover, by appropriating the negative publicity surrounding Rushdie's book, Khomeini's anti-Rushdie position gave the "cause a political dimension it had previously lacked." Khomeini's bold move effectively announced a new kind of identity politics that highlighted the tensions between Islamists and the values of the West, and simultaneously managed to "transcend the traditional frontiers of Islam."[4]

Though predominately a Sunni Muslim country, in the late 1980s Algeria represented one of the dynamic cross-roads where two divergent political projects (one working toward a fundamentalist Islam, the other trying to protect republican-style secularism) increasingly found themselves engaged in an ever-polarizing competition. Because of the tensions expressed on both sides, the reaction to Khomeini's actions and Rushdie's work were symptomatic of larger splits between secular and religious world-views. What remains unequivocal, though, is that throughout Algeria's rapid descent into the bloodbath of the 1990s, the Algerian variety of the Rushdie syndrome would be recycled again and again, destroying hundreds of intellectuals and other cultural actors (journalists, singers, athletes, etc.) offered up for slaughter by even much less learned Islamic extremists, emboldened by the innovative religious weaponry bequeathed by Khomeini. So great was the danger of this new kind of quasi-religious killing in Algeria that Rushdie himself, while still in hiding, made impassioned pleas to end it, and begged intellectuals, NGOs, and the international community to help Algerian intellectuals forced to flee from would-be assassins.

Truth to tell, despite the international support of Rushdie by other writers, very few writers within Algeria took issue with Khomeini's fatwa.[5] No doubt Algerian writers were consumed with their own internal challenges in 1989, but nevertheless the absence of a general protest was somewhat peculiar. In this context, one person stood out as perhaps the first Algerian writer to criticize Khomeini: Anouar Benmalek, a professor of mathematics at the University of Algiers and a writer. For Benmalek the Khomeini fatwa was not only theologically misguided, but, even worse, it trivialized far more pressing concerns within the Arab world in 1989, such as poverty and oppression. For this reason, Benmalek asked sarcastically if Khomeini was really serious. How could it be that against the backdrop of "great tragedies that have been known or are known today in the Muslim world, underdevelopment, illiteracy, oppression, dictatorships, famine, that all of this is nothing compared to this book: *The Satanic Verses*!?"[6]

Intellectuals and state oppression

It would have been bad enough for Algerian intellectuals if their opponents had been none but religious zealots. What made their situation truly unbearable was the state's parallel attacks on the Algerian intelligentsia, as the political situation deteriorated even before the military coup in 1992. It is clear that the Algerian state openly targeted intellectuals, especially journalists, with a campaign to discredit critics within the burgeoning free press. During the first years of the 1990s, the state censored, harassed, and even imprisoned writers with the full power of its security branches and with the support of a genuflected judiciary. Indeed, many officials and military leaders condoned the violation of human rights (including the use of torture against civilians, giving security officials carte blanche to first crush the October 1988 rioters and later the FIS),[7] and these same officials did nothing to prevent the arrests of journalists in 1992 and 1993 under bogus charges of endangering the security of the state, a feature of Algerian society that remains a problem for writers.[8]

While the intelligentsia eventually found itself squeezed from both sides (the state and radical Islamists), it was the Algerian junta that first had real power to persecute Algerian writers, as the well-respected journalist and writer Lazhari Labter has pointed out.[9] In part this is attributed to the fact that Islamists also benefited from the newly enshrined freedom of the press. Hence, the state felt doubly threatened because both secular-leaning and Islamist-leaning journalists were attempting to cover hitherto taboo topics, including state torture and the actions of Islamic terrorist groups. The fear that a meddling media could undermine the authority of the state caused the state to turn against Algerian journalists, well before terrorists began to single out those in the liberal media for assassination. Consequently, whatever the original purpose may have been, by attacking intellectuals first, the state created the conditions for radical Islamists to follow suit, rendering the liberal media especially vulnerable.

The targeting of the intelligentsia intensified following the resignation of Prime Minister Sid Ahmed Ghozali in July 1992. A moderate, Ghozali had held office since July 1992 and was followed by Belaïd Abdessalam, who remained in office until August 1993. As prime minister, Abdessalam had extraordinary power and was not afraid to use it. At the same time, he relied heavily on the military and changed the tenor of the debate over the freedom of the press, going so far as to accuse Algerian intellectuals of treason. "'The private press ... uses treason and corruption to achieve its ends. It has introduced espionage into the ranks of the [government] administration.'" Under Abdessalam, editors and journalists were arrested on trumped-up charges. For example, Mohamed Benchicou, editor of *Le Matin*, was jailed for "spreading false information" in accordance with a July 1992 law giving the government leverage over its critics in the media. Under these circumstances, according to Labter, Abdessalam's "foul" manipulations (*vacheries*) triggered a nearly complete erosion of press freedoms.[10]

It is important to point out, however, that although the state's attacks on the freedom of the press worsened under Abdessalam's draconian leadership, conditions facilitating media repression were already in place. In April 1990, the government had enacted the Information Act, or Law N. 90-7. The law mandated that any reporting on violence- or security-related issues had to originate from official government sources. This legislation criminalized criticism of the government on the grounds that it endangered national security. Moreover, Article 5 of the State of Emergency Decree issued in August 1992, Presidential Decree N. 92-320 (August), along with the government's Anti-Terrorism Decree passed in December, reinforced censorship by requiring all journalists to clear their stories with government censors before going to press. Collectively, these laws wiped out what remained of the freedoms granted in 1989 by the so-called "Hamrouche Decree" (as it was dubbed by the journalists) that had liberalized the Algerian press for the first time since independence.[11]

Censorship and arrests thereafter became routine.[12] Once journalists were identified as fair game for harassment by the junta during the early 1990s, Islamic groups followed suit. In this environment, even clandestine Islamist newspapers were used to threaten members of the liberal press. For example, *Ennafir*, an underground organ of the FIS, gave journalists 40 days to stop their "campaign of denigrating" the Islamist project.[13] That said, for Algerian writers such as Labter, it was really Abdessalam's actions and those of the government before and after him that bore a large part of the responsibility for the killing of intellectuals by Islamists.[14]

Women, sport, and shorts

The targets of the Algerian cultural war during the 1990s were not limited to the intelligentsia. The frenzy of ever-escalating intolerance caught others equally unprepared – even Olympic athletes were not immune. Without question, the two most prominent Algerian athletes were both 1,500-meter runners, and in August 1991, Hassiba Boulmerka and Noureddine Morceli both won massively impressive victories in their events at the World Championships in Tokyo.[15] Boulmerka, although not unknown, was not considered a favorite when she crossed the finish line in Tokyo, becoming the first African woman to win the World Championship in track, and Algeria's first female athlete to claim the honor of World Track and Field Champion. As Boulmerka finished her race, she screamed, grabbed her hair, and continued to scream. She later said, "I was screaming for Algeria's pride and Algeria's history, and still more."[16]

The political chaos in Algeria momentarily gave way to joyful public celebrations when Morceli and Boulmerka arrived at the airport in Algiers in August 1991. After their unprecedented double wins at the World Athletic Championships, there were so many spectators there to greet them, according to Boulmerka, that it took the "National Service to control the crowds. They threw mountains of bouquets." Thrilled by her victory, President Chadli awarded Boulmerka the Algerian Medal of Merit, the nation's highest honor, and kissed her on the forehead – to the disapproval of the Islamists. Leila Aslaoui,

Algeria's minister of youth and sport from 1991 to 1992, claimed at the time that "Boulmerka's victory," as well as Noureddine Morceli's, "was applauded by every single Algerian." Unfortunately the euphoria did not last. As *Sports Illustrated* reporter Kenny Moore noted in his story about Boulmerka and Morceli in 1992:

> Boulmerka's victory for Islamic women was a fraying rope flung across a yawning social chasm. Many Algerians, even as they cheered found their pride at odds with their religion. ... Within a few months doctrinaire imams pronounced a *kofr*, or denunciation, of Boulmerka, as un-Muslim for "running with naked legs in front of thousands of men."[17]

Initially, Minister of Sports and Youth Aslaoui tried to downplay the Islamists' hostility to Boulmerka. "It's only a minority, and you're always going to get some critics ... And anyway, she'll get over it, she's a fighter."[18] At the same time, there was a growing realization that the issue of women's participation in sport had come to illustrate an important and growing division within Algeria: between religious conservatives who opposed women like Boulmerka, and others who supported her and women's rights in general.

The attack on women in sports was not long in coming, spearheaded by the FIS. After the initial FIS electoral victories, local officials began disbanding women's sporting organizations, and the FIS also made moves to use the national government to bar women from sport. After the coup, the issue of women athletes was again taken up by the national government. Some strange contradictions emerged. For example, in a peculiar defense of Boulmerka, Aslaoui brought up the Salman Rushdie case to allay concerns that Boulmerka could offend Algerians by running in shorts: "If Rushdie has insulted the Prophet, then he must suffer the consequences."[19] Conservative Islamists united against Boulmerka precisely because she was so important to the women's movement in Algeria. As Boulmerka herself put it just before the 1992 Olympics, "I am a danger to the fundamentalists. I am a symbol to the young that our women no longer have to hide behind the veil."[20] Even Boulmerka's own father was threatened with violence if he did not publicly disown her.

As a devout but moderate Muslim woman, Boulmerka had little

patience for intolerant imams, politicians, and citizens. Nevertheless, she stated that she wished to remain apolitical and did not question the right of Islamists to govern. As she put it:

> When the FIS won the first round of the elections … I said to myself, "You can't be frightened of these people, because the majority of Algerians voted them in." I'm not scared of Islam. It's there to facilitate the lives of the people, mine included. But I am scared of the fascists who hide behind the veil of Islam in order to impose their political will. These are the people you see in Iran. But Algeria won't be like that. Our doctrinaire Muslims are too smart. They want to get along with all the Algerian people. At least I hope they do.[21]

Boulmerka also expressed her faith in the future of democracy in Algeria, and explained that for the time being, after the cancellation of the elections, she believed that President Boudiaf would do his best to steer the country through uncertain times.

On August 8, 1992, about a month after Mohamed Boudiaf's assassination, Hassiba Boulmerka became the first Algerian athlete (male or female) to win an Olympic gold medal after defeating her archrival, the Russian athlete Tatiana Dorovskikh.[22] Her victory represented a crowning achievement for Algerian sports, yet it aggravated her problems with conservative and radical Islamists. Even before the Barcelona Games, throughout 1991 and 1992, she had been forced to change her training sites to Italy and France, for fear of attack. She accepted her gold medal in Barcelona in Boudiaf's honor: "He was a brother, a father, an Algerian … Because I love him, that doesn't mean it has to mix with politics."[23] She emphasized that she did not want to "get mixed up in politics. I am just one Algerian woman trying to satisfy all the Algerian people, without exception … I don't want to make myself vulnerable."[24]

Boulmerka was indeed vulnerable, and like other athletes in Algeria and elsewhere over the next decade, after her Olympic victory she was sucked into the political arena against her will. On returning home, she found herself a continued target of Islamic fundamentalists. Some even threw rocks and spat on her in public.[25] Within a short time she had to go into hiding in France, and she later moved to the United States, to train and to avoid problems with fanatics. At the same time, the threats against her could not prevent her from becoming a role model for young women in sport. Nor did her treatment deter other Algerian girls and women from participating in sports. For example, between 1992 and 1994, over 8,000 girls and women enrolled in Algeria's athletic programs.[26] In 1995, while competing in New York, Boulmerka spoke to journalists about the problem of religious zealots in Algeria. "The number one obstacle is the fundamentalists ... Progressively, they get more dangerous. A lot of women are physically capable of becoming athletes, but psychologically they don't think so. They have to become stronger in mind, not just the body."[27]

By the time she began preparing for the 1996 Summer Olympic Games in Atlanta, Boulmerka had become one of the foremost symbols of the battle to ensure women's participation in international sport. Prior to the Atlanta Games, the French feminist organization Atlanta Plus, founded by Linda Weil-Cureil, used Boulmerka in its campaign urging the International Olympic Committee to suspend any Islamic nations that did not include women on their national teams. Weil-Cureil likened the discrimination against Muslim women in sport to "apartheid against women." She continued: "If several countries on behalf of their religion ban women from sports, they should be excluded from the Olympic movement."[28] Anita DeFrantz, a US IOC member in charge of monitoring the status of women in the Olympic movement, commented that she understood Atlanta Plus's concerns and "the large issue" that is "simple and clear. I think there are ways ... but denouncing countries and banning them is not high on my list."[29]

While it is impossible to calculate how many Algerian women and girls were scared away from sports by intolerant Islamists, not all elite athletes were so intimidated. In fact, Nouria Merah-Benida followed Boulmerka to the Olympic podium when she won a gold medal for Algeria in the 1,500-meter track event at the 2000 Sydney Games. However, despite this success, Algeria's women athletes had genuine reason to fear Islamic terrorists. For example, in July 1994 Algeria's reigning national women's judo champion, Houria Zaidat, received a message warning her to quit practicing judo. One week later, five terrorists broke down the door to her apartment in

Algiers. With herself, her mother and three siblings forced to watch, the men "wrapped" her 16-year-old brother's "mouth with masking tape," held him to the ground, and "one man slit his throat."[30] She later told a reporter of her dying brother, "I saw him trembling like a sheep." The following May, terrorists shot and killed her mother, and later, they murdered another brother. Despite this violence meant to drive her from the sporting arena, she refused to give up judo and continued to compete, wearing shorts and bright lipstick; but she carried a gun at all times.

The total cultural war

In 1993, after Hassiba Boulmerka went into exile and before Houria Zaidat's life was shattered, another part of the cultural war began. It started on March 14 with the murder of Hafid Senhadri, an outspoken critic of political Islam and member of the Algerian National Salvation Committee (a group supporting the cancellation of the elections). Known for his anti-Islamic views, he openly called for the suppression of the January 1992 election results that gave the FIS their landslide victory. Two days after Hafid Senhadri's murder, Djilali Liabes, a prominent academic and recent minister of national education (June 1992 to October 1992), was killed by radical Islamists at his home in Algiers. On March 17, Dr. Laadi Flici, a physician and prominent political candidate, was slain in the Casbah by terrorists.

These assassinations signaled the beginning of a total war against Algerian intellectuals and others whom Islamists considered legitimate targets. Journalists quickly found themselves in the forefront. The Committee to Protect Journalists records that between 1993 and 1998, 58 Algerian journalists were murdered.[31] At the same time, press freedoms continued to come under attack by the government. As Omar Bellouchet, the editor of *El Watan*, stated in an interview in 1999: "Entrenching press freedom in a country like this is a difficult business. ... You move forward, you get hit, you fall down; you get up, move forward, get hit again. It's a never-ending process. It's not something that happens in an intellectual's salon, amid the niceties of fine debate."[32]

With journalists already being pushed to the front lines of the new kind of cultural war, it was the assassination of Tahar Djaout in May 1993 that seemed to crystallize the debate. Known for his powerful and uncompromising criticism of both political Islamists and state corruption, but also for his cheerful, humorous personality, Djaout was by 1993 one of the best known and widely admired writers of his generation. Merely 39 years old, he had become renowned for his commitment to literature and democracy, and for his articulate criticisms of the military state. As a young man, he started his career at the francophone newspaper *El Moudjahid*, the paper for which Frantz Fanon had written during decolonization. After independence, *El Moudjahid* was controlled by the state and considered an official organ of the FLN. In 1980 he took a job at *Algérie-Actualité*, where he made a name for himself as an iconoclastic and energetic critic of cultural norms. Parallel to his work at *El Moudjahid* and *Algérie-Actualité*, he embarked on a successful literary career, first as a poet, then as a novelist.

When the democratic awakening began in 1988, Djaout was at first (like most Algerian intellectuals) optimistic about the liberalization of the press in 1989. This mood did not last long, and he lamented the marginalizing of intellectuals in Algeria by the state. In fact, as he put it in a January 1993 interview published in *Liberté*, the "goal" of the "strategy" "was to discredit the intellectual."[33] Noting that the state made it clear it would reintroduce heavy-handed state censorship and military abuses, he wrote openly about his concerns. He was especially vocal in his criticism of the military coup, and the government's methods of combating militant Islam. In his literary work and journalistic essays, he also deplored the rapid decline in the freedom of the press and the ever-increasing aggression toward the life of the mind. He was well aware of the risks he took in expressing himself so freely, and soon began to receive death threats. Nevertheless, in the face of menacing Islamic militants and in plain view of state censors, Djaout along with Abdelkrim Djaâd and Arezki Metref (both colleagues at *Algérie-Actualité*) founded a new francophone weekly, *Ruptures*. This journal did not shrink from castigating Islamists and the state alike:

we consider that Algeria is going through a period of decisive battles, in which every silence, every indifference, every abdication, every inch of surrendered territory can prove fatal. The year that has just ended saw freedom of expression and democracy groping along, struggling with pain, stumbling, but getting up once again and continuing to resist. ... Our hope, but also our ambition, is for *Ruptures* to become a meeting-place, a space of expression and debate for all those who are working for a democratic, open, and plural Algeria.[34]

Calling openly for a democratic and plural Algeria in 1993 placed Djaout and his colleagues in the sights of both Islamists and the military junta. To be sure, Islamists viewed his rallying-cries (written in French) as symptomatic of the forces arrayed against their project of creating an Islamic republic. Despite the obvious peril he was courting, he refused to bow to intimidation, and continued to write. His articles in *Ruptures* spelled out the danger that Islamists posed to an open society, and he also criticized the authoritarianism of the ruling elite. After the publication of his highly acclaimed novel, *Les Vigiles* (*The Watchers*) in 1991, which won the Prix Méditerranée for its frank depiction of Algeria's menacing officialdom, Djaout began work on his next novel, *Le Dernier été de la raison* (*The Last Summer of Reason*), published posthumously in France in 1999. Djaout justified his decision to engage his critics with the power of the word in the midst of a massive tug-of-war between Islamic militants and the Algerian security forces. As a husband and father, he certainly had no death wish, and carefully weighed the risks in Algeria in 1993. The following lines, from an oft-quoted poem of his, say it all: "Silence is death/And if you say nothing you die./And if you speak you die./So speak and die./And yet if you speak you die. If you keep quiet you die. So speak and die."[35]

In many ways, Djaout's stance was similar to Václav Havel's in the face of Soviet aggression in Czechoslovakia. For both men, when it came to the integrity of the life of the mind, no concessions could be made to those who wished to smother critical thinking. For Djaout, avoiding confrontation with militant Islamists in Algeria was itself a form of moral and intellectual surrender. Since the GIA had taken such a vocal stand against journalists and writers, Djaout's position represented an unequivocal rebuttal of their dogma. In the morning of May 26, 1993, Djaout was shot three times in the head as he sat in his car outside his building. After remaining in hospital for a week in a coma (during which time his fellow journalists chose to release a photograph of him on life support to the public), he died on June 2.[36]

Five days after the shooting, Algerian television broadcast a video-taped confession by the alleged driver of the hit squad, Abdellah Belabassi. Belabassi claimed to have been operating under orders from Abdelhak Layada (a member of the GIA), who had targeted Djaout because he was a "communist" and because of his "acerbic pen."[37] However, Belabassi later retracted this confession, stating that he had agreed to it only after he was tortured. He and Layada were later acquitted by the courts. Djaout's killers were never found.

On June 4, thousands of mourners came to pay their last respects to Djaout, whose body was carried on a sunny day in a flag-draped coffin to his grave in his mountain village. A long-time friend and fellow novelist, himself forced into exile by radical Islamists, Rachid Mimouni later defended Djaout's views and criticized Algeria's radical Islamists in an interview for the BBC documentary about Djaout, "Shooting the Writer." As Mimouni put it: "I think that Islam has never authorized violence. If our Prophet were alive, he would be the first to denounce those who use it to obtain power."[38]

It is impossible to overstate just how much this crime riveted intellectuals in Algeria and around the world. In direct response to the assassination of Djaout and other Algerian writers, Salman Rushdie, Václav Havel, Jacques Derrida, and Wole Soyinka founded a human rights organization called the International Parliament of Writers (IPW). The IPW was created to assist writers from around the world who lived in peril, as well as those forced to flee their homelands.[39] Hundreds of commentaries on Djaout have been written, but perhaps none as eloquent as the one Soyinka supplied for the preface to the English translation of Djaout's posthumous novel, *The Last Summer of Reason*. It includes the following paragraph:

> It is thus essential that we take note that Tahar Djaout bears witness to his own society, from within his own milieu, and in defense of

this assailed humanity. But let no one be tempted to narrow the bane of bigotry and intolerance to just one milieu from which this powerful testimony has emerged. Lucid and poignant, it is an exploration of the very phenomenon of intolerance, and its application is universal, as are the best allegories that are grounded in reality. At the same time, however, we dare not take refuge in universalisms when the victims are specific and immediate. It is not a universal principle that gets stabbed, shot, and even mutilated. It is a very specific voice, one that has made a conscious choice and died in defense of that choice. And it is only by recognizing that individuality that we are enabled to recollect, and respond to the fate of other individuals, to the fate of hundreds like Djaout, and the fate of hundreds of thousands on behalf of whom that voice has been raised, against whom the hand of atavism is also constantly raised, aiming ever more boldly for a body count that will pave the way of killers to a paradise of their imagining.[40]

Indeed, Algerian journalists and intellectuals faced hard choices in the aftermath of Djaouti's assassination. For those who opted to stay in Algeria and continue to write, the decision often meant heavy personal sacrifice, including self-imposed separation from families, so that loved ones would not be endangered in case of a direct attack on one's home. On the other hand, safety had its own drawbacks. For example, according to Ghania Mouffouk (a prominent Algerian journalist who went into exile in 1993), those who stayed were accompanied by state security minders as they worked. This "protection" hampered journalists trying to conduct interviews or to cover sensitive issues , while interviewees were reluctant to divulge information in the presence of security forces. Any journalist who declined state protection would be required to sign a document absolving the state of all responsibility for their safety. These perilous conditions caused important losses within the media. By 1995, an estimated 200 leading Algerian journalists had been forced into exile.[41]

Music and raï

The cultural war in Algeria did not stop with writers, academics, politicians, or elite athletes. It extended well into the domain of popular culture, and specifically into the music industry. Many religious conservatives regard music as forbidden, but in Algeria and in other countries like Afghanistan, radical Islamists carried their hatred for music to new levels. Algerian Islamists, in particular, grew increasingly worried about the rising popularity of *raï* music, which was becoming one of the most popular sounds on the world-music scene during the 1990s. After the FIS took power, many local FIS politicians (including those in control of Oran, the epicenter of Algerian *raï*) began to denounce this music and draw up plans to ban it. *Raï* singers were accused by the local leaders of corrupting the youth with intoxicating rhythms, irreligious and sexually explicit lyrics, and irreverent challenges to cultural norms.

Raï music evolved during the 1970s and 1980s, as an iconoclastic fusion of local popular music traditions with features of disco, played on modern Western instruments. Most of its youthful male singers, known as *"chebs,"* and women singers, or *"chabas,"* come from the city of Oran, which has been called the "Nashville of Algerian music."[42] As *raï* increased in popularity, its artists transcended national boundaries, becoming one of the most important elements of the emerging World Music scene. Its lyrics offered frank social commentary, spinning anything from the problems of romance and sexuality, unemployment, disillusionment with politics and social norms, across the airwaves of Algeria, then into France, and from France to the rest of the world. With a staggering birthrate in Algeria (an estimated 80 percent of the population was under the age of 30 in 1989), this music spoke to critical issues of the day that affected the lives of millions of young people from all social classes.

In this context, *raï* burst onto the cultural scene just as identity politics in Algeria took a critical turn for the worse.[43] By definition, *"chebs"* challenged listeners to see and to speak about their society. *Raï* originally means "way of seeing," "opinion," "point of view"; it can also mean "advice," "plan," or "engagement," and its poetry often challenged the status quo – in much the same way that rock-and-roll was viewed as a rebellion against elders and social convention during the 1950s and 1960s, or that jazz was banned by the Nazis.

Music production and distribution, unlike the press, has been and continues to be relatively amorphous. *Raï* concerts often took place in small, intimate venues, or in cabaret-like night clubs. During the 1990s, Algerian recording studios produced high-quality cassettes that were widely available and inexpensive. Many singers also produced their music in France, with major European or American labels. Among France's large North African immigrant community, *raï* music found its way into homes, discos, streets, and the airwaves to play a major part in the music industry in France throughout the 1990s. This important cross-pollination connecting recent exiles and people of North African descent to the events in Algeria fostered a dynamic and cultural exchange that energized both singers and listeners.

There were many Algerian superstars that rode the airwaves into celebrity. Perhaps the most famous singers to emerge on the global market were Cheb Khaled and Cheb Mami. Both men enjoyed enormous international success, and played with their bands at the largest venues in France and elsewhere, and their CDs enjoyed popular success. Cheb Mami is best known in the US and the UK for his collaboration with British superstar Sting, on the song "Desert Rose," which blended *raï* with Western pop music on Sting's 1999 album, *Brand New Day*. Collectively, *raï* singers offered mesmerizing lyrics and beats that combined stories of love and sorrow with a dance-crazed passion, making *raï* one of the most dynamic cultural enterprises in the world during the 1990s.

Despite or perhaps due to the success of *raï* as one of Algeria's hottest cultural exports, religious conservatives, hard-line Islamists, and local FIS officials appreciated neither the artistry nor the message of this new form of social criticism. The same could be said of those in secular seats of power, because *raï*, unlike writing, was exceedingly difficult to censor. Thus singers were freer to give their "opinion" in secular lyrics that challenged both the religious and political censors, who grew proportionately more displeased the more that *raï* made itself heard in cafés and night clubs, at public concerts and on the radio. Fundamentalists insisted that *raï* (or any secular music for that matter), with its discussion of profane things such as sex and alcohol, corrupted the youth and represented yet another impure danger imported from the West. Concerns about reactions by Islamists and the banning of *raï* by local councils along with other cultural vices, including alcohol and unveiled women, caused many leading singers to move to France, including Cheb Khaled and Cheb Mami.

One performer to emerge from the younger talented singers who did not go into exile was Cheb Hasni (Hasni Chakroun). A native of Oran, Cheb Hasni most often sang about love and youthful longing, and in 1987 he recorded his first hit, a duet, "We Made Love in a Broken Shed," with Chaba Zahouania. As his popularity increased he recorded music in which he also addressed issues of immigration (to France) and social concerns, all the while traveling and recording extensively in France. On September 29, 1994, Algeria's cultural war caught up with him as he walked down the street after singing at a club in Oran. He was shot in the neck and chest and died immediately. Following his death, there were riots in Paris and at his funeral in Oran, over 10,000 people gathered in the streets.

Immediately after Cheb Hasni's burial, Chaba Zahouania left the country, as did other singers. Those connected to the music industry and who stayed had reason to fear more violence. When asked about Cheb Hasni's murder, Khaled simply said: "People lived there [in Algeria] in terror and sadness ... they had Hasni to help them forget."[44] But they could not forget for long. In August 1995, a popular Kabyle singer, Lia Amara, was shot with her husband in Tixeraine. In September 1995, Algeria's leading *raï* producer, Rachid Baba Ahmed, was machine-gunned outside his music studio in Oran. In an interview in 1995, Khaled told *New York Times* reporter Neil Strauss that Islamists had issued death threats against him for his poetic music that they found offensive: "I know I'm at the top of the list of well-known people the fundamentalists want to kill ... I don't have any bodyguards, just tight security during concerts. Even so, I get scared." So much so that Khaled refused to return to Algeria, of which he despairingly said: "We are returning to the Middle Ages ... These people have no respect for human beings. They kill well-known people just to get publicity."[45]

Khaled did have reason to fear the situation in Algeria, as throughout 1994 hundreds of lesser-known Algerians – men, women, and children – were being murdered each month, most with their throats slit by the various GIAs. In this context, high-profile "soft targets" had become the easiest way for terrorists to hit the headlines, while silencing secular antagonists and other so-called infidels.

On September 24, 1994, just a few days before Cheb Hasni's assassination, one of Algeria's most popular but also most controversial singers, Matoub Lounès, was kidnapped near his home in Kabylia by a GIA cell. As a Kabyle pop star, Lounès was known in Algeria and France for his bitter criticisms of Islamists and the Algerian government alike. "I have my conscience," he once said. "That's why I'm not afraid, not of Democrats, not of Islamists, not of the state [*le pouvoir*]."[46] Combative and passionate, Lounès's lyrics, as well as his public comments and interviews, brought debates about Tamazight to the center of his life and work. Like many Berbers, he was outraged about the government's forced arabization programs and its refusal to integrate Tamazight into the school curriculum, even in Kabylia itself (where the majority of Berbers live). Going further than most in this cultural and language debate, though, he argued that Algeria should be made into a federation, with Kabylia joining that collection of states of its own free will. For many Algerians, even tolerant ones, his stance was as narrow and ethnocentric as that of his Arabic-only counterparts. For his supporters, however, he simply spoke the truth and gave voice to the rage of the Kabyle youth, a youth that demanded respect for its indigenous language and rejected Arab hegemony.

A week after Lounès's kidnapping, his abductors issued a communiqué declaring that they took him because he was "an enemy of God and a symbol of depravity."[47] Both the kidnapping of Lounès and the murder of Cheb Hasni were underwritten by a standing GIA fatwa against any singer considered "vulgar."[48] If Algerians had been unable to prevent the assassination of Cheb Hasni, the same was not true of Lounès, whose kidnapping galvanized the population. Knowing that he had been condemned to death by the GIA, people poured into the streets as a show of unity. In Kabylia an estimated 100,000 gathered in Tizi-Ouzou, carrying posters of Lounès and signs promising a "total war" against Islamists if he were not released.[49] For two weeks, Algerians and especially Berbers occupied the streets, demanding his release. After this unprecedented show of support from Algerians and the international community, the

GIA quite uncharacteristically released Lounès – on condition that he quit singing. His sister, Malika Matoub, was in no doubt as to why the kidnappers gave way and released the "soul" of Kabylia: "It was national mobilization and international support which saved Lounès."[50]

After he was released, Lounès described his captors as young men (with an average age of 22 or 23) who were "poor," which he explained was too common in Algeria: "... in our country, there is a lack of everything. There are no jobs and not enough food, and there is even a lack of culture." He continued: "They said I was the origin of depravity in Algeria; that young people listened to me when they should read the Qur'an. They said the Qur'an was the only truth, and that songs were sinful."[51] The 37-year-old "emir" Abou Lhimam Abdelfettah (Zdek Hocine), the mastermind behind the September 1994 kidnapping of Lounès and long-time "right-hand man" of radical Islamists like Mekhloufi Said, Hassan Hattab, and Abdelhamid Sadaoul (Abou Yahia) was finally arrested only in June 2006.

Contrary to the orders of the "emir" to retire, Lounès reaffirmed his commitment to engage his opponents and kidnappers through his song. He also spoke against Islamists in public and without restraint. However, he did go into temporary exile in France, and for the first few months at least, according to his sister, he seemed to suffer from "Stockholm syndrome," which is why he began to write of his experiences in his memoir, *Rebelle*.[52] Quickly, however, any identification with his captors faded and he become more outspoken in his criticism of them. In December 1994, at a demonstration in Paris expressing solidarity with the Algerian people, he called on France to do more, especially for those forced into exile:

> We are here to say no to the harmful progress of green fascism
> ... We are here as resistance fighters. We say no to fundamentalism, but I think that France has a role to play in all this. It ... must be firm and determined against these killers. What is happening to you here in nearby suburbs will set the France of tomorrow ablaze. Don't think that these evil forces will spare you. What France can do first of all is help democrats. It should not close its borders for good. Indeed, the forces of evil struck again in Algeria today. France has a say in the matter ...[53]

Lounès won recognition in France for his efforts to bring peace to Algeria. In December 1994 he was awarded the Prix de la Mémoire (Memorial Prize) by the French Freedom Foundation, and the following December he received the Tahar Djaout Prize – which was especially fitting, because one of Lounès's most famous songs, "Kenza" (1993), was named in honor of Tahar Djaout's daughter after her father's murder.

In 1995 Lounès published his memoir, *Rebelle*, in which he made it clear that he would continue criticizing Islamists. As he put it:

> As for the GIA, I know them like everyone else ... Everywhere in the country, these extremists enforce their laws with their weapons. There is only one word for this order: kill. Men, women, and even children die every day, victims of fanaticism ...
>
> Intellectuals and journalists were the first victims of the violence that hits everyone today. They are accused of thinking, of reflecting, of expressing themselves as free thinkers, despite the horror of the country ... Today all those who refuse to say YES and to submit are victims of terrorism.[54]

While Lounès's memoir depicted radical Islamists in Algeria as murderers who lived only for death and terrorism, he made it clear that he would not suspend his own art and activism to accommodate their hatred. In this spirit, Lounès continued to record music and to protest against the Islamists, as well as the Algerian state. After all, he argued, the Islamists had been created by the FLN because it had governed with corruption and incompetence ever since liberation. As a Berber activist and one of the leaders of the Berber cultural movement, Lounès took advantage of the almost universal goodwill toward him after his kidnapping to step up his critique of the government's language policies. He became more vocal as the government continued to enforce arabization at the expense of other indigenous languages, especially Tamazight. In his view, the arabization program was merely an extension of the violent suppression of Berber identity that had consistently been part of the government's cultural war against Berbers in Algeria. In order to fight the government, one had to become part of the "resistance," as he often put it. And resisting the Algerian state remained a central feature of his revolt. In the 1996 BBC documentary about Lounès entitled "The Rebel," he explained his artistic politics simply: "There are songs that talk about something ... There are songs and then there are songs. There are songs for regulating [life]; and there are songs that wake people up."[56]

It is important to point out that well before he was abducted in 1994, Lounès put his life on the line as an advocate for the Berber movement, and had personal reasons for hating the Algerian regime. As anthropologist Paul Silverstein notes, during the riots of October 1988, Lounès was shot five times by a policeman and left to die in the street.[55] A victim of state violence, Lounès argued that arabization simply encouraged and exacerbated Islamic fundamentalists, by fostering cultural intolerance within the legal framework of the Algerian state. Furthermore, the 1998 language law that made Algeria an Arabic-only country neutralized, if not openly contradicted, previous efforts to reach a compromise with the Berbers (including the 1996 constitutional provision to recognize "*Tamazighté*" as part of Algeria's national identity).

This scorn for government policies and the religious bigotry of the Islamists culminated in what would be Lounès's final recording. He entitled the CD *Lettre ouverte aux ...* (*Open Letter to ...*) and scheduled its release for July 5, 1998. The date was chosen both because July 5 is Independence Day in Algeria, and because it was on that day that the new Arabic-only law took effect. In this CD, he spared neither "*le pouvoir*" nor Islamic fundamentalists. The cover artwork was particularly provocative. It displayed a photograph of him saluting, under a bloodstained red crescent and star, surrounded by cartoon Algerian officials and Islamists (drawn by artist Ali Dilem) peering over his shoulders, as what looks to be a hawk-nosed policeman holds up a sign reading "Algeriassic Park."[57] Echoing the theme of national liberation and grafting that theme onto Berber politics, the first song is about freedom in Kabylia: "Ayen Ayen."[58] Determined as he was to advocate on behalf of Berbers, Lounès certainly understood the risks that such a provocative CD carried in Algeria at the height of the violence and the massacres of 1998. As he said in a TV interview before the release: "Yes, I'm still afraid. But being afraid is nothing to be ashamed of. I'd rather die for a just and noble cause."[59]

Midway through the 1998 World Cup in France and less than two weeks before the highly anticipated *Lettre ouvert aux ...* was scheduled for release, Lounès (now 42) was shot and killed in Kabylia at a fake roadblock while driving his car. His wife and two sisters were also shot and critically wounded. That same week, the men and women of three separate villages in Algeria had their throats slit in massacres carried out by Islamic terrorists.[60]

The government immediately declared that Lounès had been shot by a "terrorist group."[61] News of the assassination quickly spread to Kabylia, where riots broke out. Armed militias – now a constant feature of the countryside, because citizens' defense organizations did not believe they were adequately protected by state security forces – set up barricades and resisted Algerian riot police. In the capital of Tizi-Ouzou, angry demonstrators shot at helicopters, looted shops, attacked government offices, and set fire to the Air Algérie office. The vast majority of the people in the angry mobs believed that Lounès had been murdered by Algerian security forces. "It is not the Islamists who killed him," one youth said as he destroyed property. Other mobs shouted: "Zéroual assassin!" However, Malika Matoub maintained that the Islamists murdered her brother, and remained defiant: "They'll never kill him. He has left his songs, which will speak for him, and he is immortal. So these GIA Islamist bastards, whoever they are, will never be able to kill him." In fact, as she explained, she insisted on placing the blame on Islamists as a way of calming those angered by his assassination: "I call on the population to honor the memory of my brother in dignity, and to accompany him, in calmness, at his homecoming the day after tomorrow."[62] The violence continued for about a week in Kabylia, where protesters clashed with state forces. At Lounès's funeral on June 28, 1998, an estimated 100,000 mourners flooded the streets of Tizi-Ouzou to pay their respects to their fallen rebel.

The national and international community responded to the violence, the village massacres, and to Lounès's assassination. As Paul Silverstein notes, James Rubin (of the US State Department) called on Algerians and the government to "reject the use of violence as a political instrument."[63] The UN also sent a special commission to investigate the Algerian situation. French President Jacques Chirac denounced the assassination of Lounès as cowardly and said: "He was a man who was the voice of Algeria, loud and clear ... and I hope this voice will continue to be heard."[64] RCD leader Saïd Saadi insisted that some sort of conspiracy was at work because Lounès's assassins, as recognized by the survivors of the attack, were from local villages. Though not completely calling into question the proposition that Islamists were responsible for his murder, Saadi did say that "his death raises the problem of local complicity, because Kayblia is not a natural habitat for Islamists ... They couldn't have acted without assistance."[65] Indeed, Saadi's comments reflected a pervasive belief that the state had orchestrated the attack on Lounès, and, despite the protestations of his sister and the Algerian authorities, many Algerians, especially Berbers, continue to believe this.

Between the first abduction of Lounès in 1994 and his eventual assassination in 1998, tens of thousands of Algerians fell victim to militant Islamist attacks. Women were routinely murdered for going out unveiled; countless others became victims of gang rape and were forced by roving terrorist gangs to accept so-called temporary marriages to their captors, often remaining sequestered for years before being discarded or killed; schoolteachers had their throats slit in front of their students; entire villages (men, women, and children), some numbering in the hundreds, were killed with pick-axes and knives. In short, it seemed to be an endless season of hell on earth.

The art of terror and the transformation of violence in exile

Surprisingly, many educated Algerians have been able to hit back at this violence with art. In fact, perhaps the most remarkable aspect of the 1990s concerns the response of intellectuals to violence. Hence, if it is possible to draw anything positive at all from the horror of Algeria, it is that intellectuals, artists, and other cultural actors such as athletes have continued to engage both the state and radical Islamists with a critical determination to persevere through the violence. To be sure, many had to do so from exile, but many remained in Algeria and refused to bow to enormous pressures.

Whether from exile or from on the ground in Algeria, intellectuals stood firm against all odds, and offered their refusal to submit to the brutality of Islamist and state violence for all to see and admire in their art. In doing so, they transformed literature and the arts in inspiring ways. Today, there are hundreds of examples of writers and artists who were able to subvert destructive forces by writing about them. Thus violence transformed cultural debates, but not always in the ways that its perpetrators hoped. Why? I asked Anouar Benmalek, who went into exile in 1994, this very question when I interviewed him in Paris. Benmalek's response is crucial to understanding how violence boomeranged to become a creative cultural force in Algeria:

> The big problem for a society like Algeria's between 1988 and 1989 was self-censorship, self-censorship that was obviously cultivated by organs of repression – the army, the SM [military security], the police and so forth. This self-censorship was extremely powerful. And, paradoxically, I would say that the violence [of the 1990s], because it was limitless, in fact liberated people and writing. Why? Because people discovered that no matter what one did – one could write or not write, write with extreme caution, or throw caution to the wind – either way, they got killed. There's a poem about this by Tahar Djaout that I like a lot. It says this: "If you speak, they will kill you. If you do not speak, they will kill you. Therefore, speak and die." And that's true, because in the newspaper where I was, they killed Tahar Djaout, but they [radical Islamists] also killed the newspaper's accountant. Why? Because he worked for the newspaper. That is to say that one can be killed for reasons that are completely ridiculous. So people said to themselves, "Die just to die? Enough! We've got to write what we really think." People who had been extremely frightened no longer had any fear, because the price was the same. When they chop off your head – whether it be for some tiny little thing or for something important – it's the same thing. Paradoxically, we owe this liberty to terrorism. But a lot of people were forced to leave; a lot were forced into exile and to leave behind that which was the dearest in the world to them. As for me, I never imagined I would someday end up in France and be laid to rest in France. Never! That was never part of the plan. I was very content living in Algeria. I had a job at the university. I was involved

in the newspaper. I wrote about what I wanted, more or less. Then terrorism changed my way of life. It made me say, "So now what are you going to do? What are you going to do with yourself?" And it's at that moment when you say, "They killed my friends, and now there remains only one thing left for me – to truly say what I think." And in the Arab world, that is revolutionary.[66]

However, the fact is that revolutionary potential signaled by the end of self-censorship, as Benmalek would acknowledge, has never been fully realized.

What remains less open to interpretation is that a terrifying, vise-like cultural war played out in stereo during the 1990s, with one set of persecutors (the state) rehearsing the long-ago learned themes from the FLN's orchestra of oppression, and the other set (the radical Islamists) playing to the newer notes of Khomeini-style excess. Soon these parallel cultural wars synced and converged in a two-fold tyranny that had its own unique rhythm and logic. As this process evolved, it rendered Algeria arguably the world's most dangerous national stage on which intellectuals and other cultural actors would perform during the 1990s. After the state had moved against the Algerian intelligentsia, radical Islamists felt the urgent need to dispense summary "Islamic" justice. This meant that eventually even the courtesy of an individualized fatwa would be dropped when the GIA "emir" Sid Ahmed Mourad (also known as Djaffar Afghani) issued his own proclamation in 1993: "Our jihad consists of killing and dispersing all those who fight against God and his Prophet ...The journalists who fight against Islamism through the pen shall perish by the sword."[67] Later came the fatwa issued by Djamal Zitouni against the entire (kofr) population.

At the same time, intellectuals and artists (as groups and as individuals) were able to use the certainty and absurdity of violence as a mechanism to free them from self-censorship. But the price for Algerian society and culture was indeed heavy. Tens of thousands of Algerians, like Benmalek, moved to Europe and elsewhere because of death threats. In fact, many of the most educated and highly trained citizens fled the country between 1993 and the late 1990s. The result has been a catastrophic brain drain for Algeria. At the same time, many also refused to leave because of the violence, despite death threats. Nevertheless, the net effect of the cultural wars of the 1990s has been devastating for Algeria, which desperately needs these lost minds to help rebuild the nation. The question is, how can Algerian civil society be reconstituted without many of its most talented and engaged citizens, helping to rebuild it from the ground up?

Conclusion: a historian's reflections on amnesty in Algeria

German philosopher Friedrich Nietzsche wrote in his essay, *On the Advantages and Disadvantages of History for Life*, that historical scholarship can prove dangerous because, among other things, it impairs instincts, allows each successive generation to make claims of superiority over past ones, and compels societies to evaluate themselves with irony and cynicism. Furthermore, and in direct contrast to the conventional wisdom of our own age, Nietzsche questioned whether his contemporary generation could withstand what one might call today the weight of full consciousness. As he put it, "[a]nd so my proposition may be taken and understood: *only strong personalities can endure history; the weak are completely extinguished by it.*"[1] History is, in Nietzsche's view, something that prevents life by generating unnecessary burdens and must therefore be used only in the service of life. Lastly, perhaps Nietzsche's greatest fear regarding history is that it does not allow individuals and society the opportunity to forget.

I think it would be an understatement to say that Nietzsche probably would never have expected his views of history to be brought up in the context of an analysis of contemporary Algerian history. Nevertheless, Nietzsche's rather unconventional appraisal of history lends itself to an evaluation of President Bouteflika's recent efforts to achieve national reconciliation and thereby end the carnage in Algeria. Put more directly, in a very Nietzschian way, Bouteflika's 1999 and 2005 amnesty referendums have tried to clear a unique and equally unconventional path between absolute terror and democracy, by attempting to remove the cultural and political debris of history itself. In choosing Nietzsche's path forward, the Algerian state has decided on a course that not only denies but also negates history's utility, by prohibiting historical inquiry into the recent past. It has also threatened imprisonment and fines for those who refuse to yield to its vision. To write about Algeria's recent trauma means to take risks, as a historian or as a writer, because historical inquiry into the recent actions of the state (and the military), as well as into the violence of the radical Islamists, has been criminalized.

In this way, Algeria is seeking to overcome a terrible period of bloodletting and complex war "against civilians" by embarking on what is a glaring exception to international trends – especially when juxtaposed with South Africa's efforts to overcome the violence of apartheid. Under a provision of its 2006 legislation, which followed Bouteflika's Charter for Peace and National Reconciliation (endorsed by national referendum in September 2005), the Algerian government declared:

> Anyone who, by speech, writing, or any other act, uses or exploits the wounds of the National Tragedy to harm the institutions of the Democratic and Popular Republic of Algeria, to weaken the state, or to undermine the good reputation of its agents who honorably served it, or to tarnish the image of Algeria internationally, shall be punished by three to five years in prison and fined 250,000 to 500,000 dinars.[2]

This law supplanted the 1999 Law on Civil Concord, and clearly announced a departure from what one could call the "truth model" of reconciliation, best represented by the South African Truth and Reconciliation Commission (TRC).

In other words, it is worthwhile pointing out that the Algerian state's views on history closely resemble what Nietzsche argued a century ago: that history, if employed at all, must be employed in the service of life. From this point of view, I see Bouteflika's actions and the law passed by the Algerian parliament as clearly suggesting that history can impair future prospects of overcoming the "National Tragedy" in Algeria during the 1990s. As such, it comes close to representing a kind of secular fatwa to be used to silence any historians, journalists, and others who might "undermine" the reputation of the state, its agents, its military, and even the radical Islamists who came in from the fight.

To put Algeria's amnesty into proper historical context, it is important to recall that since the end of World War II, states that have struggled to surmount the effects of unrest, civil war, and extreme violence against civilians (including genocide) have increasingly sought some sort of political formula that balances the need for immediate peace with the need for justice.[3] Starting, perhaps ironically, in 1974 with Uganda's Commission of Inquiry into the Disappearance of People in Uganda established by President Idi Amin Dada, followed by Bolivia in 1982, Argentina in 1983, and most famously, South Africa during the mid-1990s, over 20 governments around the world have preferred a formula that incorporates truth commissions into a quest for peace.

The South African TRC undoubtedly remains the most well known, and set the international standard for transparency. However, the TRC was unique (and ultimately entirely unlike the Algerian case), because it included public testimonies from both victims and aggressors, including members of the military and security forces. The authors of the South African model could well have used a Nietzschian justification for avoiding the possible pitfalls associated with historical consciousness. However, they argued the opposite and insisted that history was not only endurable but, precisely because it had become part of society's fundamental ontological structure, it could not be overlooked.

As I read it, telling the truth was the choice that South Africans made, and telling the truth paved the way to national healing. For the architects of post-apartheid South Africa, to have a healthy society meant that victims and oppressors had to become part of history, acknowledging their participation in or relationship to past crimes. The promise of amnesty was the key incentive, but was not guaranteed, for those willing to confess even the most gruesome of crimes. And to receive amnesty, a perpetrator had to become a historical actor, in reflective and practical terms. Due to this confidence that citizens were able to endure the recounting of past atrocities, the South African hearings and testimonies were also broadcast publicly by local, national, and international media. Moreover, the TRC's chief moderators, including Archbishop Desmond Tutu and Dr Alex Boraine, as well as leading news reporters including Antjie Krog and Allister Sparks, wrote memoirs and reflections on the successes and failures of the South African truth commission and its relationship to their own lives.[4]

The reward for individual South Africans willing to coming clean on apartheid-related violence in public was amnesty. The societal reward was a possibility of closure and the opportunity to move beyond history and into a future fully aware of the past. The reward for writers prepared to record their own professional and personal views on the end of apartheid, and for historians doing their work, was nothing short of a cultural transformation.[5] In my view, the South African government correctly assessed its people's maturity and readiness to move forward through a process of truth-telling that eventually led to amnesty for thousands. But it was not a blanket amnesty. It required that one enter into a process of application, which was vetted in public; amnesty might be denied if it could not be proved that the applicant was motivated by apartheid in the commission of a crime – as in the infamous case of the killing of Steven Biko.[6]

Of the many objectives for truth commissions, none has been as important as the desire to promote national reconciliation in the post-conflict stage of political development.[7] In principle, for many societies that have recently undergone severe internal trauma, governments have found it necessary to use truth commissions and the promise of amnesty as vehicles to drive the nation forward toward national reconciliation. Many of those that combined truth commissions and amnesty were transitional democracies considered stable enough to endure a period of painful honesty, with the possibility of forgiveness.

But what happens to the idea of truth commissions when a government is still unstable? When it came to power through a military coup that suspended the democratic process? When observers and citizens continue to see it as autocratic and intolerant? When some of the regime's critics are imprisoned? When it continues to witness terrorist attacks against it? And what happens when the terrorists attacking the state are radical Islamists with direct connections to al Qaeda? In other words, what happens when we are talking about Algeria?

I have put this question to a number of respected historians, intellectuals, and artists who have thought deeply about Algeria's troubled recent past. The prominent Algerian-born French historian, Benjamin Stora, replied (in an interview I conducted in June 2007 at his home in Paris) that the "historical reference" for Algeria dates back to its war of independence against the French.[8] As he put it, despite the rapid succession of amnesties that the French awarded themselves at the end of the war, Algerians "never had an amnesty for their own violence during the war." This failure to account for their own violent excesses during the nationalist era has left important questions open and unresolved. On the other hand, the French used amnesty in order to avoid looking at themselves too closely and to avoid prosecution for heinous crimes. Hence while the French repeatedly amnestied those who fought during the French–Algerian War, those who tortured, and even those who attempted to assassinate President de Gaulle, Algerians "continued moving forward in history without ever looking back [at their own crimes]." Consequently, in Algeria "there was no amnesty, and in France there was an excess of amnesty."

Unfortunately, as Stora points out, this meant that when Algeria entered what he calls the "second Algerian war" during the 1990s, it did so without ever knowing amnesty. Hence when Algeria began to exit the trauma of the 1990s, "for the first time, Algeria asked itself how it might deal with memories of war, which had existed basically since the 1950s. It was at that moment that they were finally able to pose the question of amnesty. That is to say, to try to arrive a national reconciliation." For Stora, a historian who has written about Algeria for years and is recognized in France as the leading authority (along with Mohammed Harbi, perhaps) on Algerian history, "the classic question" one must ask "after deciding on amnesty is: is it possible to grant amnesty without prosecuting the culprits?" Here "there are two theories. One that claims that it is necessary to settle those questions [the issue of violence] with amnesty." And another that "holds that if you want to re-enter normal society, it's necessary nevertheless to name the culprits. At the very least you must designate them ..." Naturally, the "families of the disappeared" want the culprits to be "named." The "state did not want this, and neither did the Islamists." In other words, according to Stora, it comes down to a choice between "amnesia" or "remembrance."

In a 2007 Paris interview, the exiled Algerian writer Anouar Ben-malek offered a slightly different reading of amnesty in Algeria, but agreed that Algeria has sadly chosen amnesia over remembrance. Benmalek, like many Algerians I have spoken with, expressed frustration with what he called the "recurring theme" of amnesty in Algeria. He pointed out that after the riots of 1988, the Algerian state granted amnesty for those involved in the attacks on civilians. In Benmalek's words: "At each bloody confrontation there is an amnesty, and a culture of amnesia is interwoven in Algerian history. There are no lessons in Algeria. History offers no lessons, and each time it gets worse."[9] This lack of accountability has made things worse, not better in Algeria. As he pointed out, the situation went from the routine use of "torture" in 1988 (against Islamists), to "mass killings" later on "without any repercussions" and without ever bringing those guilty of heinous crimes to trial.

I also asked the novelist Malika Mokaddem about her views on the use of amnesty by Algerian authorities, during a 2007 interview I conducted with her at her home in Montpellier. As she put it:

> The problem is that law came [in 2005] without any judgment.
> There was no attempt to put into words and judge the nameless
> on their barbaric and absolutely terrible acts ... This method of
> erasing everything without ever putting into words the violence that
> the Algerians suffered and without the law passing judgment on
> people, that, I find was a terrible method. It was to put a cover on
> the violence without ever giving justice a chance. Not only were the
> fundamentalists absolved for what they had done, but they could
> also receive assistance and strut in front of others, taunting them.
> It seems pretty awful to me.[10]

The pitfalls of peace

In many ways, part of the problem with the government's recent use of amnesty is that it would have one believe that the Algerian sonderweg is so exceptional that one cannot question the state's motives. To the contrary, I believe we can and must do so, but we must first challenge our own assumptions. It is especially important today, because even if Algeria's position in the amnesty and national reconciliation debate is historically specific, it might very well become a model for other countries in the era of the war on terror.

Examining Algeria's decision to prefer amnesia in lieu of truth, which Algerian citizens endorsed in two separate national referendums, one must be willing to put aside, for an instant, one's prejudices about history and the utility of truth commissions. For historians, this very suggestion goes against the grain and is rightfully especially difficult. Algeria is a tough case, as Hugh Roberts expressed in a December 2008 interview with me, "because there are definitely questions to answer. The context here is the sheer lack of accountability in the Algerian regime. During the 1990s the military and security services were completely unaccountable. With the massacres of 1997, for example, there are some key people who have some explaining to do."[11] Thus, for the victims of military and security violence, Bouteflika's criminalization of inquiry is especially difficult to accept. That said, it is also important to test our own assumptions, if only to try to understand what is really at stake in Bouteflika's amnesty programs.

In trying to push the debate, what interests me here is the pervasiveness of what Peter Brooks has called "a confessional model" in Western culture, and especially in the work of the historian. As Brooks has put it, our "Age of Confession" has its origins in medieval Christian theology and practice. Brooks argues that our contemporary notion of confession dates from the Fourth Lateran Council in 1215, when the Roman Catholic Church mandated annual confessions. This has come to mean that "the confessional model is so powerful in Western culture that ... even those whose religion or non-religion has no place for the Roman Catholic practice of confession are nevertheless deeply influenced by the model. Indeed, it permeates our culture, including our educational practices and our law." In other words, we have come to expect it from everyone and are suspicious of those who refuse to accept it. Because of the ubiquity of this model, we now have gross and banal public forms of confession. In fact, Brooks argues, "[w]e appear today to live in a generalized demand for transparency that entails a kind of tyranny of the requirement to confess."[12]

I quote Brooks here, not to appear as an apologist for the Algerian government but in order to remind us that we, especially in the so-called West, are so conditioned by our societal expectations regarding public confession that we cannot but suspect the motives of a government willing to forgo the confessional model. We should not forget that Desmond Tutu, the architect of the TRC, was himself an Anglican prelate and was, as he noted, blending Christian notions with local African notions. Moreover, we are especially conditioned, following the great achievements of the African National Congress's approach (the TRC) in South Africa, by the reflexive assumption that governments in post-conflict periods must include confessional practices if amnesty is to be the reward of ex-combatants and killers. Without at the very least public confessions, the question of blanket amnesty is even more troubling, because such an amnesty agreement specifically precludes inquiries into the past. Nevertheless, because Algeria was a signatory to the Geneva Conventions of 1960, along with the International Covenant on Political Rights and the Torture Convention in 1989, it has a well-defined duty to look into potential violations.[13] Under international human rights law, a nation that has signed these agreements is obliged to uphold them or to let international actions against them take place.

To be sure, one of the key concerns in the application of amnesty in Algeria is that the security forces and state officials were, at first implicitly (1999) and then explicitly (2005), granted more sweeping amnesty guarantees, and this, Valérie Arnould suggests, proves the state was as much interested in shielding itself from future prosecution as it was in the question of national reconciliation. This idea of shielding the military is not new. Even post-Civil War America made provisions for granting amnesty to confederate soldiers who had rebelled against the Republic. Yet, as the Yale historian David Blight has argued in *Race and Reunion* (2001), the reconciliation process between North and South denied history partly in order to facilitate the maintenance of racial hierarchies and the creation of new forms of segregation.[14] In other words, even the US model of post-Civil War reconciliation would in the end suggest that forgetting was anything but constructive, precisely because it led to deliberately created forms of toxic oppression after the war.

Even with such problems of forgetting aside, I believe we must still be willing to examine our own assumptions about truth commissions, if only to strengthen our criticism of states that do not embrace this model. In arguing this, I need to be clear that I am not in any way supporting the trivialization of violence in Algeria. Nor am I attempting to endorse what Howard Ball has called a "culture of impunity," a phenomenon of recent years when in the face of internal courts and international declarations protecting human rights, little has been done to bring those accused of human rights violations to justice.[15]

Indeed, part of the irony of the Algerian case comes from its own position on the French military from the colonial period. With regard to that issue, the Algerian state has been entirely unambiguous. Algerian officials have argued that French military and government officials be prosecuted in the international courts as war criminals, and the Algerian state has repeatedly insisted on the need for the French government to apologize for its war crimes. To this end, the Algerian government has made good use of the works of historians, and has even gone so far as to insist that the relevant archival collections be moved to Algeria.

The decision to adopt a different stance for the events of the 1990s may be consistent, as Stora and Benmalek have suggested, with the government's efforts to sidestep uncomfortable questions about self-generating violence within society and within the government; but it does not address the issue of historical inquiry per se. In fact, in many post-conflict countries, historical inquiry has become a key ingredient of national reconciliation. Such reconciliation programs have assumed that requisite inquiry involves open access to archives and state records, as well as the use of victim testimonies (something the Bouteflika program put entirely off limits). Admittedly a major incentive for most governments to utilize truth commissions, backed up by historical and scholarly investigations during the 1990s, was the loss of international support for oppressive regimes after 1989.[16] The loss of support for such regimes meant that governments have become more accountable to their citizens and the international community, and truth commissions are often the preferred method of deploying distributive amnesty and for receiving favorable reviews among the key international powerbrokers.

We are still, however, left with the question of how historians should reply to the criminalization of historical inquiries into allegations of state violence. In other words, what has it meant to historians?

Hugh Roberts agrees that the Algerian state's position poses interesting dilemmas. As he put it when I asked him about the government's position on historical inquiry:

> Well, now you've made a shrewd observation. The question to be asked about this is how seriously is it to be taken. Maybe the answer is that it's a fall-back, it's a fail-safe. It gives the government the license to come down like a ton of bricks on someone who really does get out of line, but it won't otherwise be enforced that vigorously. It's a sort of reserve power. It's intended to reassure the military and intimidate everyone else. It may not be used that often and fall into disuse. It certainly stinks at the level of principle. You, and I, and many others could agree very vociferously on that point.

In one of the most remarkable books to come out against Bouteflika's Charter, *Algérie, le prix de l'oubli* (2005) (*Algeria, the Price of Forgetting*), Algerian journalist Souâd Belhaddad suggests that the government has never understood the effect of this violence on its citizens. Not once, she points out, have any of Algeria's heads of state, neither Liamine Zeroual nor Abdelaziz Bouteflika, ever visited one of the hundreds of sites of massacres to express their condolences to the victims in the countryside. Yet it was this helpless population that was expected to endorse this policy of amnesty. Rather than submit to the requirements of the amnesty agreement that enforces amnesia, Belhaddad offered a series of brief portraits of the victims of the violence. As she put it, "At the hour of forgetting, since the country is going to turn the page, their [the victims'] memory is still troubled; it has been forcefully inconvenienced." In speaking of the victims of violence of all kinds and those abused by the state, the Islamists, and/or the militias, she states: "It is necessary to enter into their stories, to come back to established facts to understand the tenor of forgetting that is imposed on them – and its impossibility."[17]

But is this the only real solution? Important examples of the effectiveness of truth commissions include Argentina's 1983–84 National Commission on the Disappeared, which began to investigate crimes against civilians after the fall of the military regime in 1983. In South Africa, Nelson Mandela and the African National Congress's calls to put aside "personal bitterness" and the understandable desire for revenge for the state-sponsored crimes of the past, informed worldwide policy debates over the utility of truth and reconciliation commissions. Despite the reservation in some quarters that the amnesty granted by South Africa's TRC did not adequately punish the guilty, especially the high-level state officials responsible for the crimes against humanity,[18] there has been general agreement that the TRC did prevent further bloodshed in the racially charged atmosphere of post-apartheid South Africa. The South African model was successful, in part, because the process was open and widely covered in the local and international media. In addition, the TRC was not created to deny or hide the historical past; rather it was a deliberate and public recital of, and apology for, historical crimes. The perceived success and publicity of the TRC, which encouraged open and full media coverage, transformed victims' expectations because the criminals at least had to apologize for their deeds.

The South African model is not going to be enacted in Algeria. In my view, it is not entirely clear that it could have been. Does this mean that Bouteflika was right to ensure that so many would be unaccountable for violence? It is perhaps helpful to remember that former ANC leader Winnie Mandela also refused to apologize openly for the violence she helped organize in the townships. Knowing that and knowing how important such a confession was from her, Archbishop Tutu still urged her to at least admit that something went wrong along the way; that admission would suffice for her to receive amnesty. As Tutu said: "I beg you! I beg you! I beg you! Please! You are a great person and you don't know how your greatness would be enhanced if you had to say: 'I'm sorry. Things went wrong. Forgive me.' I beg you!"[19] Proud and defiant, Winnie Mandela accepted those terms: "I am saying it is true. Things went wrong. For that, I am deeply sorry ..." So the question is: why did Bouteflika not ask his generals and the militants who opposed them to admit, at the very least, that something went wrong?

Failing that simple Winnie Mandela-like admission by the government, it is difficult to see how Algeria can truly turn the page on the 1990s. It is clear that the government believes that by turning the page before it can be written by historians, the Algerian people have more chance of success in the future. Turning a page that is blank might not help in the long run, however. On the contrary, Algeria may have set a dangerous precedent for denial. As arguably the world's most important test case for exiting from the dynamics of the "War on Terror," it is not entirely clear that it would have served as a good role model for post-conflict resolution. What is less ambiguous is that many Algerians are themselves uncomfortable with a policy that attempts to inoculate a population from violence and retribution by giving it a historical lobotomy.

Notes

Introduction

1 Warren Christopher, "A Shared Moment of Trust," National Public Radio, January 23, 2006 (npr. org/templates/story/story.php? storyId=5165229).

2 See Fawza A. Gerges, *The Far Enemy: Why Jihad Went Global* (New York: Cambridge University Press, 2005).

3 George Joffé, "Algeria: The Failure of Dialogue," in *The Middle East and North Africa 1995* (London: Europa Publications, 1995), p. 8.

4 See Sean O'Neill and Daniel McGrory, *The Suicide Factory: Abu Hamza and the Finsbury Park Mosque* (London: HarperCollins, 2006) and Jason Burke, *Al-Qaeda: The True Story of Radical Islam* (London: I.B.Tauris, 2004).

1 Building a postcolonial state

1 "Algeria: Immigration to South Africa," Embassy of the Union of South Africa, Paris, to the Secretary for External Affairs, Cape Town, April 24, 1961. South African National Archives, Pretoria, BTS 1/132/1, vol. 5.

2 For more on settler dynamics, see Alistaire Horne, *A Savage War of Peace, 1954-1962*, second edition (New York: New York Review of Books Classics, 2006).

3 See Caroline Elkins, *Imperial Reckoning: The Untold Story of Britain's Gulag in Kenya* (New York: Henry Holt and Co., 2004); Jocelyn

Alexander, *The Unsettled Land: State-Making and the Politics of Land in Zimbabwe, 1893-2003* (Athens: Ohio University Press, 2006); Roy Welensky, *Welensky's 4000 Days – The Life and Death of the Federation of Rhodesia and Nyasaland* (Roy, 1964); and Alex Von Tunzelmann, *Indian Summer: The Secret History of the End of Empire* (New York: Henry Holt and Co., 2007).

4 For the colonial period, see Patricia Lorcin, *Imperial Identities: Stereotyping, Prejudice and Race in Colonial Algeria* (London: I.B. Tauris, 1999) and for the emir Abd el-Kader, see John Kiser, *Commander of the Faithful: The Life and Times of Emir Abd el-Kader (1808-1883)* (Rhinebeck, NY: Monkfish Book Publishing, 2008).

5 See Alexis de Tocqueville, *Writings on Empire and Slavery*, edited and translated by Jennifer Pitts (Baltimore, PA: Johns Hopkins University Press, 2001) and Olivier Le Cour Grandmaison, *Coloniser, Exterminer: Sur la guerre et l'Etat colonial* (Paris: Fayard, 2005).

6 For more on this, see James D. Le Sueur, *Uncivil War: Intellectuals and Identity Politics during the French-Algerian War*, second edition (Lincoln: University of Nebraska Press, 2005).

7 See John Ruedy, *Modern Algeria: The Origins and Development of a Nation*, second

edition (Bloomington: Indiana University Press, 2005) and Benjamin Stora, *Algeria 1830–2000* (Ithaca, NY: Cornell University Press, 2001).

8 For examples of Muslim reactions to this during the colonial period, see Mouloud Feraoun, *The Poor Man's Son: Menrad, Kabyle Schoolteacher* (Charlottesville: University of Virginia Press, 2005); Messali Hadj, *Les mémoires de Messali Hadj, 1898–1938*, edited by Renaud de Rochebrune (Paris: Lattès, 1982).

9 Irwin Wall, *France, United States, and the Algerian War* (Berkeley: University of California Press, 2001), p. 252. For a classic account of the OAS see Geoffrey Bocca, *The Secret Army* (Upper Saddle River, NJ: Prentice Hall, 1968). Also see my discussion of the OAS in Ben Abro's *Assassination! July 14* (Lincoln: University of Nebraska Press, 2001).

10 See Jane Kramer's essay on the *pieds-noirs* in *Unsettling Europe* (New York: Penguin, 1990).

11 For arabization see John Entelis, *Algeria: The Revolution Institutionalized* (Boulder, CO: Westview Press, 1986), pp. 94–6.

12 James D. Le Sueur, "Arabization and Decolonization: The French Attempts to Strip Islam from Arabic Instruction at the End of Empire," in *The French Colonial Mind*, edited by Martin Thomas (University of Nebraska Press, forthcoming).

13 See Hocine Aït Ahmed, *La guerre et l'après-guerre* (Paris: Minuit, 1964). Aït Ahmed later escaped from prison in 1965 and went into exile in Switzerland.

14 See William B. Quandt, *Between Ballots and Bullets, Algeria's Transition from Authoritarianism* (Washington, DC: The Brookings Institute, 1998), ch. 2.

15 See Robert Malley, *The Call*

from Algeria: Third Worldism, Revolution, and the Turn to Islam (Berkeley: University of California Press, 1996).

16 See *Congressional Record*, 85th Congress, 1st Session, vol. 103, pt. 8 (June 21–July 10, 1957), pp. 10781–9.

17 Piero Gleijeses, *Conflicting Missions: Havana, Washington, and Africa, 1959–1976* (Chapel Hill: University of North Carolina Press, 2002), p. 31.

18 See Entelis, *The Revolution Institutionalized*. Ben Bella would remain in Algeria under house arrest for the next 15 years, after which he went into exile in Switzerland and returned to Algeria only in 1990 in order to stand for election, ironically in the nation's first multi-party presidential contest – something he had prevented while in power.

19 The Algerian historian Mohammed Harbi, who went into exile in 1965, is among the most outspoken critics of Boumediene and the FLN.

20 Henri Alleg, *Mémoire algérienne* (Paris: Stock, 2005).

21 Mafhoud Bennoune, *The Making of Contemporary Algeria, 1830–1987* (New York: Cambridge University Press, 1988), p. 120.

22 Ibid., p. 243.

23 During the colonial period, the French began oil exploration in Algeria but never imagined the wealth they would find below the sand in the Sahel region in 1956, two years into the Algerian revolution. With the discovery of the Hassi Messaoud oil field, the French (led in Algeria by the then Governor General Jacques Soustelle) immediately began plans to separate out the oil- and gas-rich areas, and by 1958 they had. Charles de Gaulle (who came to power in a military coup d'état in July) appointed Max Lejeune

as the first minister of the Sahara, which included the oil-rich parts of Algeria. During the Evian discussions that ended the war in March 1962, de Gaulle hoped to not only partition Algeria (thus keeping oil and gas holdings under French control) but also encourage other neighboring states to make claims on Algerian territory. Unsuccessful at keeping the soil, France did negotiate with the FLN representatives at Evian to continue bi-national cooperation in the development of its "subsoil" assets. This agreement translated into a legal arrangement that guaranteed French oil and gas companies the right to six years of continued exploration and development. Bennoune, *Contemporary Algeria*, pp. 49–63.

24 Bennoune, *Contemporary Algeria*, pp. 100, 122.

25 Ibid., p. 126.

26 Quandt, *Between Ballots and Bullets*, pp. 119–20.

27 Ali Aïssaoui, *Algeria: The Political Economy of Oil and Gas* (Oxford University Press, 2001), pp. 95–6.

28 Ibid., p. 1.

29 In many ways, Boumediene's ideological position sounded similar to that of India's Jawaharlal Nehru, who previously used his position within the Non-Aligned Movement to advance his own notions of anti-colonialism, industrialization, and secularism on the world stage.

30 Bennoune, *Contemporary Algeria*, p. 134.

31 Steady urbanization had quickened during the war, as France began to retaliate against Algerian nationalists with collective reprisals against civilians. Massive concentration camps were set up, euphemistically referred to as "relocation camps," in which upwards of one-fourth of the entire Muslim population were forced to reside by the French military. As Benjamin Stora notes, the population of Algiers alone increased by 85 percent during the war, and it continued to expand after independence. Stora, *Algeria 1830–2000*, p. 139.

32 By the spring of 1965, there were already over 450,000 Algerians in France. This number would continue to rise steadily and would become a complex problem for policy-makers of each nation. Among other things, it led to a decision by the Algerian government to block emigration to France in September 1973, and to the decision by the French government to pass the Bonnard Law in 1979. Both measures were extremely controversial, especially the Bonnard Law, which gave the French government authority to deport immigrant workers when their temporary resident cards were not renewed. Neither the French nor Algerian actions were sufficient to end the flow of Algerians to France, something that quickened again during the 1990s.

33 Aïssaoui, *Economy of Oil and Gas*, p. 15.

34 Ibid., p. 1.

35 Cited in ibid, p. 99.

36 Ibid., p. 100.

37 Ruedy, *Modern Algeria*, p. 234.

38 See John Ruedy, "Chérif Benhabylès and Ferhat Abbas: Case Studies in the Contradictions of the *mission civilisatrice*," *Historical Reflections*, vol. 28, n. 2 (Summer 2002): 185–201 and James McDougal, *Algeria* (New York: Cambridge University Press).

39 See Marnia Larzeg, *The Eloquence of Silence: Algerian Women in Question* (New York: Routledge, 1994).

2 The road to reform

1 William Quandt has also pointed out that, in addition to the "securitiy institutions to check dissent," during the "high tide" of Algeria's "authoritarian experiment" Boumediene also used various peaceful means to win over the average citizen. William Quandt, *Between Ballots and Bullets: Algeria's Transition from Authoritarianism* (Washington, DC: Brookings Institution Press, 1998), p. 25. For state censorship see Hafid Gafaïti, "Power, Censorship, and the Press: The Case of Postcolonial Algeria," *Research in African Literatures*, vol. 30, no. 3 (Autumn 1999): 51–61.

2 Martin Stone, *The Agony of Algeria* (New York: Columbia University Press, 1997), p. 65. Frédéric Volpi has argued that because of the brutality of the state's response to the riots, they became "fixated in the collective memory as a unitary event" and thus "introduced a symbolic breach in the historical framework of the polity." Frédéric Volpi, *Islam and Democracy: The Failure of Dialogue in Algeria* (London: Pluto Press, 2003), p. 45.

3 This was particularly critical in the problem of "food dependency," as the state had to depend on imports to sustain the population. See John Entelis, *Algeria: The Revolution Institutionalized* (Boulder, CO: Westview, 1986), pp. 132–54.

4 Michael Willis, *The Islamist Challenge in Algeria: A Political History* (New York: New York University Press, 1996), p. 109.

5 Michael Willis points out that the Islamists had been "taken by surprise by the events and took some days to formulate their response" and that Ahmed Sahnoun believed that the Islamists should not further provoke the state. Willis, *Islamist Challenge*, pp. 110–11.

6 Quoted in the documenatary *Algeria's Bloody Years*, directed by Malek Bensmaïl (New York: First Run Icarus Films, 2003).

7 Willis, *Islamist Challenge*, p. 112.

8 Interview with John Entelis, Omaha, Nebraska, April 24, 2008.

9 Omar Carlier, *Entre Nation et Jihad: Historie sociale des radicalismes algériens* (Paris: Presses de la fondation nationale des sciences politiques, 1995) and Ahmed Rouadjia, *Les frères et la mosquée: enquête sur le mouvement islamiste en Algérie* (Paris: Éditions Karthala, 1990).

10 See Václav Havel, *Open Letters: Selected Writings, 1965–1990* (New York: Vintage, 1992) and Milan Kundera, *The Unbearable Lightness of Being: A Novel* (New York: Harper Perennial, 2008).

11 Anouar Benmalek, *Chroniques de l'Algérie amère: Algérie 1985–2002* (Paris: Pauvert, 2003), p. 91.

12 For more on torture in post-independence Algeria, see Donal Reed's excellent article, "The Question of Henri Alleg," *International History Review*, 29 (September 2007): 573–386. As Reed points out, Boumediene's regime had in fact revived torture as an effective means to silence critics within the nation early during his presidency. And, Ben Bella's security forces also used it against dissidents immediately after independence.

13 For more on the history of censorship in Algeria, see Hafid Gafati's two articles: "Power, Censorship, and the Press: The Case of Postcolonial Algeria," *Research in African Literatures*, vol. 30, no. 3 (Fall 1999): 51–61; and, "Between God and

the President," *Diacritics*, vol. 27, no. 2 (Summer 1997): 59–84.

14 M. Al-Ahnaf, B. Botiveau, F. Frégosi, *L'Algérie par ses islamistes* (Paris: Editions Karthala, 1991), p. 50.

15 Ibid.

16 William B. Quandt, *Between Ballots and Bullets: Algeria's Transition from Authoritarianism* (Washington, DC: Brookings Institution Press, 1998), p. 50.

17 See Hugh Roberts, *The Battlefield Algeria, 1988–2002: Studies in a Broken Polity* (London: Verso, 2003); Quandt, *Between Ballots and Bullets*; Frédéric Volpi, *Islam and Democracy*; Willis, *The Islamist Challenge*; Stone, *The Agony of Algeria*; and Louis Martinez, *The Algerian Civil War, 1990–1998*, trans. by Jonathan Derrick (New York: Columbia University Press, 1998); and Mohammed Harbi, *L'Islamisme dans tous ses états* Paris: Arcantères, 1999); John Philips and Martin Evans, *Algeria: Anger of the Dispossessed* (New Haven, CT: Yale University Press, 2008); and Robert Malley, *The Call from Algeria: Third Worldism, Revolution, and the Turn to Islam* (Berkeley: University of California Press, 1996).

18 John Entelis long made a convincing argument about this. Interview with John Entelis, Omaha, Nebraska, April 24, 2008.

19 Camille Bonara-Waisman, *France and the Algerian Conflict: Issues in Democracy and Political Stability, 1988–1995* (Aldershot: Ashgate: 2003), p. 20.

20 Aït Ahmed had lived in exile since his escape from prison in 1966 and was thus immunized against allegations of FLN cronyism. Following his return to Algeria, he drew on broad popular support (especially among Berbers) and was generally perceived to be an ethical politician.

21 Khalida Toumi, the current minister of culture, changed her name from Khalida Messoudi to Khalida Toumi. For more on her see Khalida Messaoudi and Elisabeth Schemla, *Unbowed: An Algerian Woman Confronts Islamic Fundamentalism*, trans. Anne C. Vila (Philadelphia: University of Pennsylvania Press, 1998), and James D. Le Sueur, *Uncivil War: Intellectuals and Identity Politics during the Decolonization of Algeria*, second edition (Lincoln: University of Nebraska Press, 2005), ch. 8.

22 The Islamists' conspiratorial name for this pro-French camp was *"Hezba Franza"*, The French camp.

23 Willis, *The Islamist Challenge*, p. 135.

24 John Ruedy, *Modern Algeria: The Origins and Development of a Nation* (Bloomington: Indiana University Press, 2005), p. 253.

25 Ali Belhadj, " Un Coup de massue porté au dogme démocratique," in *L'Algerie par ses islamistes*, edited by M. Al-Ahnaf, Bernard Botiveau, and Frack Frégosi (Paris: Editions Karthala, 1991), p. 87.

26 George Joffé, "The Army in Algerian Politics and Government," in *Algeria: Revolution Revisited*, edited by Reza Shah-Kazemi (London: Islamic World Report, 1997), p. 106.

27 For more on "blowback" and negative effects of American involvement in the Middle East, see Chalmers Johnson, *Blowback: The Costs and Consequences of American Empire* (New York: Metropolitan Books, 2004).

28 Hugh Roberts, "A Trial of Strength: Algerian Islamism," in *Islamic Fundamentalisms and the Gulf Crisis*, edited by James Piscatori (The Fundamentalism Project and The American Academy of Arts and Sciences, 1991), p. 131.

29 Ibid., pp. 138–41.

30 Ibid., p. 144.

31 Quandt, *Between Ballots*, p. 54.

32 Ibid., p. 56.

33 Willis, *Islamist Challenge*, p. 180.

34 Hugh Robert, "Demilitarizing Algeria," *Carnegie Papers*, Middle East Program, N. 86 (May 2007): 12. [www.carnegieendowment.org/files/cp_86_final1.pdf]

35 See "Memorandum sur la situation du Pays et le Point de Vue de l'Armée," in Khaled Nezzar, *Mémoirs du général Khaled Nezzar* (Algiers: Chihab Editions, 1999), pp. 224–9.

36 They were released in June 2003 but prohibited from participating in politics, among other sanctions that lasted for five more years.

37 Amnesty International has led the efforts to shed light on state violence in Algeria and especially the fate of thousands of people "disappeared" by the Algerian authorities. See Amnesty International, *A Legacy of Impunity: A Threat to Algeria's Future* (London: Amnesty International Publications, 2009). [www.amnesty.org/en/library/asset/MDE28/001/2009/en/845f89f5-560a-48e1-ab63-a8328753f888/mde280012009eng.pdf]

38 Anwar Haddam has stated that Colonel Samraoui told him that the DRS intentionally encouraged and facilitated Islamic radicals in the effort to convince the population that violent acts were indeed committed by the FIS. This effort to "exploit and inculcate extremists" is confirmed in General Nezzar's memoire. Nezzar, *Mémoirs*, p. 228.

39 Willis, *Islamist Challenge*, p. 166.

40 Ibid., p. 193.

41 Even so, on that count, the FIS could and did go toe to toe with the FLN. For example, Abassi Madani was one of the original founders of the FLN and had bombed a French radio station on November 1, 1954. He spent the rest of the war in prison after his arrest in mid-November. With this in mind, Madani's own revolutionary credentials were impeccable, something that served him well as perhaps the most powerful critic of the FLN's secular and nationalist framework. Ali Belhadj, though younger, made frequent references to his father, an FLN guerrilla who fought against the French with his "Kalisnikov."

42 See *Voix des femmes*, directed by Véronique Taveau (Paris: Antenne 2, 1988).

43 Quoted in Willis, *Islamist Challenge*, pp. 219–29.

3 The kingmakers

1 See, in particular, Habib Saoudia, *La sale guerre: Le témoignage d'un ancien officier des forces spéciales de l'armée algérienne, 1992–2000* (Paris: Éditions La Découverte & Syros, 2001).

2 John Ruedy, *Modern Algeria: The Origins and Development of a Nation*, second edition (Bloomington: Indiana University Press, 2005), p. 259.

3 Mohamed Boudiaf's interview with Pascal Guimier, February 2, 1992 (fr.youtube.com/watch?v=M7RVFj_z6Sc&feature=related).

4 (fr.youtube.com/watch?v=almULUpBI9g).

5 Benjamin Stora, *La Guerre invisible: Algérie, années 90* (Paris: Presse des Sciences-Po, 2001), p. 17; Luis Martinez, *The Algerian Civil War, 1990–1998* (New York: Columbia University Press, 2000). Martinez is particularly helpful in discussing the reasons why no Islamic revolution materialized.

6 Interview with Anwar Haddam, Washington, DC, April 29, 2009.

7 Martinez, *The Algerian Civil War*, p. 59.

8 For an excellent eyewitness account of this from the partner's perspective, see Baya Gacemi, *I, Nadia, Wife of a Terrorist* (Lincoln: University of Nebraska Press, 2005).

9 Martinez, *The Algerian Civil War*, p. 62. For an excellent view of the move of the *hittistes* into the armed conflict (the GIA), see Gacemi, *I, Nadia*.

10 Ruedy, *Modern Algeria*, p. 260.

11 George Joffé, "The Army in Algerian Politics and Government," in *Algeria: Revolution Revisited* (London: Islamic World Report, 1997), p. 102.

12 Hugh Roberts, *The Battlefield Algeria, 1998–2002: Studies in a Broken Polity* (London: Verso, 2003), p. 168.

13 See Khalida Messaoudi, *Unbowed: An Algerian Woman Confronts Islamic Fundamentalism. Interviews with Elisabeth Schemla* (Philadelphia: University of Pennsylvania Press, 1998).

14 Lyes Larbi, *L'Algérie des généraux* (Paris: Max Milo Editions, 2007), p. 141.

15 Robin Wright, "West Sounds the Alarm as Algerian junta falters," *Los Angeles Times*, November 23, 1992.

16 Martinez, *Civil War*, p. 72.

17 Michael Willis, *The Islamist Challenge in Algeria: A Political History* (New York: New York University Press, 1996), p. 269.

18 Lawrence Wright, *The Looming Tower: Al-Qaeda and the Road to 9/11* (New York: Knopf, 2006), p. 190.

19 Interview with Anwar Haddam.

20 Messaoudi, *Unbowed*, p. 131.

21 Martin Stone, *The Agony of Algeria* (New York: Columbia University Press, 1997), p. 114.

22 See Joffé, "The Army in Algerian Politics," p. 110.

23 Ruedy, *Modern Algeria*, p. 265.

24 This theory had already been proven wrong when the exiled FIS leader, Anwar Haddam, declared that he renounced violence around the same time that Saïd Saadi was urging "armed resistance" against the regime. See Benjamin Stora, *Algeria, 1830–2000: A Short History* (Ithaca, NY: Cornell University Press, 2004), p. 217.

25 For the full platform see www. algeria-watch.org/farticle/docu/platform.htm.

26 William B. Quandt, *Between Ballots and Bullets: Algeria's Transition from Authoritiarianism* (Washington, DC: Brookings Institution, 2000), pp. 71–2.

27 Abdennour Ali-Yahia, *Algérie: Raisons et déraison d'une guerre* (Paris: L'Harmattan, 1996), p. 7.

28 Quandt, *Between Ballots and Bullets*, p. 72.

29 Ibid., pp. 72–3.

30 Stone, *Agony of Algeria*, p. 137.

31 Ruedy, *Modern Algeria*, p. 268.

32 Ibid., p. 77.

33 Roger Cohen, "Military Tightens Grip in Algeria Election," *New York Times*, June 7, 1997.

34 "Under Western Eyes: Violence and the Struggle for Political Accountability in Algeria: Interview with Hugh Roberts," *Middle East Report*, no. 26 (Spring 1998): 41.

35 Many have accused the Algerian security forces of being behind many of the massacres. This issue aside, the fact is, as Hugh Roberts states clearly, that the government did not have "accountability." Hugh Roberts, *The*

Battlefield Algeria, p. 41. In fact, Roberts points out that "[t]he central shortcoming of the Algerian state has been and remains today the fact that the formal distribution of political responsibility does not correspond to the actual distribution of power ..." Hence, when it comes to accusations of military involvement in the massacres, it is difficult not to believe that there was at least some level of involvement, because the security forces and the government itself cannot be held accountable.

36 Habib Souaïdia, *La sale guerre: Le témoignage d'un ancien officier des forces spéciales de l'armée algérienne, 1992–2000* (Paris: Éditions La Découverte & Syros, 2001). As one of the officers in charge of counter-terrorism, Souaïdia was responsible for infiltrating radical Islamist cells. He wrote openly about the military's efforts to manipulate Algerian terrorists and about military involvement in the massacres after he went into exile in France in April 2000, where he requested and received political asylum. In France he named names, and laid out detailed charges that included torture, rape, disappearing, and other crimes against his military colleagues. And for that he was found guilty in 2002 by an Algerian court of "demoralization of the military," a crime for which he was sentenced *in absentia* to 20 years. He now lives in exile in France.

37 For an excellent article on this, see Adam Shatz, "Algeria's Ashes," *New York Times Book Review*, July 18, 2003.

38 See Mohammed Samraoui, *Chronique des années de sang* (Paris: Éditions Denoël, 2003; Abdelkader Tigha with Philippe Lobjois, *Contre-espionnage algérien: Notre guerre contre les islamistes* (Paris: Éditions

Nouveau Monde, 2008); and Sid Ahmed Semiane, *Au refuge des balles perdues: Chronique des deux Algéries* (Paris: La Découverte, 2005). Also see Habib Souaïdia, *Le procès de "La Sale Guerre": Algérie: Le général-major Khaled Nezzar contre le lieutenant Habib Souaïdia* (Paris: La Découverte, 2002). Tigha, who went into exile in France, was involved in intelligence and counter-terrorism, and detailed the security operations that involved working directly with the GIAs, including the high-profile kidnapping of Trappist monks in 1996, which he claims was originally staged by his superiors in an effort to undermine the GIA publicly. Like Tigha, Mohammed Samraoui published a book, *Chronique des années de sang* (2003) from exile (in Germany), that outlined the activities of Algerian authorities during the 1990s. In his account, Samraoui claims to have witnessed torture, extralegal killings, and a host of other crimes committed by authorities, including orders to carry out assassinations of key FIS leaders. Semiane, a journalist in Algeria during the 1990s, gave unique insights into the government's efforts to use the media to manipulate and distort representations of radical Islamists. In particular, in his book *Au refuge des balles perdues* (2005), Semiane describes how the government printed fake GIA communiqués in the Algerian press throughout the conflict, with intent to undermine and destabilize the radical and political Islamist movements.

4 The Bouteflika era

1 In 1998 Zeroual had decided to allow a UN fact-finding mission to evaluate the violence, in order to allay fears in the international com-

munity about the state's role in the violence.

2 "President calls on army to support civil concord," BBC Summary of World Broadcasts, July 6, 1999. (Translated from Arabic by BBC.)

3 Edward Cody, "Algeria's President Charges at Peace; Leader Promises Radical Change," *Washington Post*, September 24, 1999, A 23.

4 John Ruedy, *Modern Algeria: The Origins and Development of a Nation*, second edition (Bloomington: Indiana University Press, 2005), p. 276.

5 "Abdelkader Hachani," *The Economist*, December 4, 1999.

6 "Leader of Banned Islamic Group in Algeria is Slain by Gunman," *New York Times*, November 23, 1999, A5.

7 Immediately after Hachani's assassination, conspiracy theories abounded. The government blamed the assassination on 26-year-old Fouad Boulemina, accused of being a GIA member. The authorities claimed Boulemina had been found with the murder weapon and Hachani's personal identity documents. Boulemina was prosecuted and sentenced to death, but then released. Later, in 2003, the FIS claimed that an Algerian security officer had informed FIS leaders that Hachani was assassinated by the government.

8 For more on violence against women see Catherine Lloyd, "From Taboo to Transnational Political Issue: Violence against Women in Algeria," *Women's Studies International Forum*, 29 (2006): 453–62.

9 See in particular this excellent documentary: *Algeria's Bloody Years*, directed by Malek Bensmaïl, Patrice Barrat, and Thierry Leclère (New York: Icarus Films, December 2003).

10 European Parliament, "Human rights: Situation in Algeria," Minutes of 19/01/2001- Final Edition [B5-00666, 0083 and 0086/2001].

11 Ruedy, *Modern Algeria*, p. 279.

12 Hugh Roberts, *The Battlefield Algeria, 1988–2002: Studies in a Broken Polity* (London: Verso, 2003), p. 293.

13 Ibid., p. 281.

14 Benflis served as the campaign manager for Bouteflika's 1999 election.

15 Roberts, *Battlefield Algeria*, p. 218.

16 William B. Quandt, "US and Algeria: Just flirting," *Le Monde Diplomatique*, July 2002 (mondediplom. com/2002/07/08algeria).

17 Article on Morocco.

18 "Algerian President Committed to Economic, Political Reforms," Xinhua General News Service, July 13, 2001.

19 Most notable is the controversy that emerged following the publication of Habib Souaïdia's *La sale guerre* (Paris: La Découverte, 2001).

20 Of particular interest is Jeremy Keenan's work. See Jeremy Keenan, "The Banana Theory of Terrorism: Alternative Truths and the Collapse of the 'Second' (Saharan) Front in the War on Terror," *Journal of Contemporary African Studies*, 25, 1 (January 2007): 31–58.

21 Iraq, which was invaded by the US and its allies that same month, would become especially important in this context because by 2005, it was estimated that roughly one quarter of foreigners fighting against coalition forces were from Africa and that most of these had passed through the Sahel. With these estimates, the Sahel moved to the center stage in an international conflict.

22 "Visiting US official calls for transparent presidential elections," BBC Monitoring Middle East, October 26, 2003.

23 In 2005, NATO's European Command sponsored the next phase of partnership with African forces by creating the Trans-Sahara Counter-terrorism Initiative (TSCI). This five-year, $500 million initiative brought together Saharan Morocco, Algeria, Chad, Niger, Senegal, Mali, Mauritania, Nigeria, and Tunisia in a coordinated effort to combat terrorism. As part of the TSCI, Operation Flintlock represented the first coordinated military training of over 3,000 soldiers from these countries. Overseen by the US military with a force of approximately 1,000 troops, Flintlock represented an important milestone in African–US military relations and was held a model for future coordinated military efforts in the new war on terror.

24 Evidence of the first major failure of this coordinated military effort appeared in February 2009, after the American military's efforts to help Uganda crush the Lord's Resistance Army led to massacres in the Congo. See Jeffrey Gettleman and Eric Schmitt, "U.S.-backed raid fails, and Congo rebels run wild," *International Herald Tribune*, February 6, 2009 (www.iht.com/articles/2009/02/06/africa/07congo.php).

25 See Jeremy Keenan, "Collapse of the Second Front," *Foreign Policy in Focus*, September 26, 2006. For example, Keenan has argued that given the fact that Iraqi leader Ahmed Chalabi was able to carry off a stunning charade that fooled US intelligence officers in the lead-up to the war against Saddam Hussein, it is not beyond imagination that Algerian double agents could dupe the military with a staged kidnapping that went awry. However, interesting as this conspiracy thesis is, and difficult as it may be to confirm, Keenan's real insight is to reveal the degree to which the US military presence has radicalized the local population (www.fpif.org/fpiftxt/3544).

26 The most visible outcome was the formation on February 7, 2007 of AFRICOM, the joint DoD–State Department initiative that shifted strategic planning for Africa away from the NATO command structure in Germany to a stand-alone Africa command (also housed in Stuttgart, Germany). Through AFRICOM, the US promotes "military-sponsored activities, and other military operations to encourage a stable and secure African environment in support of US foreign policy" (www.africom.mil/AboutAFRICOM.asp).

27 David S. Cloud, "Rumsfeld's Algeria Agenda: Arms Sales and Closer Ties," *New York Times*, February 13, 2006.

28 "Rumsfeld describes deeper ties with Algeria," *International Herald Tribune*, February 12, 2006.

29 Elaine Sciolino, "France seeks new role after opposing a war against Baghdad," *International Herald Tribune*, March 31, 2003.

30 Lara Marlow, "A presidential election campaign, Algerian-style," *Irish Times*, March 25, 2004.

31 "Powell urges honest Algeria elections," United Press International, December 4, 2003.

32 For more on Khalida Toumi, see James D. Le Sueur, *Uncivil War: Intellectuals and Identity Politics during the Decolonization of Algeria* (Lincoln: University of Nebraska Press, 2005).

33 Phone interview with Hugh Roberts, December 15, 2008.

34 "Bouteflika en Bechar hier," *Liberté* (Algeria), August 29, 2005.

35 For the text see hrw.org/english/docs/2006/03/01/algeri12743.htm.

36 Lyes Larbi, *L'Algérie des généraux* (Paris: Max Milo Editions, 2007), p. 207. Also see the excellent analysis in Hugh Roberts, "Demilitarizing Algeria," *Carnegie Papers*, Middle East Program, N. 86 (May 2007) (www.carnegieendowment.org/files/cp_86_final1.pdf).

37 Ed Blanche, "Algeria: the power within; President Bouteflika clips the wings of Algeria's long-powerful military," *The Middle East*, May 1, 2006.

38 Cited in Ed Blanche, "Algeria."

39 "A Flawed Charter," *The Economist*, October 8, 2005.

40 See web.amnesty.org/library/index/engmde280102005.

41 Craig Whitlock, "Algerian Program Offers Amnesty, but Not Answers about Past," *Washington Post*, September 17, 2006.

42 Interview with Besma Kerracha, originally published in *El-Khabar*, December 19, 2006. Reprinted as "Algerian Islamist dissident refugee in US wants to return home," in BBC Monitoring International Reports, December 21, 2006.

43 John Philipps, "Two-Term Limit Abolished by Lawmakers," *Washington Times*, November 13, 2008.

44 Telephone interview with Hugh Roberts, December 15, 2008.

45 "Algerian president forgives farmers' debts," Associated Press Financial Wire, February 29, 2009.

46 "Stop the Denial, Disclose the Truth," Amnesty International, March 30, 2009 (www.amnesty.org/en/for-media/press-releases/algeria-stop-denial-disclose-truth-20090330).

47 "FIS leader says 'determined' to be candidate in Algerian presidential election," BBC Worldwide Monitoring, October 19, 2008.

48 "Historic Islamist leader urges Algeria vote boycott," Yahoo! News Canada, February 24, 2009 (ca.news.yahoo.com/s/afp/090224/world/algeria_vote_fis).

49 "75.25 % de taux de participation dont 90.16 % pour Bouteflika," *El Watan*, April 11, 2008 (www.elwatan.com/75-25-de-taux-de-participation). However, there were widespread allegations of voter fraud, despite Bouteflika's decision to allow for outside election monitors to follow the results. And there were regions, especially in Kabylia, that had a very modest turnout. See "Faibles taux de participation," *El Watan*, April 10, 2009 (www.elwatan.com/Faibles-taux-de-participation).

50 Cited in Ahmed Aghrout and Yahia H. Zoubir, "Introducing Algeria's President-for-Life," *Middle East Report Online*, April 1, 2009 (www.merip.org/mero/mero040109.html).

5 Energy and the economy of terror

1 See Naomi Klein, *The Shock Doctrine: The Rise of Disaster Capitalism* (New York: Picador, 2007).

2 Development of global capitalism from the 1970s thus relied heavily on a Friedman-inspired approach, which in turn gave rise to a whole neo-conservative movement flanked by loyal lieutenants and global capitalists, including and perhaps most especially the very men who engineered and oversaw the the occupation of Iraq in 2003.

3 Klein, *Shock Doctrine*, p. 13.

4 For the most egregious example of this absurd approach, see Francis

Fukuyama, *The End of History and the Last Man* (New York: Free Press, 1992).

5 Ibid., p. 291.

6 Clement M. Henry, "Crisis of Money and Power: Transitions to Democracy?" in *Islam, Democracy, and the State in North Africa*, edited by John P. Entelis (Bloomington: University of Indiana Press, 1997).

7 "Nostalgic about the bad old days," *The Middle East* (4), July 1, 1993.

8 This quid pro quo loan could not, however, offset the catastrophic losses in oil revenue. For example, between 1991 and 1992, the declining price of oil caused the nation to lose more than $1 billion, bringing its GDP down from $11.9 billion to $10.9 billion.

9 Phillip C. Naylor, *France and Algeria: A History of Decolonization and Transformation* (Gainesville: University of Florida Press, 2000), p. 174.

10 John Entelis, "The Political Economy of an Algerian Institution," *The Middle East Journal*, vol. 23, no. 1 (Winter 1999): 23.

11 John Ruedy, *Modern Algeria: Origins and Development of a Nation*, second edition (Bloomington: Indiana University Press, 2005), p. 272.

12 Ibid., p. 101.

13 Naylor, *France and Algeria*, p. 175.

14 Ali Assaoui, *Algeria: The Political Economy of Oil and Gas* (Oxford: Oxford University Press, for the Oxford Institute of Energy Studies, 2001), p. 100.

15 John Entelis, "The Political Economy", p.18.

16 Ibid., p. 24.

17 Naylor, *France and Algeria*, p. 181.

18 Ibid.

19 Cited in ibid., p. 183.

20 Camille Bonora-Waisman, *France and the Algerian Conflict: Issues in Democracy and Political Stability, 1988–1995* (Burlington, VT: Ashgate Publishing Company, 2003), p. 41.

21 Naylor, *France and Algeria*, pp. 192–3.

22 Ibid., p. 196.

23 Ruedy, *Modern Algeria*, p. 271.

24 Francis Ghiles, "Algerian debt takes on a surreal aspect: fears over the country's political stability cloud an encouraging report from the IMF," *Financial Times*, September 13, 1994.

25 Alan Friedman, "Risk Seen to Funds if Government Falls to Islamic Fundamentalists: France and the IMF Press Aid for Algeria," *International Herald Tribune*, January 10, 1995.

26 For an excellent study of immigration politics in France see Jérôme Valluy, *Rejet des exiles: le grand retournement du droit de l'asile* (Bellecombe-en-Bauges: Éditions du Croquant, 2009).

27 Lounis Aggoun and Jean-Baptiste Rivoire, *Françalgérie: crimes et mensonges d'États* (Paris: La Découverte, 2004), pp. 403–4.

28 Bonora-Waisman, *France and the Algerian Conflict*, p. 129.

29 Friedman, "Risk Seen to Funds."

30 Nick Tabakoff, "Calm in the war zone is Camdessus lifestyle," *South China Morning Post* (Hong Kong), September 22, 1997: 4.

31 Bruce Barnard, "EU's Maghreb Policy Largely Fear-Driven," *Journal of Commerce*, March 28, 1994, 9a.

32 Mark H. Hayes, "Algerian Gas to Europe: The TransMed Pipeline and the Early Spanish Gas Import Projects," Geopolitics of Gas Working Paper Series, Program on Energy and

Sustainable Development at Stanford University, and James A. Baker III Institute for Public Policy, Working Paper #27 (May 2004), p. 22.

33 "Nostalgic about the Bad Old Days."

34 "Algeria: Recent Economic Developments," International Monetary Fund, IMF Staff Country Report No. 00/105 (August 2000), p. 50.

35 See Timothy Williams, "Few Bidders to Develop Iraqi Oil and Natural Gas Fields," *New York Times*, Global Edition, Global Business (June 30, 2009).

36 "Algerian crisis leaves no room for comfort," *Financial Times Energy Newsletter*, April 1, 1994.

37 "Algeria: Country Profile," *African Review World Information*, August 30, 2000.

38 "The Forces of the Private Sector," IPR Strategic Services Database, February 27, 2000.

39 "A vote for transparency as Algeria opens up," *FT Energy Newsletter*, January 26, 2001.

40 For a superb analysis of Algerian conspiracy theories, see Paul A. Silverstein, "An Excess of Truth: Violence, Conspiracy Theorizing and the Algerian Civil War," *Anthropological Quarterly*, vol. 75, no. 4 (Fall 2002): 643–74.

41 Roger Cohen, "A Chance to Try to End an Agony," *New York Times*, February 2, 1997.

42 Cameron R. Hume, *Mission to Algiers: Diplomacy by Engagement* (New York: Lexington Books, 2006), p. 79.

43 "Algeria: Review," *Middle East Review of Information*, July 1999.

44 Rachid Khiari, "AFR: train bombing kills 18; main gas pipeline bombed," AAP Newsfeed, February 24, 1998.

45 Emma Ross, "UK: Algerian exiles say authorities responsible for massacres," AAP Newsfeed, January 23, 1998.

46 *Oil & Gas Journal*, January 12, 1998.

47 "Algeria: Country Profile."

48 "A vote for transparency as Algeria opens up," *FT Energy Newsletter*, January 26, 2001.

49 "Oil prices swell trade surplus," *MEED Quarterly Report: Maghreb*, January 31, 2001.

50 Ruedy, *Modern Algeria*, p. 274.

51 Abdelaziz Testas, "Algeria; Puzzles in Algeria's Development Strategy," *Africa News*, August 18, 1999.

52 Ruedy, *Modern Algeria*, p. 274.

53 "Algeria – Confusing E&P Regime & Tax," *APS Review Oil Market Trends*, February 5, 2007.

54 "Billions for Upstream," *Africa Energy Intelligence*, January 11, 2006.

55 "Algeria," *World of Information Africa Review of Information*, July 30, 2007.

56 "Billions for Upstream."

57 "Algeria Oil Revenue Hits $59B," *International Oil Daily*, December 26, 2007.

58 "Algeria's energy minister says oil revenues to be around 80bn," BBC Worldwide Monitoring, October 6, 2008.

59 Youcef Bedjaoui, Abbas Aroua, and Méziane Aït-Larbi, eds, *An Inquiry into the Algerian Massacres*, forewords by Noam Chomsky and Lord Eric Avebury (Geneva: Hoggar, 1999), p. 979.

60 Ibid., pp. 985–6.

61 Tony Geraghty, "Guns for Hire: Rambo or White Knights," *Sunday Express*, September 23, 2007.

62 On February 14, 1996, the London-based Arab-language newspaper, *Al Hayat*, noted that a GIA leader, Abu Abdul Rahman Amin,

had promised to kill both foreign and domestic gas and oil workers if they continued going to their jobs.

63 One recent exception occurred on December 6, 2006, when terrorists attacked a vehicle convoy carrying nine American employees of the Halliburton subsidiary, Brown & Condor-Root, a company involved in energy and construction projects in Algeria. The Algerian driver was killed and the nine employees wounded.

64 This point is made repeatedly in Bedjaoui et al., *Inquiry into the Algerian Massacres*.

65 Ibid., p. 973.

66 "Kidnappings reap millions in Algeria," UPI, May 20, 2008.

67 Luis Martinez, *The Algerian Civil War, 1990–1998* (New York: Columbia University Press, 2000), p. 184.

68 Ibid., pp. 185–9.

69 Ibid., p. 188.

6 A genealogy of terror

1 See Brynjar Lia, *Architect of Global Jihad: The Life of Al-Qaida Strategist Abu Mus'ab al-Suri* (New York: Columbia University Press, 2008), and Alison Pargeter, *The New Frontiers of Jihad: Radical Islam in Europe* (Philadelphia: University of Pennsylvania Press, 2008).

2 Ahmed Rachid, *The Taliban* (New Haven, CT: Yale University Press, 2001), p. 130.

3 Michael Willis, *The Islamist Challenge in Algeria: A Political History* (New York: NYU Press, 1996), p. 268. Other historians date the first attacks by mujaheddin as having occurred in 1991. See Lia, *Architect of Global Jihad*.

4 Lawrence Wright, *The Looming Tower: Al-Qaeda and the Road to 9/11* (New York: Random House, 2006), p. 124.

5 Quoted in Willis, *Islamist Challenge*, p. 285.

6 Ibid., p. 283.

7 "All Things Considered," National Public Radio, 4:30 pm EST, December 17, 1993: Transcript # 1334-2.

8 Quoted in Evan F. Kohlmann, "Two Decades of Jihad in Algeria: the GIA , the GSPC, and Al-Qaida," NEFA Foundation, May 2007.

9 Willis, *Islamist Challenge*, p. 329.

10 Anwar Haddam confirmed this in a recent interview with the author. Interview with Anwar Haddam, Washington, DC, April 29, 2009.

11 Willis, *Islamist Challenge*, p. 328.

12 Luis Martinez, *The Algerian Civil War 1990–1998* (New York: Columbia University Press, 2000), pp. 201, 91.

13 Roland Jacquard, *In the Name of Osama Bin Laden: Global Terrorism and the Bin Laden Brotherhood* (Durham, NC: Duke University Press, 2002), p. 67.

14 Sean O'Neill and Daniel McGrory, *The Suicide Factory: Abu Hamza and the Finsbury Park Mosque* (London: Harper Perennial, 2006), pp. 112–13.

15 Wright, *The Looming Tower*, p. 190.

16 Telephone interview with Hugh Roberts, December 15, 2008.

17 Daniel Pipes and Patrick Clawson, "Anwar N. Haddam: An Islamist Vision for Algeria," interview in *Middle East Quarterly*, September 1996, vol. III, issue 3 (www.meforum.org/article/316, accessed 9/11/2008).

18 Ibid.

19 In my April 29, 1999 interview with Anwar Haddam, he made it clear that the GIA was made up of a collection of groups, some of which

were controlled by ex-FIS colleagues who resigned from the FIS in order to continue the struggle against the military regime. According to him, not all of the GIAs shared the same violent agenda, and the particular groups he supported limited their violence to attacking agents of the state.

20 Ayman al-Zawahiri, "Knights under the Prophet's Banner," in *Al Qaeda in Its Own Words*, edited by Gilles Kepel and Jean-Pierre Milelli, trans. Pascale Ghazaleh (Cambridge, MA: Harvard University Press, 2008), pp. 194–5.

21 Willis, *Islamist Challenge*, p. 277.

22 Mark Dejevsky, "Algerian group blamed for Paris bombings," *Independent*, August 21, 1995.

23 "Algeria: Zeroual Pronounces Dialogue Dead," *Middle East Economic Digest*, July 21, 1995.

24 Simon Freeman, "Court backs extradition for 1995 Paris bombing suspect," Times Online, November 17, 2005.

25 John W. Kiser, *The Monks of Tibhirine: Faith, Love, and Terror in Algeria* (New York: St. Martin's Press, 2002), p. 213.

26 "World News Briefs; 7 French Trappist Monks Kidnapped in Algeria," *New York Times*, March 28, 1996.

27 Kiser, *The Monks*, p. 232.

28 These two French agencies often had conflicting approaches to the Algerian crisis, and they disagreed over the very constitution of the GIA during this crisis. For example, the DGSE believed that the GIA was a structured organization and would act reasonably if it could find a French partner with whom it could negotiate; whereas the DST believed that the GIA was too decentralized to

work with an interlocutor. Kiser, *The Monks*, p. 230.

29 Florence Aubenas and José Garçon, "Tibéhirine, un silence de dix ans; Des proches des sept moines assassinés dénoncent la collusion entre Paris et Alger," *Libération*, March 25, 2006.

30 France did not grant him asylum for his testimony, and left him to be held in a detention center in Bangkok.

31 Arnaud Dubus, "Abdelkader Tigha lâché par la France," *Libération*, December 23, 2002.

32 Martin Evans and John Phillips, *Algeria: Anger of the Dispossessed* (New Haven, CT: Yale University Press, 2007), p. 231.

33 Samraoui's account is vital for understanding the role of the DRS during the 1990s in Algeria. As the second in command of the anti-terrorism campaign, his depiction of the state's role in the violence is perhaps the most important written. See Mohammed Samraoui, *Chronique des années de sang* (Paris: Denoël, 2003).

34 Evans and Phillips, *Algeria*, p. 224.

35 O'Neill and McGrory, *The Suicide Factory*, pp. 114–15.

36 Ibid., p. 126.

37 Ibid., pp. 130–5.

38 Omar Nasiri, *Inside the Jihad: My Life with Al Qaeda. A Spy's Story* (New York: Basic Books, 2006), p. 58.

39 Ibid., p. 252.

40 Ibid., pp. 79–80.

41 Ibid., p. 28.

42 Ibid., p. 285.

43 See Lia, *Architect*.

44 Ibid., p. 231.

45 Steve Coll, *Ghost Wars: The Secret History of the CIA, Afghanistan, and Bin Laden, from the Soviet Invasion to September 10, 2001* (New York: Penguin Press, 2004), p. 260.

46 Lia, *Architect*, pp. 112–14.

47 Coll, *Ghost Wars*, p. 260.

48 Ibid., p. 261.

49 Lia, *Architect*, p. 115.

50 As Lia notes, al-Suri was clear about his mission with the GIA: "My position was that I should assist the GIA as best I could, especially in the field of external media, provide advice and consultation to its leadership inside Algeria, gather supporters around it, and attempt to reach the inside to participate in the field." Quoted in Lia, *Architect*, p. 153.

51 Ibid., pp. 128–53.

52 Abdel Bari Atwan, *The Secret History of al Qaeda* (Berkeley: University of California Press, 2008), p. 229.

7 The future of radical Islam

1 Omar Ashour, "Islamist De-Radicalization in Algeria: Success and Failures," *The Middle East Institute Policy Brief*, no. 21 (November 2008): 6, 7.

2 Ibid., pp. 1–10.

3 "GIA leader accuses rival armed groups of helping army," BBC Summary of World Broadcasts, May 7, 1998. Translation from Arabic of *Al-Hayat* article.

4 "Armed Islamist group widens its territorial influence," BBC Summary of World Broadcasts, May 4, 1999.

5 Dominique Thomas, *Le Londonistan: la voix du djihad* (Paris: Éditions Michalon, 2003), p. 167.

6 On March 27, 2000, the Algiers newspaper, *Le Matin*, reported that Hassan Hattab had contacted the Algerian authorities and was negotiating possible amnesty agreements. However, according to Sid Ahmed Semiane, a whistle-blowing Algerian journalist, many of these GIA communiqués published in *Le Matin* and other dailies were fabricated by the journalists and Algerian security service officers in order to undermine the GIA. See Sid Ahmed Semiane, *Aux refuge des balles perdues: Chronique des deux Algéries* (Paris: La Découverte, 2005).

7 Rohan Gunaratna, *Inside Al Qaeda: Global Network of Terror* (New York: Berkeley Books, 2003), p. 166.

8 Olivier Roy, *Globalized Islam: The Search for the New Ummah* (New York: Columbia University Press, 2004), pp. 304–7.

9 Lorraine Adams, "The Other Man: For months the feds contended that Abdel Ghani Meskini was the key to unlocking the millennial terrorist bomb plot. But was he mastermind or dupe?" *Washington Post*, May 20, 2001 (Final Edition).

10 Josh Meyer, "Border arrest stirs fear of terrorist cells in the US," *Los Angeles Times*, March 11, 2001. Ressam's testimonies eventually led to the conviction of two other Algerian terrorists in Canada, Samir Ait Mohamed and Mokhtar Houari, and to the US federal grand jury indictment of Abdelmajid Dahoumane (along with Ressam himself) for crossing the border in a "conspiracy to 'destroy or damage structures.'" See Lorraine Adams, John Lancaster, and Philippe German, 'Algerian Charged in Bombing Plot Aids FBI Probe," *Washington Post*, January 21, 2000.

11 Bill Schiller, "Bomb Plot Charged 3rd for Canada," *Toronto Star*, December 13, 2001.

12 Ibid.

13 Timothy Egan, "A Nation Challenged: The Convicted Terrorist," *New York Times*, September 27, 2001.

14 Chris McGann, "Ressam likely witness against captured al Qaeda leader," *Seattle Post-Intelligencer*, April 3, 2002.

15 Rod Mickleburgh, "Ressam jailed for 22 years; Judge first salvo at Bush officials for handling of terror suspect," *Globe and Mail* (Canada), July 28, 2005.

16 "Algeria: UK envoy says security services 'brutal', disregard human rights," BBC Worldwide Monitoring, September 4, 2002.

17 Paul Gallagher, "Algerian militants the main terror threat to Britain, experts warn," *Scotsman*, January 16, 2003.

18 Giles Tremlett, "Terror thrives in Algeria's climate of bloody conflict," *Guardian* (London), January 17, 2003.

19 Isambard Wilkinson, "Explosives cache 'part of al-Qa'eda network in Europe' Spain," *Daily Telegraph* (London), January 25, 2003.

20 Niz Al-Aly, "Politics-Algeria: Islamic Upsurge Breaks Fragile Calm," IPS-Interpress Service/Global Information Network, January 10, 2003.

21 Hattab had already begun to talk about negotiating with Algerian authorities and, unlike his successor, had begun to have reservations about al Qaeda. He eventually gave himself up in September 2007, and applied for amnesty.

22 "Algeria: GSPC Leader Hattab Replaced by man 'close' to al-Qa'idah," BBC Monitoring International Reports, October 10, 2003.

23 Evan F. Kholmann, "Two Decades of Jihad in Algeria: The GIA, GSPC, and Al-Qaeda," NEFA Foundation (May 2007) (www. nefafoundation.org/miscellaneous/ nefagspc0507.pdf).

24 Abdel Bari Atwan, *The Secret History*, second edition (Berkeley: University of California Press, 2008), p. 232.

25 Salima Mellah and Jean-Baptiste Rivoire, "El Para, the Maghreb's Bin Laden," *Le Monde diplomatique*, February 2005 (monde diplo.com/2005/02/04algeria).

26 "Algeria: Tourist Kidnappers Demand Ransom; six hostages very sick," BBC Monitoring International Reports, August 4, 2003.

27 Mark Huband and Hugh Williamson, "Schroeder vows to help find hostage-takers," *Financial Times* (London), August 20, 2003.

28 Tony Paterson, "Libya claims lead role in negotiations that freed Sahara hostages," *Independent*, August 20, 2003.

29 Craig Smith, "Chad Rebel Group Says It Holds Qaeda-Linked Terrorist," *New York Times*, October 1, 2008.

30 Ibid.

31 Craig Whitlock, "Taking Terror Fight to N. Africa Leads U.S. to Unlikely Alliances," *Washington Post*, October 28, 2006.

32 Alex Belida, "US General: Libya Could Become Participant in Fight Against Terrorism," *Voice of America News*, April 2, 2004.

33 Whitlock, "Taking Terror Fight to N. Africa."

34 "Islamist group leader vows war to the death," BBC Monitoring International Reports, January 10, 2004.

35 "Algeria: GSPC threatens US, UK, French, other countries' interests," BBC Monitoring International Reports, February 17, 2004.

36 "Overseas Relations: North Africa – Charges and Sentences," *Africa Research Bulletin*, May 1, 2004.

37 Shaun Waterman, "Analysis: Algeria bombs show al Q strength," UPI, August 22, 2008.

38 "An Interview with Abdelmalek Droukdal," *New York Times*, July 1, 2008. (For full text see www.

nytimes.com/2008/07/01/world/
africa/01transcript-oukdal.html?_
r=1&pagewanted=print.)

39 Raffi Khatchadourian, "Pursuing Terrorists in the Great Desert: The U.S. Military's $500 Million Gamble to Prevent the Next Afghanistan," *Village Voice*, January 24, 2006 (www.villagevoice.com/2006-01-24/news/pursuing-terrorists-in-the-great-desert/4).

40 Ibid.

41 Atwan, *The Secret History*, p. 235.

42 "Interview with Abdelmalek Droukdal," *New York Times*.

43 See Jeremy Keenan, "Alternative Truths and the Collapse of the Second (Saharan) Front in the War on Terror," *Journal of Contemporary African Studies*, vol. 25, no. 1 (January 2007): 31–58.

44 Phone interview with Hugh Roberts, December 15, 2008.

45 "Algerian Islamists blast former emir for supporting reconciliation," BBC Monitoring International Reports, February 12, 2005. From the GSPC's standpoint, Hattab was now the equivalent of Ahmed Shah Masud, the pro-Western, anti-Soviet Afghan resistance fighter killed by al Qaeda suicide bombers in Afghanistan on September 9, 2001.

46 "Algeria group claims Mauritania attack," UPI, June 6, 2005.

47 Mauritania's supreme court finally cleared the men of all charges on July 27, 2007.

48 "Mauritania's Coup Isolates it, Improving the Jihadist Position," *Defense and Foreign Affairs Strategic Policy*, August 2005.

49 "Junta Declares General Amnesty for Political Prisoners," *Africa News*, September 5, 2005.

50 "Algerian group said contacting al-Zarqawi to target French," BBC Monitoring International Reports, July 4, 2005.

51 For more on the headscarf controversy in France, see John R. Bowen, *Why the French Don't Like Headscarves: Islam, the State, and Public Space* (Princeton, NJ: Princeton University Press, 2008) and Joan Wallach Scott, *The Politics of the Veil* (Princeton, NJ: Princeton University Press, 2007).

52 "Algerian Rebels Said to Reject Amnesty," *New York Times*, October 2, 2005.

53 John Ward Anderson, "France Says Extremists are Enlisting Its Citizens; Police Assert Some Trained in Middle East Could Attack Paris," *Washington Post*, October 19, 2007.

54 Ibid.

55 "10 charged with aiding radical Islamic group," *International Herald Tribune*, November 24, 2005.

56 "Algeria's al-Qaida Franchise," *Counterterrorism and Homeland Security Reports*, Summer 2006, vol. 13, nos. 3, 1.

57 "Al-Qaida-linked group behind attack in Algeria," *The Record* (Kitchener-Waterloo, Ontario), December 12, 2006.

58 "Interview with Abdelmalek Droukdal," *New York Times*.

59 "Algeria – Terrorists Change Name to Highlight al-Qaida Link," *Periscope Daily Defense News Capsules*, January 29, 2007.

60 "Al-Qaida's plan to hit French poll," *Sunday Mail* (Australia), February 11, 2007.

61 See Marc Sageman, *Leaderless Jihad: Terror Networks in the Twenty-First Century* (Philadelphia: University of Pennsylvania Press, 2008).

62 Robert A. Pape, *Dying to Win: The Strategic Logic of Suicide Terrorism* (New York: Random House, 2005).

63 Interview with Hugh Roberts.

64 Craig Smith, "Within striking distance of Europe, a jihad rises in North Africa," *International Herald Tribune* (Paris), February 21, 2007.

65 Ibid.

66 Jason Motlagh, "Analysis: GSPC regroups in Italy," UPI, February 18, 2006.

67 Craig Smith, "At least 23 die in 2 terrorist bombings in Algeria," *International Herald Tribune*, April 12, 2007.

68 "Maghreb Al-Qa'idah group 'leader' calls for more suicide attacks; Text of report by Qatari-Al-Jazeera satellite TV on 8 May," supplied by BBC Worldwide Monitoring, May 9, 2007.

69 "Algeria: Editorial blasts Al-Jazeera over treatment of domestic terrorism" [text of report by Algerian newspaper *Liberté* website on May 10], BBC Worldwide Monitoring, May 20, 2007.

70 Ed Blanche, "Salafist splits: Al Qaeda plans to establish a new network across the Maghreb are threatened by growing fracture within Algerian core group," *The Middle East*, no. 385, January 1, 2008.

71 "Zawahiri urges attacks on Western targets in North Africa" (AFP), November 3, 2007 (afp.google.com/article/AlegM5gwwodPc1:WA WogDNpTOpFoMr96Ww).

72 Hassane Meflahi, "2nd Algeria bomb in Deys kills 28 coast guard officers," *Washington Post*, September 9, 2007.

73 Katrin Bennhold and Craig Smith, "Car bombings in Algiers kill as many as 60," *International Herald Tribune*, December 11, 2007.

74 Michael Moss, Souad Mekhennet, Eric Schmitt, Elaine Sciolino, and Margot Williams, "In Algeria, insurgents gain a lifeline from Al Qaeda," *International Herald Tribune*, July 1, 2008.

75 "Al Qaeda says it was behind Algeria bombing," *International Herald Tribune*, October 1, 2008.

76 "GIA, GSPC, AQMI, échec d'un combat purement national," interview with Louis Caprioli, *El Watan* (Algiers), October 11, 2007. (Website accessed October 8, 2008.)

8 Killing the messengers

1 Koenraad Elst, "Postscript," in *The Rushdie Affair: The Novel, the Ayatollah, and the West* by Daniel Pipes (New York: Transaction Publishers, 2004), p. 258.

2 Gilles Kepel has most forcefully made this claim in his superb study, *Jihad: The Trail of Political Islam* (Cambridge: Harvard University Press, 2003), p. 186.

3 Ibid., p. 190.

4 Ibid., pp. 189–90.

5 For international reaction of writers, see Anouar Abdellah, ed., *For Rushdie: Essays by Arab and Muslim Writers in Defense of Free Speech* (New York: George Braziller, 1994) and Steve MacDonogh, ed., *The Rushdie Letters: Freedom to Speak, Freedom to Write* (Lincoln: University of Nebraska Press, 1993).

6 Anouar Benmalek, *Chroniques de l'Algérie amère: Algérie 1985–2002* (Paris: Pauvert, 2003), p. 94.

7 For earliest evidence of the criticism of the state's use of torture, see *Cahier noir d'octobre* (Algiers: Comité National Contre la Torture, 1989).

8 Mohamed Benchicou, one of the most critical opponents of the government, is a particularly salient case. As the director of *Le Matin*, Benchicou criticized the military government, and in 2004 he published *Bouteflika, un imposteur algérien*

(Paris: Picollec, 2004), a scathing critique of Abdelaziz Bouteflika. He was jailed for this. See Suzanna Ruta, "Stifling Free Press: For critics of Algeria's regime, a jail cell awaits," *International Herald Tribune*, August 11, 2004. For more by Mohamed Benchicou on his experiences, see his: *Journal d'un homme libre* (Paris: Éditions Riveneuve, 2008) and *Les Geôles d'Alger* (Paris, Éditions Riveneuve, 2007).

9 Lazhari Labter, *Journalistes algériens entre le bâillon et les balles* (Paris: L'Harmattan, 1995). In particular, see chapters "L'Aventure intellectuelle" and "La Presse sous haute surveillance."

10 Ibid., pp. 48–51.

11 Ghania Mouffouk, *Être journaliste en Algérie 1988–1995* (Paris: Reporters Sans Frontières), p. 26.

12 In October 1922, the francophone newspaper *Liberté* was suspended for the first time for five days, on the grounds that it violated the law. After reporting on an important terrorist attack committed by militant Islamists on January 3, 1993, journalists writing for *El Watan* (a major French-language daily) were arrested for endangering state security.

13 Mouffouk, *Être journaliste*, p. 56.

14 Labter, *Journalistes algériens*, p. 61.

15 Morceli, a clear favorite, also won the men's World Indoor 1,500-meter championship in 1991 and was named athlete of the year in 1993 by *Track and Field Magazine*.

16 Kenny Moore, "A Scream and a Prayer," *Sports Illustrated*, August 3, 1992: 48.

17 Ibid.: n. 14.

18 Pat Butcher, "Keep on Running," *Guardian*, January 11, 1992.

19 Ibid. Unfortunately, on October 17, 1994, Islamists assassinated Aslaoui's husband, a dentist, employing the same logic.

20 Jeff Powell, "The gazelle on final lap of a running battle to lift tyrants' veil," *Daily Mail*, August 5, 1992.

21 Moore, "A Scream," p. 53.

22 In winning the 1,500-meter event at the Barcelona Olympic Games, she became the second African woman, after Moroccan 400-meter hurdler Nawel El Moutawakel (gold medalist at the Los Angeles Games and now a Moroccan IOC member), to win a gold medal.

23 Filip Bondy, "Algeria's Boulmerka Outruns her Limits," *New York Times*, August 9, 1992.

24 Jay Weiner, "Algeria's Boulmerka sets her own pace to 1,500 victory," *Star Tribune*, August 9, 1992.

25 Jere Longman, "Pressure Beyond the Track for Algerian Women," *New York Times*, February 12, 1995.

26 Robert McG. Thomas Jr. "Runs, She Is Making History," *New York Times*, February 3, 1994.

27 Longman, "Pressure Beyond the Track."

28 Elizabeth Levitan Spade, "Women Athletes Grapple for Olympic Equality," *Christian Science Monitor*, March 24, 1995.

29 Interview with Anita DeFrantz, Los Angeles, June 27, 2005. DeFrantz, the US athlete who led the charge against President Jimmy Carter's decision to boycott the 1980 Olympic Games, had come to the conclusion that diplomacy was a much more effective tool for engaging debates of this nature.

30 Youssef M. Ibrahim, "As Algerian Civil War Drags On, Atrocities Grow," *New York Times*, December 28, 1997.

31 See www.cpj.org/news/1999/
AlgeriaKilled.html.

32 John F. Burnes, "Algerian
Journalists Assert their Indepen-
dence Just by Surviving the Purges,"
New York Times, April 3, 1999.

33 Interview by J.L. with Tahar
Djaout, *Liberté*, January 26, 1993.

34 Cited in Julija Šukys, *Silence
is Death: The Life and Work of Tahar
Djaout* (Lincoln: University of
Nebraska Press, 2007), p. 22.

35 Tahar Djaout, *The Last Summer of Reason* (Lincoln: University of
Nebraska Books, 2007), p. xvi.

36 *L'Opinion* published the
shocking photograph on May 28–9,
1993 in order to graphically illustrate
the crime.

37 Cited in Šukys, *Silence is
Death*, p. 29.

38 "Shooting the Writer,"
documentary produced by Catherine
Seddon, presented by Salman Rushdie, BBC2, 08/12/1993.

39 Václav Havel served as the
IPW's second president, later
followed by Nobel Laureate Wole
Soyinka and the American writer,
Russell Banks.

40 Wole Soyinka, "Foreword: A
Voice that Would not Be Silenced," in
Djaout, *The Last Summer of Reason*,
p. xxviii.

41 Mouffouk, *Être journaliste*,
pp. 112–14.

42 Nora Boustany, "For Raï,
There's No Oasis in Algeria; After the
Murders of Two Colleagues, Musi-
cians Choose Between Living in Exile
and Fear," *Washington Post*, July 2,
1995, Sunday Final Edition.

43 Marc Schade-Poulsen, *The
Social Significance of Raï: Men and
Popular Music in Algeria* (Austin:
University of Texas Press, 1999), p. 14.

44 Boustany, "For Raï, There's No
Oasis."

45 Neil Strauss, "Pop Music;
Singing of a Beloved Homeland,
Fearful of Going Home Again," *New
York Times*, April 30, 1995.

46 (www.dailymotion.com/
related/x2qkv8_tahar-djaoutshoot-
ing-the-writer-fin_politics/video/
xqrup_httplouneslekabyleskyblog-
com_events).

47 "GIA says 'moudjahidine' were
responsible for kidnapping of singer
Matoub Lounès," BBC Summary of
World Broadcasts, October 4, 1994.

48 "Top Algerian pop star
murdered," *Hollywood Reporter*,
September 30, 1994.

49 Paul A. Silverstein, "'The
Rebel is Dead. Long Live the Martyr!'
Kabyle Mobilization and the Assas-
sination of Lounès Matoub," *Middle
East Report*, 208 (Fall 1998).

50 "GIA release singer Matoub
Lounès with message calling for
Kabyle support," BBC Summary of
World Broadcasts, October 13, 1994.

51 "Voices from the Casbah tell
of a 'hidden war,'" *Observer*, January 1, 1995.

52 Malika Matoub, *Matoub Lounès, mon frère* (Paris: Albin Michel,
1999), p. 161.

53 "Demonstration in 'solidarity'
with Algeria held in Paris," BBC Summary of World Broadcasts, December
5, 1994.

54 Lounès Matoub, *Rebelle* (Paris:
Stock, 1995), pp. 213–15.

55 Silverstein, "'The Rebel is
Dead'" (www.merip.org/mer/mer208/
mer208.html).

56 For an extract of BBC documentary, see openvideo.dailymotion.
com/video/x1k1l–matoub-lounes
reportage-bbc-news.

57 Cover art for Matoub Lounès,
Lettre ouverte aux ... (Paris: Virgin
Records, 1998).

58 Matoub, *Mon frère*, p. 194.

59 Charles Trueheart, "Pop Singer's Killing Roils Algeria; Matoub Lounes Was Critic of Both Sides in Bloody Civil War," *Washington Post*, June 27, 1998.

60 Silverstein, "'The Rebel is Dead.'"

61 Abdelmalik Touati and Victoria Brittain, "Angry Berbers go on rampage after radical singer's murder," *Guardian* (London), June 27, 1998.

62 Matoub, *Mon frère*, p. 200.

63 Quoted in Silverstein, "'The Rebel is Dead.'"

64 Craig R. Whitney, "Lounes Matoub, 42, Is Killed; Sang to Promote Berber Cause," *New York Times*, June 27, 1998.

65 Lara Marlowe, "Thousands mourn assassinated singer," *Irish Times*, June 29, 1998.

66 Interview with Anouar Benmalek (Paris, June 10, 2007).

67 Cited in Julija Šukys, "Language, the enemy: Assia Djebar's response to the Algerian intellocide," *Journal of Human Rights*, vol. 3, issue 1 (2004): 117.

Conclusion

1 Friedrich Wilhelm Nietzsche, *On the Advantages and Disadvantages of History for Life* (New York: Hackett Publishing Company, 1980), p.30.

2 See hrw.org/english/docs/2006/03/01/algeri12743.htm.

3 See, for example, Elazar Barkan, *The Guilt of Nations: Restitution and Negotiating Historical Injustices* (New York: W. W. Norton, 2000); Priscilla B. Hayner, *Unspeakable Truths: Confronting State Terror and Atrocity. How Truth Commissions around the World are Challenging the Past and Shaping the Future* (New York: Routledge, 2001); Martha Minow, *Between Vengeance and Forgiveness: Facing History after Genocide and Mass Violence* (Boston, MA: Beacon Press, 1980); Geoffrey Robinson, *Crimes Against Humanity: The Struggle for Global Justice* (New York: The New Press, 1999); Ruti G. Teitel, *Transnational Justice* (New York: Oxford University Press, 2000).

4 See Alex Boraine, *A Country Unmasked: Inside South Africa's Truth and Reconciliation Commission* (New York: Oxford University Press, 2001); Antjie Krog, *Country of My Skull: Guilt, Sorrow, and the Limits of Forgiveness in the New South Africa* (New York: Three Rivers Press, 1999); Allister Sparks, *Beyond the Miracle: Inside the New South Africa* (Chicago, IL: University of Chicago Press, 2003); Desmond Tutu, *No Future without Forgiveness* (New York: Image, 2000).

5 Antjie Krog's *Country of My Skull* is particularly relevant here.

6 Hayner, *Unspeakable Truths*, pp. 43–4.

7 Ibid., p. 15.

8 Interview with Benjamin Stora, Paris, June 23, 2007.

9 Interview with Anouar Benmalek, Paris, June 10, 2007.

10 Interview with Malika Mokaddem, Montpellier, August 5, 2007.

11 Phone interview with Hugh Roberts, December 15, 2008.

12 Peter Brooks, *Troubling Confessions: Speaking Guilt in Law and Literature* (Chicago, IL: University of Chicago Press, 2000), pp. 2–4.

13 Valérie Arnould, "Amnesty, peace and reconciliation in Algeria," in *Conflict, Security & Development*, vol. 7, issue 2 (June 2007): 227–53.

14 See David W. Blight, *Race and Reunion: The Civil War in American Memory* (Cambridge, MA: Belknap Press, 2001).

15 Howard Ball, *Prosecuting War Crimes and Genocide: The Twentieth-*

Century Experience (Lawrence: University of Kansas Press, 1999), p. 5.

16 Ibid., p. 4.

17 Souâd Belhaddad, *Algérie, le prix de l'oubli, 1992–2005* (Paris: Flammarion, 2005), pp. 14–15.

18 See Terry Bell and Dumisa Buhle Ntsebeza, *Unfinished Business: South Africa, Apartheid, and Truth* (Observatory, South Africa: Redworks, 2001).

19 For Winnie Madikizela-Mandela's testimony online, see www.sabctruth.co.za/windows.htm.

Index